THE PHILOSOPHER'S AUTOBIOGRAPHY

A Qualitative Study

Shlomit C. Schuster
Foreword by Maurice Friedman

PRAEGER

Westport, Connecticut
London

Library of Congress Cataloging-in-Publication Data

Schuster, Shlomit C., 1951–
The philosopher's autobiography: a qualitative study / Shlomit C. Schuster ; foreword by Maurice Friedman.
p. cm.
Includes bibliographical references and index.
ISBN 0-275-97789-7 (alk. paper)
1. Philosophy—Authorship. 2. Philosophers—Biography—History and criticism. 3. Autobiography. 4. Psychoanalysis and philosophy. I. Title.
B52.7.S38 2003
190—dc21 2002070868

British Library Cataloguing in Publication Data is available.

Library of Congress Catalog Card Number: 2002070868
ISBN: 0-275-97789-7

First published in 2003

Praeger Publishers, 88 Post Road West, Westport, CT 06881
An imprint of Greenwood Publishing Group, Inc.
www.praeger.com

Printed in the United States of America

The paper used in this book complies with the Permanent Paper Standard issued by the National Information Standards Organization (Z39.48–1984).

10 9 8 7 6 5 4 3 2 1

The author and publisher gratefully acknowledge permission for use of the following material:

Schuster, Shlomit C. "Bedside and Philosophically Oriented Clinical Practice." *Journal of Radical Psychology* 2, 1 (2001). Available at: <http://www.radpsy.yorku.ca/vol2-1/bedside.htm>. June 2002.

Schuster, Shlomit C. "Philosophical Autobiography." In *Encyclopedia of Life Writing*, edited by M. Jolly, 706–707. London: Fitzroy Dearborn, 2001.

Schuster, Shlomit C. "Revisiting *Hope Now* with Benny Lévy: A Note on the 1996 English Edition of *Hope Now*." *Sartre Studies International* 4, 1 (1998): 63–75.

Schuster, Shlomit C. "Sartre's Freud and the Future of Sartrean Psychoanalysis." *Israel Journal of Psychiatry* 35, 1 (1998): 20–30.

Schuster, Shlomit C. "Sartre's 'Words' as a Paradigm for Self-Description in Philosophical Counseling." In *Perspectives in Philosophical Practice*, edited by W. van der Vlist, 20–34. Doorwerth: Dutch Society for Philosophy Practice, 1997.

For my parents
For all they are,
and for their love and goodness.

Vita Nuova

I stood by the unvintageable sea
Till the wet waves drenched face and hair with spray,
The long red fires of the dying day
Burned in the west; the wind piped drearily;
And to the land the clamorous gulls did flee:
Alas! I cried, my life is full of pain,
And who can garner fruit or golden grain,
From these waste fields which travail ceaselessly!
My nets gaped wide with many a break and flaw
Nathless I threw them as my final cast
Into the sea, and waited for the end.
When lo! a sudden glory! and I saw
The argent splendour of white limbs ascend,
And in that joy forgot my tortured past.

Oscar Wilde

Contents

Foreword

Maurice Friedman

Dr. Shlomit Schuster has written another groundbreaking book, following up on her earlier book *Philosophy Practice: An Alternative to Counseling and Psychotherapy*, the first full-length book in English on this subject. Her new book, *The Philosopher's Autobiography: A Qualitative Study*, is a unique study that makes a significant contribution to such diverse fields as philosophy, psychology, biography, sociology, and cultural history.

The scholarship that undergirds this book is breathtaking, but what Dr. Schuster has done on the basis of this scholarship is even more breathtaking. None of the many works she cites has accomplished what she has. Building on her earlier book, Dr. Schuster lays the foundation of this one by a thorough examination of the meeting of philosophy and autobiography and the special problems and issues that this meeting raises.

Schuster also elaborates on the meeting and "mismeeting" of autobiography and psychoanalysis, offering in the place of the traditional Freudian reductionist approach a psychology of her own that does not remove the reality of the author into the interpsychic or try to demonstrate that the present and the future are determined by childhood upbringing and unconscious complexes. Instead, she presents a philosophical psychological approach, influenced by R. D. Laing and others, that gives ample due to personal decision and the congruence, continuity, and changes of personal existence.

Particularly impressive are the three long chapters on the autobiographical writings of Augustine, Rousseau, and Sartre. These are carried over, with major revisions, from Schuster's doctoral dissertation for the Hebrew University of Jerusalem (on which, incidentally, I worked with her for a number of years). That she can do justice to three such different figures from such different time periods and cultural contexts is impressive indeed, especially given her knowledge of both the life and the full range of works of each figure. Still more impressive, however, is the exciting and thoroughly readable way in which she has brought these figures to life. Her presentation and analysis of Jean-Paul Sartre in this context is truly outstanding. I believe the readers of this book will be grateful to her, as I was, for rescuing Sartre from the popular image of him as an extreme existentialist individualist and bringing out the socialism and concern for reciprocal relationships that marked his later writings and his later years.

In her epilogue, Shlomit Schuster deftly presents just what is necessary from the autobiographies of John Stuart Mill, Søren Kierkegaard, and Bertrand Russell to rescue them from the reductionist readings that have been given them and to bolster her conclusion that the self-understanding in all the philosophical autobiographies is in no way inferior to Freudian psychoanalytical understandings. She demonstrates with authority that each of these thinkers in philosophizing was also establishing consistency with his real self.

This is, in short, an original, significant, and exciting book that deserves and hopefully will find a wide readership.

Acknowledgments

The crucial ideas of this book and the chapters on Augustine, Rousseau, and Sartre are based on my Ph.D. dissertation, "Philosophical Autobiography: A Commentary on the Practice of Philosophy," which I wrote at the Hebrew University of Jerusalem, 1990–1997. Although these chapters were considerably revised to be part of this book, it seems right to me to thank all those who were helpful at one stage or another in promoting my dissertation labor, among whom were Jacques Schlanger, Avishai Margalit, and Marcel Dubois. I am particularly grateful to Maurice S. Friedman (San Diego State University) for having been a very kind and helpful advisor. I thank also George Stern (Australian National University) for reading and giving encouraging advice on chapters I wrote more recently.

I thank the editors of the books and the journals in which sections of this book have been published for their permission to republish these texts with some minor changes.

Last, but not least, I would like to thank the commissioning editor, Elisabetta Linton, and others at Praeger Publishers, the Greenwood Publishing Group, as well as the copy editor, Seth Reichgott, of the John Beck Production Group, for their interest and assistance in contributing to the realization of *The Philosopher's Autobiography*.

CHAPTER 1

Philosophical Autobiography

> William [James] kept diaries and at one time made the very revealing confession to Henry Adams that "autobiographies are my particular line of literature, the only books I let myself buy outside of metaphysical treatises."
>
> Robert F. Sayre, *The Examined Self*

This book is an introduction to the relatively new genre of philosophical autobiography. Though this unique genre existed throughout the ages, it did not receive the recognition that, for example, hagiography received. Only during the last century did a few scholars begin to regard the autobiographies of philosophers as a distinct type. Moreover, this is the first book solely dedicated to the subject of philosophical autobiography, the finest example of philosophical life writing.

In this chapter I outline *The Philosopher's Autobiography* and present a general introduction to this genre. I describe characteristics of philosophical autobiography and show how this type of life writing developed. Also, I survey and list different examples belonging to this category and examine research involving these autobiographies. Chapter 2 is a selection from several representative narratives extending from antiquity to postmodernity: Plato, Marcus Aurelius, Abelard, Al-Ghazali, Dante, Erasmus, Hume, Kahlil Gibran, Simone Weil, Hazel E. Barnes, and Alfred I. Tauber. I examine how philosophy and self-reflection are specified in these texts. However, I intend this book to be more than a survey of a genre, and I extensively analyze in it three philosophical self-narratives as qualitative research samples and case studies in philosophical psychoanalysis (Chapters 4, 5, and 6).

In Chapter 3 I show the meaning of philosophical psychoanalysis different from the philosophical interpretation of psychoanalysis as presented by Richard Wollheim, Jonathan Lear, and other psychoanalytically informed philosophers or philosophically oriented psychoanalysts. I present philosophy "in itself" as a method for a different kind of psychoanalysis: the analysis of the self and its development from a philosophical perspective. I show as well the philosophical origins of qualitative research and its relationship to psychoanalysis.

Though qualitative research originated in phenomenological philosophy, nowadays mainly social scientists practice qualitative research. Qualitative researchers from diverse disciplines publish hundreds of papers and books yearly, using or explaining qualitative methods. Yet the public and many professionals remain quite ignorant about this flourishing alternate way of obtaining knowledge. I turn to qualitative research as a philosophical method. Justifying it as more than merely a scientific method may promote its use in the humanities as well.

Chapters 4, 5, and 6 are essays on the autobiographies of Augustine, Rousseau, and Sartre: We are introduced to these life stories from a philosopher's perspective. Mainly, but not only, their subjective voices reveal to us their lived experience and intellectual achievements. The chapters are divided into three sections. Each section presents an analysis of the dynamics of philosophical living, thinking, and writing, while comparing and contrasting these with inner changes accomplished in a successful psychoanalysis.

In Chapter 4 I describe Augustine's *Confessions* as a philosophical text in which Augustine narrates his philosophical development and shows how philosophy shaped his life. Through analyzing other writings of Augustine, I question the consistency of these works with the philosophy of his autobiography. The chapter is divided into subsections: "Philosophical Confessions," "Philosophical Reflections, Theology, and Autobiography," and "Psychoanalysis Informed by Philosophical Rebirth."

I apply a corresponding strategy in Chapters 5 and 6. Chapter 5 has the following subdivisions: "The Philosophical Self-Portrait," "Philosophy as Autobiography," and "Psychoanalysis from Nature's Perspective."

In Chapter 6, I analyze Sartre's *Words* under the subtitle "A Philosophical Narrative for All." This section is followed by "Philosophy as Literary and Political Engagement" and "Psychoanalysis on the Writer's Couch." In this chapter I show how Sartre used his own brand of psychoanalysis in becoming the radical philosopher he wanted to be.

Finally, in the epilogue, I reflect on self-renewal or change, and on the likelihood of persons attaining different selves through combining philosophical psychoanalysis with narrative writing. I illuminate these issues through conclusions drawn from former chapters, while comparing these to the dynamics of consistency and continuity in the autobiographies of John Stuart Mill, Søren Kierkegaard, and Bertrand Russell.

Philosophical autobiography proper need not describe the life of a so-called professional philosopher, though most philosophical autobiographies have been written by such philosophers. Sometimes the recognition of the biographer as a philosopher has been obscured by other eminent professional skills, such as those of the theologian, politician, novelist, and so on. Nevertheless, the philosophical bent of mind and philosophical style of writing in such autobiographies remain obvious (e.g., in St. Augustine, Benjamin Franklin, and Jean-Paul Sartre).

According to the *Dictionary of World Literary Terms*, "The autobiography proper is a connected narrative of the author's life, with stress laid on introspection."[1] Over the last forty years the subject of autobiography has been a flourishing field of academic studies, and more elegant and elaborate definitions are abundantly available. An excellent essay on defining autobiography is Robert F. Sayre's "The Examined Self Reexamined."[2] In the context of my inquiry into philosophical autobiography, clarifying definitions of "autobiography proper" seems an aside. I consider this minimal denotation of autobiography as a working definition to elaborate further about the main topic of inquiry as sufficient.

In her classic work, *The Autobiography*, Anna Robeson Burr listed autobiographies according to professions and made a special listing for a few philosophers and scientists.[3] There she included the philosophers Avicenna, Giordano Bruno, René Descartes, Desiderius Erasmus, Al-Ghazali, Solomon Maimon, John S. Mill, Herbert Spencer, and Giambattista Vico.[4] Furthermore, Burr categorizes certain other philosophers under other professions; for example, David Hume is found among the historians.

Georg Misch, author of another classic work, *A History of Autobiography in Antiquity*, analyzes the development of autobiography in the ancient philosophical and religious movements.[5] He describes the philosophical disclosure of personality in Cicero's letters and the self-portrayals of Seneca, Epictetus, and Marcus Aurelius.

Throughout the ages philosophers have been inclined to write about their own philosophical lives, but it was only in the last half of the twentieth century that the term "philosophical autobiography" was first coined by William C. Spengemann in *The Forms of Autobiography: Episodes in the History of a Literary Genre* to indicate a particular genre.[6] Karl Jaspers was the first and so far the only philosopher who used for his self-narrative the title *Philosophical Autobiography*. However, there are autobiographic works with titles such as *Philosophical Letters* (Voltaire, Peter Chaadaev), *Confessio Philosophi* (Gottfried Wilhelm Leibniz), *A Philosophic Memoir* (Abigail L. Rosenthal), and *Philosophical Meditations* (Robert Nozick).

Spengemann considers as authentically philosophical those individuals who wrote their lives with a skeptical slant. It is doubtful whether the historical aspects of the self are real; the real self is founded metaphysically: in allegory, metaphor, God, nature, or even opium. Spengemann discerns three genres in autobiography, and all these are manifest in Augustine's *Confessions* as historical, philosophical, and poetical autobiography. The first genre is typical for antiquity, the philosophical model for the eighteenth century, and the poetic narrative is the norm in modernity. Spengemann's reference to Carlyle as having used the concept "philosophico-poetic autobiography" might suggest his source of inspiration for creating these three genres. Unlike Burr and Misch, Spengemann finds the profession of the philosopher—or philosophizing in general—not the main indicator for the philosophical genre. Characteristic is the additional metaphorical meaning of the autobiographers' experiences, as found in Wordsworth's *Prelude* or De Quincey's *Confessions of an English Opium-Eater*.

Paul de Man, in a somewhat similar way, suggests that life not only produces autobiography but that, as an additional dimension, "the autobiographical project may itself produce and determine the life."[7] Unlike Spengemann, Man finds it problematic "to define and to treat autobiography as if it were a literary genre among others," let alone considering a genre such as philosophical autobiography. Nevertheless, Jacques Derrida observed that Man's allegorical reading of texts is "on the one hand, the Hegelian concept of allegory . . . on the other hand, it is also Hegelian philosophy as allegory."[8] But unlike Hegelian absolute knowledge, Man's reading of narratives paradoxically leads away from self-knowledge obtained through self-scrutiny.

Martin Warner, in "Philosophical Autobiography, St. Augustine and John Stuart Mill," finds, in contradiction to the additional metaphorical meaning of the life story as characteristic for Spengemann's view, that philosophical autobiography is recognizable in the relation between self-description and personal persuasion. He describes examples of such a tie in the autobiographies of Augustine and Mill:

> A model of man which is integrated with the author's perception of his own self in the light of past experience. This integration provides a point of reference for understanding that experience, and hence may constitute a significant element in any cumulative case which seeks to defend (or attack) the model in question. The connection between "Know thyself" and one's overall metaphysical standpoint may not be so dated as is sometimes thought.[9]

Warner's view signifies through its broad perspective of philosophical thought as significant for the philosophical life narrative a recoinage of the term philosophical autobiography in its widest sense.

Genevieve Lloyd observes that she owed much of her interest in philosophical autobiography to Warner's paper. But instead of a "model of man," she finds as a common thread running through the autobiographies of Augustine, Rousseau, and Sartre the attempt to create a "fictional self": "the attempt of a living self to make an object of itself, to grasp itself as a complete being without paying the cost of death."[10]

I claim in "On Philosophical Self-Diagnosis and Self-Help" that many philosophical autobiographies are characterized by a dynamic relationship between philosophical conviction and the philosopher's praxis.[11] There, and in Chapters 4, 5, and 6 of this book, I describe philosophical autobiographies as documents typically providing two kinds of information: how philosophical thought processes influence the praxis of the philosopher, and how life situations influence philosophical thought processes. Nevertheless, such a dynamic dual pattern is not necessarily a vicious circle, or a priori existent.

In "Can Philosophy Speak about Life?" Ilham Dilman sees the pursuit of philosophy itself as a form of engagement: an engagement of the whole person, not just his or her intellect. Philosophy as a marriage "changes the life and perspective of the person who takes it seriously, including his perspective on his own personal problems. And this, indeed, would constitute a change in the person who takes philosophy seriously."[12]

Of course, one can conceive of a professional philosopher who philosophizes—in spite of disliking philosophy—only to earn his or her living. Consequently, a philosopher "in spite of him- or herself" philosophizes only during working hours, and preferably deals with subjects that deny a relationship between philosophy and life. Such philosophizing can be compared with any other professional activity, such as that of a chemist, dentist, or butcher. The professional activity of a chemist would have no bearing on the meaning or content of his or her autobiography: A chemist's autobiography is not written as a chemical formula, nor does it use chemical symbolic language to produce a "chemical autobiography."

One cannot compare philosophy, as done by most philosophers, with a rigidly detached professional activity. Not to love "the love of wisdom" but nevertheless to pursue it is, to put it as delicately as possible, an ambivalent and paradoxical endeavor.

Philosophers are usually characterized by a serious dedication to philosophy. And such dedication, "given the character of its questions, may amount to a spiritual reorientation—as Socrates tells us it did for him. Such a transformation is more than a change in the philosopher's understanding . . . it is a change in *him*, in his mode of existence and, therefore, in his very being."[13] The seriously engaged philosopher writing about his or her life writes a philosophical autobiography, since philosophy and the philosopher's way of living and writing are inseparable. Two contemporary philosophers, Bryan Magees and Abigail L. Rosenthal, seem to provide further evidence for this claim by having written their life narratives with the explicit aim of showing how ideas influenced their lives.[14] Nevertheless, philosophical reflection as a free, critical, and creative mental activity comprises only the potential for transcending habitual and slavish trends of cognition.

Different from my view are the views of R. G. Collingwood and Wilhelm Dilthey: They find that historical cognition of the self and philosophy cannot be detached. In *An Autobiography*, Collingwood claims a necessary rapprochement between philosophy and history. In his view the philosophical and the autobiographical are one: Philosophy is a historical investigation into the principles a person is unaware of. Dilthey similarly finds philosophy a hermeneutical "Verstehen," a historical, biographical, or autobiographical practice.[15]

An important contribution to the contemporary practice of philosophical autobiography has been made by Paul A. Schillp, the founding editor of the Library of Living Philosophers. At present the Library of Living Philosophers series is edited by Randall E. Auxier.[16] In this series, twentieth-century philosophers were asked to write an autobiographical essay as an important feature of their work. The outcome so far of this initiative is more than twenty-five volumes, containing autobiographic essays by George Santayana, Alfred North Whitehead, G. E. More, Bertrand Russell, Albert Einstein, Sarvepalli Radhakrishnan, Karl Jaspers, C. D. Broad, Rudolf Carnap, Martin Buber, C. I. Lewis, Karl Popper, Brand Blanshard, Jean-Paul Sartre, Gabriel Marcel, W. V. Quine, Georg Henrik von Wright, Charles Hartshorne, A. J. Ayer, Paul Ricoeur, Paul Weiss, Hans-Georg Gadamer, Roderick M. Chisholm, and P. F. Strawson. Some of these philosophers produced, apart from their essay in the Library of Living Philosophers, other autobiographical works as well (see listing further on).

Schillp wrote an autobiography in which he reflects on the great minds he encountered: Albert Einstein, Sarvepalli Radhakrishnan, Karl Jaspers, Martin Buber, Ernest Cassirer, and Brand Blanshard.[17] Another collection of autobiographical essays by philosophers has been edited by James R. Watson, and contains the work of twenty-two contemporary American philosophers (e.g., John D. Caputo, Thomas R. Flynn, David M. Rasmussen, and Hugh J. Silverman).[18]

Following is a listing of more philosophical autobiographies. What characterizes the authors of this group of heterogeneous documents is that they attained academic degrees in philosophy and/or demonstrated their talents as philosophers in their writings. Despite the conventional differentiation between the autobiography proper and other autobiographic writings, I include in the main body of autobiographies listed some diaries, journals, memoirs, letters, novels, interviews, and autobiographic essays that seem to me of philosophical and autobiographical significance. My motive for not making too strict a division between the many stylistic forms of philosophical self-narratives is that apparently the essential description of the philosopher's life one expects to find in philosophical autobiography has been conceived by some philosophers as best expressed in a stylistic form different from autobiography proper.

At first glance, some of the autobiographers choose names for their works that do not indicate an autobiographic intention, but upon a closer look the titles chosen often characterize in a single phrase a complete life project. For others the name "Memoirs" or "Journal" is a cover title for their letters. And letters are sometimes autobiography or function as such. Other philosophical autobiographical writings are a mixture of biographical and historical data, or contain so much philosophizing that autobiography per se seems of minor importance. The latter can particularly be said of many apologies: The life worth writing about is mainly, or even only, the author's metaphysical life.

In the listing here I present the names of the authors in alphabetical order. Though titles of the autobiographical writings are all given in italics, not all were published as books. Some of these titles have been published as essays in books by these authors, or are found as a foreword or introduction to their works. Other texts may appear as essays in books about these philosophers, or in their collected works, or as essays in magazines and journals:

Abélard, Peter (1079–1142): *The Story of My Misfortunes*, Apuleius (123–170): *Apologia Apuleius*, Adams, Henry (1838–1918): *The Education of Henry Adams*, Adler, Mortimer J. (1902–2001): *Philosopher at Large* and *A Second Look in the Rearview Mirror*, Adorno, Theodore (1903–1969): *Minima Moralia: Reflections from Damaged Life*, Alexander, Samuel (1859–1935): *Memoir*, Al-Ghazali (1058–1111): *Confessions*, Alighieri, Dante (1265–1321): *Vita Nuova*, Althusser, Louis (1918–1990): *The Future Last Forever*, Amiel, Henri Frédéric (1821–1881): *Journal Intime*, Andreas-Salomé, Lou (1861–1937): *Lebensrückblicke*, Antoninus, Marcus Aurelius (121–180): *To Himself*, Aristides, Marcianus (second century): *Apologia*, Artaud, Antonin (1896–1948): *Fragments of a Diary from Hell*, Augustine, Saint (354–430): *The Confessions*, Babbage, Charles (1791–1871): *Passages from the Life of a Philosopher*, Barclay, Robert (1648–1690): *Apology for the True Christian Divinity*, Barnes, Hazel E. (1915–): *The Story I Tell Myself: A Venture in Existential Autobiography*, Barthes, Ronald (1915–1980): *Ronald Barthes by Ronald Barthes*, Beauvoir, Simone de (1908–1986): *Memoirs of a Dutiful Daughter, The Prime of Life, Force of Circumstance, All Said and Done, Adieux: A Farewell to Sartre*, Ben Gershon of Rosheim, Rabbi Joseph (1478–1554): *Sefer ha Mikneh*, Benjamin, Walter (1892–

1940): *Moscow Diary* and *Reflections: Essays, Aphorisms and Autobiographical Writings*, Berdyaev, Nikolai Alexandrovitch (1874–1948): *Dream and Reality: An Essay in Autobiography*, Berlin, Isaiah (1909–1997): *Personal Impressions* and *Conversations with Isaiah Berlin*, Bernard of Clairvaux, Saint (1090–1153): *Apology to William of St. Thierry*, Boethius (470–525): *The Consolation of Philosophy*, Bok, Sissela (1934–): *Alva Myrdal: A Daughter's Memoir*, Breton, André (1896–1966): *Conversations: The Autobiography of Surrealism*, Buber, Martin (1878–1965): *Meetings: Fragments of an Autobiography*, Canetti, Elias (1905–1994): *The Tongue Set Free*, *The Torch in My Ear*, and *The Play of Eyes*, Caro, Rabbi Joseph Ben Ephraim (1488–1575): *Maggid Mesharim*, Cavell, Stanley (1926–): *A Pitch of Philosophy: Autobiographical Exercises*, Chaadaev, Peter I. (1794–1856): *Philosophical Letters* and *Apology of a Madman*, Cioran, Emil (1911–1995): *Les Continents de L'Insomnie*, Coleridge, Samuel T. (1773–1834): *Biographia Literaria*, Copleston, Frederick C. (1907–1994): *Memoirs of a Philosopher*, Croce, Benedetto (1866–1952): *An Autobiography*, Cusa, Nicholas of (1401–1464): *Apologia doctae ignorantiae*, Daly, Mary (1928–): *Outercourse: The Be-Dazzling Voyage*, D'Arcy, Martin C. (1888–1976): *Laughter and the Love of Friends*, Deleuze, Gilles (1925–1995): *Negotiations*, Derrida, Jacques (1930–): *Memoires for Paul de Man*, Descartes, René (1596–1650): *Discourse on Method* and *Meditations*, Du Bois, William E. B. (1868–1963): *The Autobiography of W.E.B. Du Bois: A Soliloquy on Viewing My Life from the Last Decade of Its First Century*, Einstein, Albert (1879–1955): *The World as I See It* and *Out of My Later Years*, Eizik of Komarno, Rabbi Isaac (1806–1874): *The Secret Diary*, Eliade, Mircea (1907–1986): *Autobiography*, Emerson, Ralph Waldo (1803–1882): *Journal and Miscellaneous Notebooks*, Erasmus, Desiderius (1466–1536): *Compendium Vitae*, Feyerabend, Paul (1924–1994): *Killing Time*, Flew, Antony (1923–): *Apologia Pro Philosophia Mea*, Foucault, Michel (1926–1984): *Self-Portraits: The Minimalist Self*, *Critical Theory/Intellectual History*, and *An Aesthetics of Existence*, Fox, George (1624–1691): *Journal*, Franklin, Benjamin (1706–1790): *Autobiography of Benjamin Franklin*, Friedman, Maurice S. (1921–): *The Covenant of Peace: A Personal Witness* and *Touchstones of Reality*, Gibran, Kahlil (1883–1931): *A Self-Portrait*, Gide, André (1869–1951) *If It Die* and *The Journals of André Gide*, Godwin, William (1756–1836): *Autobiography*, Goethe, Johann Wolfgang von (1749–1832): *Poetry and Truth: From My Own Life*, Goodman, Paul (1911–1972): *Five Years: Thoughts during a Useless Time*, Gramsci, Antonio (1891–1937): *Letters from Prison*, Gregory, Saint (213–275): *Oratio Panegyrica*, Gurdjieff, George I. (1872–1949): *Meetings with Remarkable Men*, Hartshorne, Charles (1897–): *The Darkness and the Light: A Philosopher Reflects Upon His Career*, Heidegger, Martin (1889–1976): *Vita*, Herbert of Cherbury, Baron Edward (1583–1648): *The Life of Edward Lord Herbert of Cherbury, Written by Himself*, Herder, Johann Gottfried (1744–1803): *Journal of My Travels in the Year 1769*, Herzen, Alexander (1812–1870): *My Past and Thoughts*, Hobbes, Thomas (1588–1679): *Thomae Hobbesii Malmesburiensis Vita carmine expressa*, Honderich, Ted (1933–): *Philosopher: A Kind of Life*, Hook, Sidney (1902–1989): *Out of Step: An Unquiet Life in the 20th Century*, Horkheimer, Max (1895–1973): *Aus der Pubertät: Novellen und Tagebuchblätter*, Hume, David (1711–1776): *My Own Life*, Huxley, Thomas Henry (1825–1895): *Diary of the Voyage of H.M.S. "Rattlesnake"* and *Life and Letters of Thomas Henry Huxley*, Ibn Khaldun (1332–1395): *Al-Tasrif*, Isocrates (436–338 B.C.E.): *Antidosis*, Jaki, Stanley L. (1924–): A Mind's Matter: An Intellectual Autobiography, James, Henry (1843–1916): *A Small Boy and Others* and *Notes of a Son and Brother*, James, William (1842–1910): *The Letters of William James*, Jones, Mary Harris (1830–1930): *Autobiography of Mother Jones*, Justinus, Saint Flavius (100–165): *Dialogue with the Jew Tryphon*, Kafka, Franz (1883–1924): *The Diaries: 1910–1913*, Kenny, Anthony John Patrick (1931–): *A Path from Rome*, Keyserling, Hermann A., Count von (1880–1946): *The Travel Diary of a Philosopher*, Kierkegaard, Søren (1813–1855): *The Journals of Søren Kierkegaard*, Koestler, Arthur (1905–1983): *Dialogue with Death, Scum of the Earth, Arrow in the Blue, The Invisible Writing*, and *The God That Failed*, Kropotkin, Peter (1842–1921): *Memoirs of a Revolutionist*, Kuhn, S. Thomas (1922–1996): *The Road since Structure: Philosophical Essays, with an Autobiographical Interview*, Leibniz, Gottfried Wilhelm (1646–1716): *Confessio Philosophi*, Leiris, Michel (1901–1990): *Manhood* and *The Rules of the Game*, Lévi-Strauss, Claude (1908–): *Tristes Tropiques*, Lévinas, Emmanuel (1906–1995): *Signature*, Lewis, Clive Staples (1898–1963): *The Pilgrim's Regress*, Loyola, Saint Ignatius of (1491–1556): *Reminiscences and Spiritual Diary*, Lukács, Georg (1885–1971): *Georg Lukács: An Autobiographical Sketch*, Luxemburg, Rosa (1871–1919): *The Letters of Rosa Luxemburg*, Mahan, Asa (1799–1889): *Autobiography: Intellectual, Moral, and Spiritual*, Maimon, Salomon (1754–1800): *Salomon Maimon: An Autobiography*, Maine de Biran, François-Pierre (1766–1824): *Journal Intime*, Malraux, André (1901–1976): *Antimémoires*, Mann, Thomas (1875–1955): *Tagebücher*, Marcel, Gabriel (1889–1973): *Metaphysical Journal*, McGinn, Colin (1950–): *The Making of a Philosopher: My Journey Through Twentieth-Century Philosophy*, Merton, Thomas (1915–1968): *The Seven Storey Mountain* and *The Other Side of the Mountain*, Mill, John S. (1806–1873): *Autobiography*, Molcho, Salomon (1500–1532): *Hayyot Kaneh: Hazon Shelomo Molkho*, Montaigne, Michel (1535–1592): *The Essays*, More, Saint Thomas (1478–1535): *Apology*, Newman, John H. (1801–1890): *Apologia pro Vita sua*, Nietzsche, Friedrich (1844–1900): *Ecce Homo*, Nozick, Robert (1938–2002): *The Examined Life: Philosophical Meditations*, Palmer, George Herbert (1842–1933): *Autobiography of a Philosopher*, Pascal, Blaise (1623–1662): *Pensées*, Petrarch, Francesco (1304–1374): *Secretum*, Plato (428–348 B.C.E.): *The Seventh Letter*, Priestley, Joseph (1833–1904): *Autobiography of Joseph Priestley*, Rand, Ayn (1905–1982): *Journals of Ayn Rand*, Raymond, Aron (1905–1983): *Memoirs*, Read, Sir Herbert (1893–1968): *The Contrary Experiences*, Ricoeur, Paul (1913–): *Critique and Conviction*, Rolland, Romain (1866–1944): *Mémoires*, Rosenzweig, Franz (1886–1929): *Diaries and Autobiographic Fragments*, Rousseau, Jean-Jacques (1712–1778): *The Confessions*, Russell, Bertrand (1872–1970): *Autobiography*, Sade, Marquis de (1740–1814): *Letters from Prison*, Said, Edward (1935–): *Out of Place: A Memoir*, Saint-Simon, Claude-Henri de Rouvroy, Comte de (1760–1825): *His Life, Written by Himself*, Santayana, George (1862–1952): *Persons and Places: The Autobiography of George Santayana* and *Apologia Pro Menta Sua*, Sartre, Jean-Paul (1905–1980): *The Words* and *War Diaries*, Scholem, Gershom (1897–1982): *From Berlin to Jerusalem*, Schurman, Anna Maria van (1607–1678): *Eucleria*, Schweitzer, Albert (1875–1965): *Out of My Life and Thought: An Autobiography*, Segur, Count Louis Philippe de (1753–1830): *Memoirs and Recollections of Count Louis Philippe de Segur*, Sellars, Wilfrid (1912–1989): *Intellectual Autobiography*, Seuse, Heinrich (1295–1366): *Vita*, Shusterman, Richard (1949–): *Next Year in Jerusalem?*, Sidney, Algernon (1622–1683): *Memoirs of His Life and an Apology*, Sontag, Susan (1933–): *Pilgrimage* and *Conversations with Susan Sontag*, Spencer, Herbert (1820–1904): *An Autobiography*, Stein, Gertrude (1874–1946): *The*

Autobiography of Alice B. Toklas, Stein, Saint Edith (1891–1942): *Life in a Jewish Family: Her Unfinished Autobiographical Account*, Steiner, Rudolf (1861–1925): *Story of My Life*, Suso, Henry (1295–1366): *The Life of Blessed Henry Suso by Himself*, Swedenborg, Emanuel (1688–1772): *The Journal of Dreams*, Tauber, Alfred I. (1947–): *Confessions of a Medicine Man*, Tertullian (165–220): *Apologeticum*, Tillich, Paul J. (1886–1965): *My Search for Absolutes*, Tocqueville, Alexis, Comte de (1805–1859): *Recollections of Alexis de Tocqueville*, Tolstoy, Count Leo Nikolayevich (1828–1910): *Childhood, Boyhood, Youth*, Trotsky, Leon (1879–1940): *My Life*, van der Post, Sir Laurens (1906–1996): *The Admiral's Baby*, Vasconcelos, José (1882–1959): *A Mexican Ulysses*, Vico, Giambattisto (1668–1744): *The Autobiography of Giambattisto Vico*, Vital, Rabbi Hayyim (1542–1620): *Book of Visions*, Voltaire, Francois Marie Arouet de (1694–1778): *Philosophical Letters*, Warnock, Baroness Mary (1924–): *Mary Warnock, a Memoir*, Watts, Alan W. (1915–1973): *In My Own Way: An Autobiography*, Weil, Simone (1909–1943): *Spiritual Autobiography*, White, Morton G. (1917–): *A Philosopher's Story*.

A variant of the philosophical autobiography is its pseudo form. For example, Socrates's *Apology* was written by Plato, and *The Life of Avicenna* by Jorjani (Sorsanus), a disciple of Ibn Sina (Avicenna). More recently, Kenneth Laine Ketner produced *His Glassy Essence: An Autobiography of Charles Sanders Pierce*.

Another subgenre is the philosophical quasi autobiography, in which the ideas, or the life of the author, are concealed but still expressed through a fictional or another actual person. Such are Mary Hays's *Memoirs of Emma Courtney*, Elizabeth Hamilton's *Memoirs of Modern Philosophers*, Montaigne's *Apologie de Raimond Sebond*, Thomas Carlyle's *Sartor Resartus: The Life and Opinions of Herr Teufelsdröckh*, and Santayana's *The Last Puritan: A Memoir in the Form of a Novel*. Albert Camus's posthumously published *The First Man* is also such an autobiographical novel. In contrast with Sartre's *Words*—also an autobiographical novel—Camus does not present us with names of significant persons in his childhood, such as his mother and his teacher. But Catherine, Camus's daughter, finds *The First Man* "completely autobiographical. The mother he describes is the woman I knew, and she was exactly as he describes her. And this teacher [Monsieur Germain] really existed."[19]

Ben-Ami Scharfstein considers the writings of some psychotics to resemble those of philosophers. He even suggests that psychotics "can be philosophers." Examples of "philosophical psychotic" autobiographies are D. P. Schreber's *Memoirs of My Nervous Illness* and M. Sechehaya's *Autobiography of a Schizophrenic Girl*.[20]

In addition to these subgenres is the sheer fictional form of philosophical autobiography—or in critics' jargon, philosophical autobiofiction—such as found in Oliver Goldsmith's *The Citizen of the World*.

Although the listing here may appear encyclopedic, it is not an all-inclusive or conclusive listing. Since writing philosophical autobiographies is obviously a universal and perennial activity, I regret the absence of examples from African, Asian, American, and Australian traditional cultures. Although the influence of traditional cultures may not have been encouraging to self-disclosure, examples of uncommon self-descriptions are likely to be found. For example, the lack of autobiographies in the ancient and medieval Judaic tradition originates in a striving for personal humility; self-narration and idolization apparently were considered synonyms.[21] Two twentieth-century Asian autobiographies that became part of the Western philosophical autobiographic tradition are Mahatma Gandhi's *An Autobiography: The Story of my Experiments with Truth* and Paramahansa Yogananda's *Autobiography of a Yogi*.

My range of expertise and inquiry is confined to the Western realm of influence. Moreover, my listing is selective. In spite of today's trend to regard Freud's autobiography as philosophical, I did not include his autobiography or those of two other great psychoanalysts, Carl Jung and R. D. Laing. On the other hand, I include some metaphysically, literary, and politically inspired accounts. Though these seem to me to be philosophical texts, others may consider these autobiographies as just being on the fringes of philosophy, or as literary, spiritual, political, or theoretically informed texts only (e.g., Gide's *If It Die*, Merton's *The Seven Storey Mountain*, or Luxemburg's *Letters*). Likewise, some may judge the greatness of an autobiography—meaning its "right" to be indexed here—by standards of the greatness of the philosopher. Yet my intention with this listing is not to evaluate or rank these texts as the best available, but to show how broadly life-writing is practiced by philosophers of diverse traditions and nationalities.

Then there is the "end-of-philosophy" trend: Only the term "ethics" remains relevant and functional, and in postmodern self-narratives the words "critic" and "intellectual" supersede the term "philosopher."[22] Richard Freadman, for example, uses the term "reflective autobiography" in *Threads of Life: Autobiography and the Will*. Freadman's definition of the reflective autobiography would fit quite a few instances of philosophical autobiography as well:

> Autobiography in which there is a significant and sophisticated component of reflection on the meaning and larger implications of the life being written, and of life in general; and in which there is a significant sense of reflective, critical distance between the attitudes and assumptions of the autobiographer, and the attitudes and assumptions that were/are prevalent in her or his cultural–ideological milieu.[23]

It is not surprising that some of the reflective autobiographies about the condition of the human will that Freadman examines are written by philosophers (e.g., Louis Althusser, Simone de Beauvoir, and Arthur Koestler).

It remains to be said that with so many worthy philosophical autobiographies available, one can only marvel at the fact that very few researchers have discovered this genre so far.

As the subtitle of this book indicates, I propose not a quantitative but a qualitative study. Nevertheless, I find it appropriate to present a profile of the genre showing it as numerous as well: In this chapter I indexed more than a hundred and fifty autobiographic writings by philosophers. With the purpose of showing this genre also as a field of inquiry, I comprehensively survey some recent research entailing several of these autobiographies.

Until now most researchers scrutinizing the autobiographies of philosophers—mainly the well-known ones of Augustine, Mill, Rousseau, Nietzsche, and Sartre—neglected the importance of the fact that these authors were philosophers. These narratives have seldom been analyzed within the context of the authors' work or as philosophical texts. Moreover, quite a few academic philosophers are doubtful about the value of their colleagues' autobiographies as a contribution to the discipline of philosophy. Most research done in this field is found in other disciplines, such as language studies and comparative literature.

Though some philosophers maintain that all philosophizing emanates from the philosopher's life, in general the philosopher's autobiography is not given an equal status to other philosophical writings. A regular exception seems to have been made for Augustine's *Confessions*, Descartes's *Discourse on Method and Meditations*, and Sartre's *Words*; these autobiographical works are frequently found in philosophy course bibliographies.[24] If these autobiographies are acknowledged as philosophy, why not canonize so many other excellent philosophical autobiographies?

Michael Davis turns my question around by showing philosophy to be autobiography. Nevertheless, he does not find that "every philosopher is, perhaps without realizing it, simply rendering his idiosyncratic view of the world in a universal form . . . [but] rather that it is not really possible to philosophize without making the conditions for the possibility of one's own activity the deepest concern of this activity."[25] Davis's central theme in *The Autobiography of Philosophy* is the connection between the nature of philosophy and the nature of the human soul. He observes that the autobiographical character of philosophy is most obviously found in Greek philosophy, in Nietzsche and in Heidegger.

Though Plato and Nietzsche also wrote conventional autobiographic texts, it is not to these texts that Davis turns to show that by being authentically in the world, Plato, Aristotle, Nietzsche, and Heidegger stand autobiographical in the world. He demonstrates at length that Heidegger's "Introduction" to *Being and Time*, Nietzsche's *On the Genealogy of Morals*, Aristotle's *Metaphysics*, Book I, and Plato's *Lysis* are appropriate texts to show philosophy as autobiography.

These texts are contrasted with the conventional autobiographical texts of Rousseau and, in particular, with *The Reveries of the Solitary Walker*. Davis's strategy for showing this last text as philosophy is by demonstrating that *The Reveries of the Solitary Walker* "amounts to a philosophical account of the human soul and of philosophy that places Rousseau firmly in a tradition beginning at least with Plato and Aristotle and still present in Nietzsche and Heidegger."[26]

Donald P. Verene and Anton Donoso uphold similar claims as Davis concerning "philosophy as autobiography."[27] Peter Suber's course, *Philosophy as Autobiography: Psychologistic, Reductive & Non-Immanent Readings of Philosophy*, seems to accentuate a corresponding angle of the philosophy–autobiography complex.[28]

Susan Sontag observes in "'Thinking against Oneself': Reflections on Cioran" that one of the responses to the breakdown of the philosophical system making of the nineteenth century was "a new kind of philosophizing: personal (even autobiographical), aphoristic, lyrical, anti-systematic. Its foremost exemplars: Kierkegaard, Nietzsche, Wittgenstein." She finds Cioran "the most distinguished figure in this tradition."[29]

In a different manner, Jo-Ann Pilardi argues for philosophy to have become autobiography in *Simone de Beauvoir Writing the Self: Philosophy becomes Autobiography*. Pilardi analyzes the concepts of "self" and "other" in Beauvoir's early writings and major work (*The Second Sex*), and compares these with Beauvoir's self-descriptions in her autobiography. She finds that the philosophical analysis of self in Beauvoir's autobiography has greater significance.[30]

I quote Jacques Derrida's position on understanding autobiographical work as follows: "You cannot think the name or names of Friedrich Nietzsche, you cannot *hear* them before the reaffirmation of the hymen, before the alliance or wedding ring of the eternal return. You will not understand anything of his life, nor of his life and works, until you hear the thought of the 'yes, yes.'"[31] This leads Derrida to a particular kind of logic, a grammar of thinking, a language of biography we must learn before we can understand a life. In "The Logic of Living Feminine," the opening section of *The Ear of the Other: Otobiography, Transference, Translation*, Derrida says no to the logic of biographical novels, psychobiographies, and the "autos" of autobiographies as the signature par excellence on the life and work of authors. He proposes a new type of analysis for the biography of philosophers and exemplifies it with his reading of Nietzsche's work. This analysis is not only concerned with understanding *Ecce Homo*, but is also a reflection on biography and autobiography in general.

Reading Derrida made me wonder if one can read autobiography only as biography, with the exception perhaps of the autobiographer himself or herself. And, likewise, in the process of writing this book it appeared to me that writing about philosophical autobiographies is sometimes akin to writing philosophical biography. Lois W. Banner presents a different, psychologically informed argument when she considers that through empathizing with the biographical subject, the biographer cannot "keep his or her own autobiography distinct from the biography being written."[32]

The genre of philosophical biography seems as little researched as its autobiographical consort, but interest in it is increasing. Notable articles on philosophers and biography are Danny Postel's "The Life and the Mind," Timothy Madigan's "Philosophical Biographies," and Richard Freadman's "Genius and the Dutiful Life: Ray Monk's *Wittgenstein* and the Biography of the Philosopher as Sub-genre." An early paper on philosophical biography was published in 1992. Its authors, Edward H. Madden and Marian C. Madden, describe this genre as a flourishing practice in the United States, from the colonial days onward. Yet a critical appraisal of the genre is lacking: "Philosophers have given insufficient attention to conflicting views about what should count as legitimate philosophical biography; in contention we find the classical view, psychobiography, and milieu analysis, all having diametrically opposed presuppositions from which they start."[33]

The aim of the Maddens is to structure systematically selected American biographies into the three subgenres mentioned earlier. They prefer among these types a golden mean, and locate the exemplary blend of philosophical biography in Gerald Myers's *William James: His Life and Thought*.

In another article, "The Biographers: Can We Learn Anything Important from the Biographies of the Great Philosophers?" Julian Baggini interviews three biographers of philosophers. He uncovers some definitions and insights on this neighboring and sometimes overlapping field to philosophical autobiography. Ray Monk, the biographer of Bertrand Russell and Ludwig Wittgenstein, considers philosophical biography a special kind of life narrative. He beliefs that "a philosophical biography is one which takes as its task the understanding of a person's thought through, so to speak, getting inside their mind. This approach can be taken with regard to anyone whose thought seems interesting, whether that thought is expressed in philosophy, poetry, fiction, music or whatever." Margaret Gullan-Whur, biographer of Baruch Spinoza, holds the unorthodox view that biography's so-praised objectivity actually proves the biographer to be an unreflecting and nonanalytical narrator. She finds that "paradoxically, the more philosophically a biography is written, the more we encounter meddling, author-centered material." Ben Roger, biographer of A. J. Ayer, indicates a difficulty that seems to be particularly ignored by most psychoanalytically inclined biographers. Rogers agrees that understanding texts in the context of a life creates a better understanding of the texts, at least if one does not commit the so-called genetic fallacy. The biographer should know to differentiate "between what motivates a writer and the arguments that he or she presents, which stand on their own ground."[34]

In a biographical essay on Walter Benjamin, "Under the Sign of Saturn," Susan Sontag states, "One cannot use the life to interpret the work. But one can use the work to interpret the life."[35] Apparently Benjamin was absorbed with this matter in his polemic essay on Goethe's *Elective Affinities*.

A book I cite as a philosophical biography is Alan Sheridan's *André Gide: A Life in the Present*. Sheridan claims to have lost faith in theories that explain a life, finding theories such as theology, psychoanalysis, Marxism, or their more sophisticated contemporary incarnations all fictions. "This abandonment of general explanations does not preclude, of course, the holding of all manner of views about human activities, but these should arise out of the particular, indeed, perhaps, be confined to the particular." This would create a more complex view of the subject of biography, "just as one gets to know, or not to know, a friend."[36]

Similar to the autobiography researchers surveyed so far, Toril Moi, in *Simone de Beauvoir: The Making of an Intellectual Woman*, finds it necessary to take the philosophy of Beauvoir seriously in understanding her autobiography. Moi's critique of some of the biographies on Beauvoir published so far precisely pertains to their lack of philosophical contexts, although she considers that usually traditional biography comes closer than literary criticism to showing the significance of its subject. She finds "critical biography" not the right term for her analysis and description of Beauvoir, which she names a personal genealogy: "Personal genealogy assumes that every phenomenon may be read as a text, that is to say as a complex network of signifying structures." According to this approach, "There can be no methodological distinction between 'life' and 'text.'"[37] It is clear that Moi's interest in Beauvior is not primarily as the subject of autobiography, but in Beauvoir as intellectual woman.

Last but not least, Amélie Oksenberg Rorty seems to have developed a skeptical understanding of our subject. She finds that

> Philosophers' autobiographies help demystify claims to a special access to truthful insight. They express hesitations, uncertainties, appeals for help,

struggles to find an appropriate method of discovery or a persuasive rhetorical genre. They reveal the common plight of all serious inquiry; but they also express—often in an encoded, indirect, hesitant way—a philosopher's struggle to think, to define and exhibit the process of thinking.[38]

In addition to these references, the following books include one or several chapters on philosophical autobiographies, or present a view relevant to understanding this genre: Peter Brooks's *Troubling Confessions,* Janice Carlisle's *John Stuart Mill and the Writing of Character,* Stuart Z. Charmé's *Meaning and Myth in the Study of Lives: A Sartrean Perspective,* Elizabeth De Mijolla's *Autobiographical Quests: Augustine, Montaigne, Rousseau, and Wordsworth,* Paul John Eakin's *Touching the World: Reference in Autobiography,* James D. Fernandez's *Apology to Apostrophe: Autobiography and the Rhetoric of Self-Representation in Spain,* Avrom Fleishman's *Figures of Autobiography,* Pierre Hadot's *Philosophy as a Way of Life,* Genevieve Lloyd's *Being in Time: Selves and Narrators in Philosophy and Literature,* George Lukács's *The Historical Novel,* Paul de Man's *The Rhetoric of Romanticism,* Suzanne Nalbantian's *Aesthetic Autobiography,* Gareth B. Matthews's *Thought's Ego in Augustine and Descartes,* Jonathan Reé's *Philosophical Tales,* Michael Sheringham's *French Autobiography Devices and Desires,* Hugh J. Silverman's *Textualities: Between Hermeneutics and Deconstruction,* Eugene L. Stelzig's *The Romantic Subject in Autobiography: Rousseau and Goethe,* John Sturrock's *The Language of Autobiography,* and Donald Verene's *The New Art of Autobiography.*

Please note, as with the listing of philosophers' autobiographies, this list of references is also selective and not conclusive. Many of the authors referred to in this chapter's note 2 have also written a chapter or more on an autobiography by a great philosopher. Augustine's *Confessions,* in particular, is seldom overlooked.

Although I like to believe that this book on philosophical autobiography is a relevant contribution to its genre, it needs to be stressed that it is an introduction. To conclude my prologue on the topic: Philosophical autobiography is a narrative self-questioning of the self, its social context, and existence at large. As the critical inquiry into the self and its times, the philosophical self-narrative is a creative and alternative way of looking at and understanding the human inner world in its context. Philosophers throughout the ages looked at themselves and their world through their own philosophical perspectives. It may help us to envision that future times and circumstances will bring with them radical new self-understandings when we perceive that new philosophical self-conceptions, self-narratives, and ways of living are related. Though to a certain extent self-narratives and self-perception are dependent on times and circumstances, it still is and remains the critical inquiry into the self and life that initiates constituent changes in the perception of self and the "self as itself," independent of time areas, circumstances, and ways of being.

NOTES

1. *Dictionary of World Literary Terms*, 1970 ed., s.v. "autobiography."

2. Sayre refers in this introduction to eminent theorists such as Roy Pascal, James Olney, Robert Butler, John Morris, Stephen Shapiro, Jean Starobinsky, Georges Gusdorf, Philippe Lejeune, Elizabeth Bruss, and Janet Varner Gunn. Robert F. Sayre, "The Examined Self Reexamined," in *The Examined Self: Benjamin Franklin, Henry James, Henry Adams* (Madison: University of Wisconsin Press, 1988). Not only does one find reflections on and definitions of autobiography in the works of these authors, but the great philosophical autobiographies (Augustine, Mill, Rousseau, and Sartre) are often discussed by these theorists as well. An alternative and new source for definitions of autobiography is the *Encyclopedia of Life Writing*, 1st ed. (London, Fitzroy Dearborn, 2001).

3. Anna Robeson Burr, *The Autobiography* (Boston: Cambridge University Press, 1909).

4. Although Anna Robeson Burr's work is a very good source book, nevertheless the existence of autobiographies by Avicenna and Giordano Bruno is questionable. On the Avicenna pseudoautobiography see further on in this chapter. The only reference I was able to find to the possible autobiography of Bruno was found at "I DOCTOR JORDANO BRUNO NOLANO," available at: <http://digilander.iol.it/giordanobruno1600/autobiografia.htm> (last accessed March 2001). Professor Paul Richard Blum, an eminent Bruno scholar, identified this text as fake and obscure, and partly taken from Bruno's statement at court (see original in Vincenzo Spampanato, *Vita di Giordano Bruno*). However, Blum states in an e-mail to me that there are autobiographical elements in Bruno's writings, such as his "De immenso." Blum discusses these autobiographic elements in a chapter of his book *Philosophenphilosophie und Schulphilosophie*.

5. Georg Misch, *A History of Autobiography in Antiquity*, vols. 1–2 (London: Routledge, 1949–1950).

6. William C. Spengemann, *The Forms of Autobiography: Episodes in the History of a Literary Genre* (New Haven, Conn.: Yale University Press, 1980).

7. Paul de Man, "Autobiography as De-Facement" in *The Rhetoric of Romanticism* (New York: Columbia University Press, 1984).

8. Jacques Derrida, "Mnemosyne," in *Memoires for Paul de Man* (New York: Columbia University Press, 1986).

9. Martin Warner, "Philosophical Autobiography, St. Augustine and John Stuart Mill," in *Philosophy and Literature*, ed. A. Phillips Griffiths (Cambridge: Cambridge University Press, 1984).

10. Genevieve Lloyd, "The Self as Fiction: Philosophy and Autobiography," *Philosophy and Literature* 10 (1987): 183.

11. Shlomit C. Schuster, "On Philosophical Self-Diagnosis and Self-Help: A Clarification of the Non-Clinical Practice of Philosophical Counseling," *International Journal of Applied Philosophy* 12, 1 (1998): 37–50.

12. Ilham Dilman, "Can Philosophy Speak about Life?" in *The Impulse to Philosophise*, ed. A. Phillips Griffiths (Cambridge: Cambridge University Press, 1992), 109–123.

13. Ibid., 122–123.

14. Bryan Magees, *Confessions of a Philosopher: A Personal Journey through Western Philosophy from Plato to Popper* (New York: Modern Library, 1999); Abigail L. Rosenthal, *Conversions: A Philosophic Memoir* (Philadelphia: Temple University Press, 1994).

15. R. G. Collingwood, *An Autobiography* (London: Oxford University Press, 1939); Wilhelm Dilthey, *Selected Writings* (Cambridge: Cambridge University Press, 1976).

16. Full details on the volumes published by the Library of Living Philosophers is available at: <http://www.sui.edu/~philos/llp/publ.html> (last accessed July 2000).

17. Paul A. Schilpp, *Reminiscing: Autobiographical Notes* (Carbondale: Southern Illinois University Press, 1995).

18. James R. Watson, ed., *Portraits of American Continental Philosophers* (Bloomington: Indiana University Press, 1999).

19. Russell Wilkinson, "Solitaire et Solidaire: Interview with Catherine Camus about Albert Camus' The First Man," *Spike Magazine*, Internet journal, available at: <http://www.spikemagazine.com/0397camu.htm> (last accessed July 2000).

20. Ben-Ami Scharfstein, *The Philosophers, Their Lives and the Nature of Their Thought* (New York: Oxford University Press, 1980), 378, 472.

21. According to the entry "Biography and Autobiography" in the *Encyclopedia Judaica* (1st ed.), this literary genre was completely unknown among Jews in ancient times. Exceptions are the Book of Nehemiah, Josephus's *Vita*, and some hagiographic works. Likewise, in medieval times autobiographies were practically unknown, although historiography written as personal experience became an accepted literary expression (Maimonides's letters, for example).

22. Some recent studies in ethics, criticism, and autobiography are Leona Toker, ed., *Commitment in Reflection: Essays in Literature and Moral Philosophy* (New York: Garland, 1994); H. Aram Veeser, ed., *Confessions of the Critics* (New York: Routledge, 1996); Angel G. Loureiro, *The Ethics of Autobiography: Replacing the Subject in Modern Spain* (Nashville, Tenn.: Vanderbilt University Press, 1999); and Dominic Rainsford and Tim Woods, eds., *Critical Ethics: Texts, Theory and Responsibility* (New York: St. Martin's Press, 1999).

23. Richard Freadman, *Threads of Life: Autobiography and the Will* (Chicago: University of Chicago Press, 2001), 327–328.

24. I was pleasantly surprised to find several courses on philosophical autobiography. In the academic year 1996–1997 Boston College (philosophy department) offered a course entitled "Philosophical Autobiography." In this course Vanessa P. Rumble examined with her students the understanding of human nature as found in the autobiographies of St. Augustine, Rousseau,

Nietzsche, and Maya Angelou (see <http://www.bc.edu/iehome>, last accessed July 2000). Professor Hugh Silverman, at Stony Brook University, New York, has been teaching philosophical autobiography since the 1980s. He taught this course also at the University of Warwick and the University of Nice. Readings for the course were Montaigne, Sartre, de Beauvoir, Mill, Russell, Barthes, Levi-Strauss, and others. Professor Sissela Bok gave courses in Ethics at Harvard and Brandeis Universities using in her classes autobiographical works by Augustine, Theresa of Avila, Mill, Tolstoy, Margaret Mead, and Gandhi. In the academic year 2000–2001 the Anglia Polytechnic University (European philosophy and literature department) offered at its Cambridge campus a course titled "Autobiography: Confession, Sincerity and Authenticity." Key texts in this course were by Rousseau, Camus, Maya Angelou, and Marguerite Duras. Some other texts named for this seminar were by J. S. Mill, Gosse, Sartre, and Beauvoir. The course aimed at examining "the meaning of the autobiographical or confessional project in terms of literary and philosophical ideas of the self and the extent to which autobiography is fictive or historical" (see <http://www.anglia.ac.uk/dso/catalogue/EPH2036.html>, last accessed July 2000). For Peter Suber's course, "Philosophy as Autobiography: Psychologistic, Reductive & Non-Immanent Readings of Philosophy," see note 28.

25. Michael Davis, *The Autobiography of Philosophy: Rousseau's The Reveries of the Solitary Walker* (Lanham, Md.: Rowan and Littlefield, 1999), 2, 6.

26. Ibid., 7.

27. Donald P. Verene, "The Limits of Argument: Argument and Autobiography," *Philosophy and Rhetoric* 26, 1 (1993): 1–8; Anton Donoso, "Philosophy as Autobiography: A Study of the Person of Miguel de Unamuno," *Personalist* 49 (1968): 183–196.

28. Suber taught this course in the spring of 1999–2000 at the philosophy department of Earlham College. Quotations and a bibliography belonging to this course are found at the course's Web page: <http://www.earlham.edu/~peters/courses/meta/autobio.htm#bibliography> (last accessed December 2001).

29. Susan Sontag, "'Thinking against Oneself': Reflections on Cioran," in *Styles of Radical Will* (New York: Farrar, Straus, Giroux, 1969), 78.

30. Jo-Ann Pilardi, *Simone de Beauvoir Writing the Self: Philosophy becomes Autobiography* (Westport, Conn.: Greenwood Press, 1999).

31. Jacques Derrida, *The Ear of the Other: Otobiography, Transference, Translation*, tr. Peggy Kamuf, ed. Christie V. McDonald (New York: Schocken Books, 1985), 13.

32. Lois W. Banner, "Biography and Autobiography: Intermixing the Genres," *a/b: Auto/Biography Studies* 8, 2 (1993): 162.

33. Edward H. Madden and Marian C. Madden, "Philosophical Biography: The American Scene," *Transactions of the Charles S. Pierce Society: A Quarterly Journal in American Philosophy* 28 (1992): 609, 635; Danny Postel, "The Life and the Mind," *The Chronicle of Higher Education*. Available at: <http://www.chronicle.com/free/v48/i39/39a01601.htm> (last accessed June 7, 2002); Timothy J. Madigan, "Philosophical Biographies," *Philosophy Now* 35 (2002): 26–28; Richard Freadman, "Genius and the Dutiful Life: Ray Monk's *Wittgenstein* and the Biography of the Philosopher as Sub-genre," *Biography* 25, 2 (2002): 301–342.

34. Julian Baggini, "The Biographers: Can We Learn Anything Important from the Biographies of the Great Philosophers?" *The Philosophers' Magazine* 7 (1999): 14–15. Also available at TPM on-line: <http://www.philosophers.co.uk/current/biography.htm> (last accessed March 31, 2001).
35. Susan Sontag, *Under the Sign of Saturn* (New York: Doubleday, 1991), 111.
36. Alan Sheridan, *André Gide: A Life in the Present* (Cambridge: Harvard University Press, 1999), xvii.
37. Toril Moi, *Simone Beauvoir: The Making of an Intellectual Woman* (Oxford: Blackwell, 1994), 3, 4, 7.
38. Amélie Oksenberg Rorty, "Witnessing Philosophers," *Philosophy and Literature* 22, 2 (1998): 327.

CHAPTER 2

Philosophy, Self-Reflection, and Life-Writing

> I am accused of causing young people to acquiesce in subjectivity. Maybe, for a moment. But how would it be possible to eliminate all the phantoms of objectivity that act as an audience, etc., except stressing the category of the separate individual. Under the pretext of objectivity the aim has been to sacrifice individualities entirely. That is the crux of the matter.
>
> Søren Kierkegaard, *The Diary of Søren Kierkegaard*

In every other philosophical autobiography and similar autographic statements, the relation between philosophy, self-reflection, and life-writing tends to surface differently. Authors' reasons for writing an autobiography often have a dominant sway over the style and content of the work. Philosophers have written autobiographical texts with the purpose of defending their philosophy, explaining their philosophical way of life, or with some other intentions, such as presenting an exemplary life or attaining self-understanding and transformation. In this chapter I conceptualize several philosophical autobiographies to show how differently the threads of philosophy, self-reflection, and self-narration can be knotted together. In contrast to most other readings of these autobiographical texts, I accentuate the autobiographer's description of the role of philosophy within his or her life.

THE SEVENTH LETTER

An illustrious ancient text in defense of philosophy is Plato's "Seventh Letter."[1] In this farewell letter to Dion's relatives and friends in Sicily, Plato justifies himself for having instructed Dion and Dionysius in philosophy. It also contains instructions to Dion's friends about the philosophical–political path to be taken in their situation at that time.

Plato conveys his personal development and experiences as key factors in explaining his own conduct in Sicily. As a youth he was particularly attracted to public and political life. His preparation for public and political life had been predominantly through the teachings of Socrates. He discloses in this letter how severely affected he was by the trial and death of this teacher.

At first, Plato withdrew completely from public and political life. He became interested in political affairs again only after a change occurred in the Athenian government. Nonetheless, his political ambitions were and remained considerably subdued.

Plato describes how, through continuously watching the policies of state, he became strengthened in his idea that only through the right rule of philosophy can justice be done to the public and to the individual. In spite of this conviction, he consciously adopted a strategy of waiting for an opportune moment for involvement in public and political life.

Plato reports his three journeys to Sicily. His motives for these visits were purely in obedience to his conscience and in allegiance to reason and justice. Although "the opportune moment" seems to have arrived when Plato was invited to instruct Sicily's rulers, it was still not an invitation to establish a utopia. Plato's attempts at instructing Dionysius in true philosophy and virtue failed, due to Dionysius's wrong comprehension of philosophy. Another cause for Plato's failure is attributed to the negative influences of persons at Dionysius's court.

That Dion, a convert to Plato's philosophy, had been exiled from Sicily added to the graveness of the situation. When Dion impetuously returned to the island, he was murdered by two false friends. Plato's apology aims to articulate that Dion died a noble death. The events at Sicily may appear to others—most of all to Plato's fellow citizens, the Athenians—as bizarre. But in light of Socrates's trial and condemnation, Plato sees Dion's murder as that of a Socratic-like victim.

As a consequence of this failed mission, Plato's initial belief is strengthened anew; only under specially favorable circumstances can political philosophy be applied to the ruling of states. Dion's relatives and friends are counseled to take this lesson to heart. The apologetic letter intends to show not only Plato's virtuous philosophy as true against Dionysius's false attempts to philosophize; it also shows Plato's philosophy as conservative and not revolutionary in its practice. The latter appears here as a consequence of the trauma Plato suffered through Socrates's death. The "Seventh Letter" reveals Plato's political thought as pragmatic at best, but one could also consider it to disclose a slightly opportunistic side of Platonian utopianism.

THE MEDITATIONS

Another early text in this genre is "The Meditations" or, as Marcus Aurelius Antoninus named it, "To Himself."[2] Except for its opening pages it is not clear why "To Himself" can be considered autobiographical in the usual sense of the word. The main body of the text consists of philosophical advice on how to live a virtuous life. Nevertheless, one should keep in mind that when Marcus Aurelius addresses himself with these maxims on the good life, many of the moral and character issues he dwells on are obviously not just universal problems. These issues seem particularly to be representative of matters he needed to address in his own interior world. For example, "About what am I now employing my own soul? On every occasion I must ask myself this question, and inquire, what have I now in this part of me which they call the ruling principle? and whose soul have I now?"

Leaving aside these speculations about Marcus Aurelius's soul—that is, the major part of "To Himself" for what they are, I will only focus on the definite autobiographical section as found in the openings pages of "To Himself."

Here he renders homage to the persons who taught him the virtuous life. He recalls his great-grandfather, grandfather, parents, and brother for having taught him a particular virtue or moral lesson. In a similar vein he remembers his tutor and other teachers—that is, those who taught him philosophy: Rusticus, Apollonius, Maximus, and Alexander the Platonist—for a particular virtuous teaching, or for having been good examples. From Rusticus, Apollonius, and Maximus he received a "clear and frequent impression about living according to nature, and what kind of life that is."

Marcus Aurelius practiced what he received as good teachings, and claims to be happy to be able to imitate those virtuous lives. Thus, by presenting this inventory of virtues obtained, he actually portrays a developmental historical account of his own character.

Marcus Aurelius renders most praise to his father and to the gods, although he does not boast of having obtained the lofty character traits ascribed to these last two. Nevertheless, he records at length his indebtedness to them. In the two pages assigned to his father, virtues and only virtues are described. For example, his father was mild of temper, without vainglory, possessing perseverance, overcoming a passion for boys, being faithful to his friends, ever ready to listen to others, not superstitious, not greatly attached to life, acting according to the institutions of his country, and so on.

Present-day memories of a parent cannot differ more strikingly from the account of Marcus Aurelius. Likewise, Aurelius's meditations differ strikingly from most confessional autobiographies, which in general do not disregard failures in others or in the author's own character. I suggest that instead of disregarding this glorification of the significant persons in Aurelius's development as pure vanity—or maybe even as a "narcissistic" gloss—we may like to infer that Aurelius purposefully chose to write as he did. His style is an edifying tactic: In "To Himself" he declares that he finds nothing as morally uplifting and joyful as meditating on a virtuous life. Aurelius's autobiographical and biographical act is a moral exercise.

HISTORIA CALAMITATUM

Peter (or Pierre) Abélard's *Historia Calamitatum* (*The Story of My Misfortunes*) is, like Plato's autobiographical text, a long letter.[3] It has been compared with Augustine's *Confessions*, although its aim has more in common with Boethius's *The Consolation of Philosophy*. Boethius described in this autobiographical book how he found comfort in his sufferings (imprisonment) through a dialogue with the metaphorical image of a majestic lady, whom he identifies as Philosophy and calls his nurse.[4]

Abélard's consolation differs from Boethius's: Abélard considers the comfort given through words of wisdom inferior to the comfort obtained through knowledge of the actual sufferings of others. He hopes that by recording his own sufferings, others may discover that their sufferings are as nothing when compared to his.

Abélard starts the *Historia Calamitatum* with a description of how as a young man he was attracted to "logical reasoning" more than to any other kind of philosophy. He compares himself with one of the ancient peripatetics because he had traveled all over France in search of schools where logic was taught outstandingly. But years thereafter, he traces the start of all his misfortunes precisely to one of these excellent schools: the school of the distinguished dialectician William of Champeaux in Paris. At the beginning of Abélard's relationship with Champeaux, Abélard was a well-liked new student. Nevertheless, Champeaux changed his attitude after having been frequently attacked by Abélard in disputations, which were won by Abélard. Champeaux is said to have envied Abélard, particularly when the latter's fame spread and the student established a school of his own through his teachings.

But then, for several years, Abélard has to withdraw from his teaching post to his native Britanny due to an illness. When he returns to Paris, he finds that the teaching position he held has been given by

Champeaux to his opponent.

It seems then providential that Abélard, during his illness, had become interested in theology, possibly through parental influences on him. When he finds his teaching position in Paris occupied, he decides to take up theological studies with Anselm of Loan, another prominent teacher.

In theology Abélard soon demonstrates his excellence as well, and soon starts to teach theology in addition to philosophy. He then returns to Paris, where he begins to instruct numerous students. Fame and prosperity become part of his daily life. Abélard observes that his success makes him feel as if he is the only philosopher in world. He traces his digression from his habitual chastity, and his loss of control of his sexual life, to the mental and emotional state brought on by his new renown and affluence. He finds himself lost in pride and sensuality.

Abélard interprets the continuity of his story of misfortunes as the cure for "the diseases" of pride and sensuality: namely, his affair with Heloïse, her pregnancy, their marriage, Heloïse taking the nun's veil, Abélard's castration by Heloïse's angry family members, and Abélard becoming a monk.

Heloïse's initial objection to marriage is said to have originated in a particular philosophical–theological idea about married life being a distraction and burden for a wise person. In her attempt to persuade Abélard not to marry her she refers to the single lives of the Hebrew Nazarites, the followers of Elias, St. Paul, St. Jerome, St. Augustine, and the virtuous lives of Cicero and Seneca. However, Abélard decides that morality and the honor of Heloïse's family obliges them to get married. Heloïse's wish is fulfilled only after their short-lived marriage.

Abélard considers that the essential lessons he had to learn had been expressed in sayings of Augustine and Seneca. Augustine stated in his *Confessions* that the wise are so called not so much for their erudition as for their virtuous lives, and Seneca recommends philosophers to give up everything else for philosophy.

The final decision of the couple to retreat to a monastic way of life makes an end to their sensual passions and renews their dedication to the "path of the wise," but this is not the end of Abélard's sufferings. Abélard, as a newly religious zealot, severely criticizes the worldly ways he encounters among his fellow monks. He accuses his monastic order of scandalous living, and this makes him quite unpopular among fellow monks and other Christians. As a last refuge, he chooses the life of a hermit and, in his new found hermitage, "The Paraclete," he returns to teaching. He sees himself as a follower of the Pythagoreans and Plato, who also founded their schools in solitary desert places, remote from city life. Questions from his students inspire him to write a tract. This tract on the unity and trinity of God becomes extremely popular, but it is a new cause for persecution. The tract is condemned by the Church Council and burned, in spite of Abélard's showing that it did not contain any dogma contradicting that of the Church.

Abélard describes the persecution by his fellow monks and other clergy: They would even have killed him if they had had the chance. Life in a distant country among non-Christians seems preferable. Abélard finishes narrating his never-ending troubles by quoting from the Psalms, the New Testament, and St. Jerome, to convince his readers that hatred and persecution are natural to those who please God.

At first he interprets his sufferings as being caused by his own pride and sensuality. After having been "cured" of what he describes as his sins, he believes that his remaining sufferings are caused by the unrighteousness of others. The moral of the story is that he and others should be encouraged by all sufferings, since all will "work together for good to them that love God."

THE DELIVERANCE FROM ERROR

Al-Ghazali's "Confessions," or "The Deliverance from Error," was written about the same time as the *Historia Calamitatum*, but in the region Abélard dreamed of fleeing to.[5] Al-Ghazali was educated at Nishapur and Baghdad. He was one of the great thinkers of the Arab world and influential among Jewish and Christian philosophers in the Middle Ages. He can be considered Islam's "antiphilosopher" par excellence, since after Al-Ghazali "philosophy as a major discipline of study disappeared from the Islamic world, except for Persia."[6]

Al-Ghazali explains in his confessions the central place he gives to Sufism within Orthodox Islam. His confessions are a reply to a "brother in the faith" who is interested in knowing Al-Ghazali's experiences. More precisely, Al-Ghazali is asked why he stopped teaching at Baghdad University and years later resumed teaching at Nishapur.

To answer these questions, Al-Ghazali sets out to summarize his search and research in the vast ocean of theology and philosophy, from the time of his boyhood until he wrote "The Deliverance from Error" (i.e., a few years before his death). He delineates in his reply the different issues that guided his search.

He tells of having been struck by the contradictions found in trying to separate truth from falsehood. The goal in his studies became to ascertain "the basis of certitude." The account of how he arrives at certainties in life is the astonishing chronicle of how a philosophical question can bear on a person's inner life and development. Al-Ghazali discovers that he cannot trust the evidence of reason more than that of the senses, and he becomes even more doubtful when he reflects on the state of consciousness in sleep. He is particularly interested in the idea that there are different states of consciousness, and that there might be a state of consciousness in which people can know absolute truth (i.e., truth based in experience that was not obtained through the senses or reason). This state of consciousness he compares to the condition the Sufis call "hal" or ecstasy. In such a state of suspension of sense perception the Sufis claim to have access to a realm of visionary insight beyond the realm of the intellect.

Although Al-Ghazali had been till then a convinced skeptic, Sufism incites in him a state of crisis or, as he calls it, an unhappy state, which lasts for several months. He understands that he must test the claims of Sufism through personally experiencing these teachings, yet he remains in doubt about Sufism's primary assumptions for proving truth. He describes his healing from this "mental malady" to a sovereign act of God: The light of God penetrated his heart.

This experience causes him to research afresh among Scholastic theology, philosophical systems, and Sufism. He describes his research findings and relates these to some of his outstanding writings (e.g., *The Destruction of the Philosophers*, *The Just Balance*, and *Alchemy of Happiness*).

Through studying the methods and teachings of Sufism it becomes clear to him that study alone is not sufficient for reaching the spiritual stage these teachings point to. To reach that stage of purity and moral perfection one needs "transport, ecstasy, and the transformation of the moral being." Al-Ghazali then understands that he has to free himself from personal attachments, from worldly living. He has the insight that his motives for teaching at the University of Baghdad are based on a vain desire for personal glorification, and that he lacked in seeking God's honor.

For six months he feels torn between a desire to give up his respectable teaching job and the fear of losing his material belongings and a professional, secure future. He was so thoroughly disturbed by this inner conflict that he lost his speech, had stomach problems, and even stopped eating and drinking entirely. His physicians considered that the illness was caused by a great sadness, and the cure would depend on terminating the cause of dejection.

Al-Ghazali figures that through this illness God made it easy for him to sacrifice his possessions and position. He pretends to go on the pilgrimage to Mecca, although he intends to travel to Syria and never to return. In the Mosque of Damascus he lives a solitary life for two years, practicing the devotion and exercises learned from Sufi masters. However, unlike most Sufi neophytes, who are in personal contact with their teachers, Al-Ghazali writes about having been instructed through Sufi *writings* only (e.g., through the works of Abu Talib of Mecca, Hareth el Muhasibi, Junaid, Shibli, and Abu Yezid Bustami). He continues from Damascus to Jerusalem, Mecca, Medina, and Hedjaz.

When he returns to Iran after ten years of solitude and meditation, he is able to assure others from his personal experiences that "the Sufis are the true pioneers on the path of God." He finds that returning to family life with its daily cares disturbs his meditative calm. Nevertheless, he continues at irregular times the practice of having devotional ecstasies. He concludes "The Deliverance from Error" with a philosophical analysis of the reality of inspiration and its importance for humankind. He credits Sufism with having taught him several valuable certainties, of which he names in particular the "knowledge of the true nature of inspiration."

COMPENDIUM VITAE ERASMI ROTERODAMI

About 400 years after Al-Ghazali, Desiderius Erasmus, a Catholic philosopher from The Netherlands, likewise rejected Scholastic philosophy and theology. But unlike Al-Ghazali's turn to mysticism, Erasmus turned to ancient philosophy and humanistic studies. Erasmus wrote an "inventory" of his life that is best read in the context of the letter of which it is a section.[7]

The "Compendium Vitae" starts with a sentence in Greek stating, "The life is to be kept secret." The letter, including the short autobiography, is addressed to Conradus Goclenius. Goclenius is asked in this letter to take care not only of Erasmus's literary legacy and posthumous reputation, but also receives directions on how to disburse Erasmus's heritage.

We know from this letter why Erasmus wrote the "Compendium Vitae," and why he wanted it to be kept secret. Erasmus describes himself as being surrounded by treacherous and base persons who should have as little knowledge as possible about him during his lifetime. Erasmus finds his life to be an "Iliad of ills." It seems to him that nobody was born more unhappy than he.

He has very few friends as faithful as Goclenius. Although Erasmus is confident of having obtained the Pope's favor and protection, he knows that he not only has admirers but also enemies among Catholics and Protestants. Erasmus finds living among his fellow Christians quite unbearable; he complains about being slandered and spied on. His life is endangered from time to time, but he is most concerned about his posthumous reputation. This latter issue seems to have been the main reason why he wrote his biographical profile.

Erasmus writes in the "Compendium Vitae" about his life in a very detached manner. That he chooses to write about himself in the third-person singular instead of using the intimate first-person singular might indicate his feelings toward the public he wrote the "Compendium Vitae" for; that is, the multitude of his enemies and the misinformed. His friends, however, know him in person, and through personal letters to them.

Erasmus begins the "Compendium Vitae" by narrating his descent. He reveals details about the family to which he was born: His parents never married, his father became a priest, and his grandmother was responsible for bringing him up. The father considered his son's education so important that Erasmus was sent to elementary school at the age of four. Both Erasmus's parents died during the plague, when he was about thirteen years old.

Erasmus's caretaker decides that instead of going to university the boy should become a monk. Erasmus had no dislike for religion, but he loathed joining the religious life. Yet years later he is drawn into the monastic life through a friend named Cornelius. Cornelius, a member of the monastic order at Emmaus (Steyn), showed the life in his order as ideal. In particular, it seemed perfect for helping Erasmus to realize his early objective of studying. After a while, the young Erasmus understood that the order he considered joining was not quite ideal: "He made preparations to leave before his profession, he was restrained partly by natural shyness, partly by threats and partly by necessity."

Yet he makes his monastic profession, and after his entry he travels through Europe and becomes acquainted with several of the Church's primates. Erasmus is repelled by the theological doctrines and attitudes he encounters in these religious courts. He fears that his critical spirit will undermine the theological foundations of the Church and he will end up as a heretic.

Erasmus also describes his weak health—he suffered easily from fevers throughout his life—and he presents a character sketch of himself: "His character was straightforward, and his dislike of falsehood such that even as a child he hated other boys who told lies, and in old age even the sight of such people affected him physically."

The only book he mentions from his entire opus is the *Adagia*, which was published in Venice when he was about forty years old.

In spite of his contempt for high office and his love for leisure and liberty, he becomes a councillor to Emperor Charles V. This seems to have brought about a major change in Erasmus's life, at which he hints: "The principle behind his [Erasmus's] change of costume he has explained in the first of the pamphlets in which he answered the attacks of Lee." In the continuation of the "Compendium Vitae" he confesses that only after the age of fifty was he able to retaliate against those that attacked him, but always he remains courteous.

The more one reads Erasmus's short autobiographic text, the stronger becomes the impression that much of his interesting life story remains hidden; it could not be written down by him. Clear hints to his secrecy are sentences such as "Among his friends he spoke freely—too freely sometimes." Erasmus considers his zeal for promoting the study of the humanities the main reason for being attacked by so many enemies. The "Compendium Vitae" ends with the words: "The sad business of Luther had brought him a burden of intolerable ill will; he was torn in pieces by both sides, while aiming zealously at what was best for both."

I conclude that the first sentence of the "Compendium Vitae," "The life is to be kept secret," might be more revealing than the text following it. It is not only an instruction to his friend, but a warning to all those who will read the "Compendium Vitae." The life of Erasmus remains best known through the correspondence with his friends, and not through the "Compendium Vitae." It seems obvious to me that Erasmus's fear of accusations of heresy kept him from writing openly about his life, including conveying frankly his philosophical development and convictions in the formal autobiographical statement. His anxiousness was such that he feared the letter containing the "Compendium Vitae"—which he sent to Goclenius with all possible precaution—would be intercepted by his enemies.

Nevertheless, the text discloses the harsh conditions a critical philosopher was likely to encounter during the Reformation's high season. Erasmus phrases this condition to his confidant, Conradus Goclenius: "As for my own position, I can tell you it is fairly confused. I have to cope here with desperate people—real furies they are."

VITA NUOVA

Plato and Erasmus are not the only authors of philosophical autobiographies who felt restrained in revealing their life stories or their philosophy for political, religious, social, cultural, or other reasons. Another example of revealing and concealing aspects of the philosopher's life is found in the *Vita Nuova*: Dante Alighieri is anxiously concealing the identity of the lady he loves.[8]

In this extremely original text Dante combines poetry, prose, philosophy, and theology with autobiography. The book is dedicated to the poet Guido Cavalcanti, "his first friend." Dante married at about the age of twenty, but his wife seems not to have been the chosen subject of the passions described in the *Vita Nuova*. The recipient of Dante's great love remains hidden. From the many names named in the book the name of Beatrice is chosen as a pseudoname for his beloved. Next to the characters of Beatrice and Dante there is another dominant character in the narrative: the Lord of Love. This character might only be an allegorical figure invented by Dante for the sake of expressing the sensations he observed in himself. The Lord of Love does not necessarily personify another male character, as one might easily suppose from a Freudian perspective. The Lord of Love and Beatrice are separate characters; nevertheless, they are intrinsically related. Beatrice is identified with Love; she is even named Love in some paragraphs of the *Vita Nuova*. Another name for the Lord of Love is "Lord of all virtues." And his lordship differentiates himself from Dante in the following self-definition: "I am like the centre of the circle, equidistant from all points on the circumference, but you are not."

To remind us, and to accentuate, that we don't know who Beatrice is, the description of the object of Dante's affection undergoes additional transformations: Love for "Lady Bice" turns into love for several other ladies. Mark Musa maintains that Beatrice is one person, but a person associated with the miraculous (the Trinity, the Virgin Mary, and so on). Musa also notes that "pretended devotion to another woman was a common device of the troubadour poets."

The narrative of the *Vita Nuova* consists mainly of the description of the meetings—real and imaginary—that Dante has with Beatrice. The narrative presents in poetry, prose, and critical (philosophical) analysis how these events had a forceful and lasting influence on Dante's emotional, mental, and spiritual life.

Dante and Beatrice first meet each other when they are both nine years old, and their second meeting is nine years later. Through their first meeting—basically no more than a glance that the two children gave each other—love takes control of Dante's soul. Dante interprets this experience in categories derived from Albert Magnus's *De Spiritu et Respiratione*. The first encounter with Beatrice creates in him such purity of heart that for the rest of his life his affections will be always ruled "by the trusted counsel of reason."

During their second encounter, Beatrice's greeting induces in Dante a spiritual state he characterizes as "the very summit of bliss" and "intoxication." The state of ecstasy following the encounter leaves him a "marvelous vision" of the Lord of Love holding Beatrice in his arms. However, the ecstatic vision also includes a saddening prophetic facet; later on one understands that it foretold Beatrice's untimely death. Two other deaths lead up to—scheme, as it were—the tragic end of the love of Dante's life: the death of a "young lady of exceedingly kind aspects" and that of Beatrice's father.

However, in comparison to Dante's mourning over these two deceased persons, Beatrice's sudden refusal to greet him at their third meeting causes greater affliction. Whereas Beatrice's greeting aroused in Dante exultation and spiritual vision, the absence of the anticipated greeting induces great sadness. But a dream revelation resolves why Beatrice refused to greet him. Dante's transfiguration of the object of his love appears to have misled even Beatrice into thinking that Dante "did harm" to one of the women he met on his travels. Guided by this revelation, Dante is inspired to write a ballad. He declares in these verses—but actually the words are not his, but from Love's own person—that he is and always will be Beatrice's faithful servant.

In Chapter 20 there is a word play referring to Dante's friend Cavalcanti, who asks Dante for a definition of love. In reply, Dante describes in a short sonnet the nature of love: The heart is the center where love latently dwells till the power of love is brought into action by "a worthy lady's beauty."

A few days after the death of Beatrice's father, Dante himself becomes seriously ill for nine days. During the last day on his sickbed he starts thinking of Beatrice and becomes delirious through the idea that she might be dead as well. Visions of angels and the dead Beatrice make him desire to be united with her even more. But Dante wakes up from these dark visions, and not long thereafter is cured from his illness and composes a poem (a *canzone*) about his dark precognition.

These events trigger in Dante further reflections on Love. In Chapter 25 we are presented with a discussion on this topic: Dante denies that Love exists "as if it were a thing in itself," or as a body. Instead of being an intellectual or bodily substance, it is "an accident in substance." He refers to the Philosopher (i.e., Aristotle), from whose perspective it would appear that the word "Love" is used in the *Vita Nuova* as if it were a substance, a body: "Love" moves, it comes, it is in locomotion, hence it is a body. Dante explains that he uses the word "Love" not in this Aristotelian sense; its use should be understood within the tradition of classical Latin poetry, although he writes in the vernacular. He shows through examples from Virgil, Lucan, Horace, Homer, and Ovid that these poets spoke "to inanimate objects as if they possessed sense and reason and have made them speak to each other, and that they did this not only with real things but also with unreal things." Like these poets, the vernacular poets of Dante's day should be able to give an account of "the dress of an image or rhetorical coloring" and be able to explain the true meaning of poetic imagery (i.e., its allegorical nature).

Whereas all poems in the *Vita Nuova* are love poems in praise of Beatrice and Love, Dante's great sadness and mourning over Beatrice's death is an additional sentiment introduced in the last fifteen chapters of the book.

A new vision of Beatrice, in which Dante seems to see her as when they first met, convinces him that no one else can ever replace her. This spiritual revelation causes Dante to repent of having allowed himself to be tempted by someone else not long after Beatrice's death. He expresses regret over the "very gracious lady" who had appeared in his life, and whose compassionate looks he had found difficult to resist. But he dedicates himself anew, and now completely, to the love of his youth.

According to Musa, Dante gave in a later work (i.e., *Convivio*), an allegorical explanation of this "very gracious lady" as symbolizing philosophy. In the same endnote Musa refers to Boethius's *Consolation of Philosophy* as Dante's "first investigation" in philosophy.

Coinciding in the *Vita Nuova* and the *Consolation of Philosophy* is the combination of poetry with prose writing. But unlike Boethius's "Lady Philosophy," who can be understood by reason, Dante cannot grasp with his mental powers the nature of Beatrice. Dante refers to the second book of the *Metaphysics*, in which Aristotle shows that in general the "mind functions in relation to those blessed souls [such as Beatrice's] as the weak eye does in relation to the sun." Musa comments here that Dante knew "the Philosopher" through St. Aquinas.

The book ends with a climactic, "miraculous" vision of Beatrice, which persuades Dante to write more on his blessed lady in a "more worthy fashion." The outcome of this resolution is found in *The Divine Comedy*.

This prophetic and visionary book, which Dante named *Commedia*, is often considered his autobiography constructed as a spiritual voyage. There is an autobiographical touch to the story in that Dante meets on his trip the authors he admires, friends, enemies, acquaintances, family, and even his beloved Beatrice. But apart from recalling these persons, and perhaps also the portrayal of how meeting these and other persons affect him, there seems to be no further explicit biographic disclosures about Dante or his life.

The account of the journey is based on an event in Dante's life that took place during Easter in 1300. Dante began transcribing this experience into poetry about eight years later, and worked on it about twelve years. In contradistinction to the *Vita Nuova*, the narrative of *The Divine Comedy* takes place mainly in other worldly realms (Hell, Purgatory, and Paradise).

In Limbo, the upper part of Hell, Dante meets the philosophers Aristotle, Socrates, Plato, Diogenes, Anaxagoras, Thales, Empedocles, Heraclitus, Cicero, Seneca, and Zeno. Time and ephemeral continuity seems only to exist in the span of four days in which Dante travels through Purgatory. Thereafter he enters Paradise, where he meets Augustine, Bonaventure, and Anselm; these philosophers have their abode in the fourth Angelic order of Paradise. If one takes Dante's comedy seriously, one is led to conclude that Paradise is a place without exit. In spite of the persecution and exile Dante experienced during the years he worked on *The Divine Comedy*, his spirit is kindled "by the love which moves the sun and the other stars," and apparently sojourns in an estate imbued with divine delight. Dante formulated the aim of *The Divine Comedy* as "to remove those living in this life from their state of misery, and to lead them to a state of happiness."[9]

Soon after Dante's completion of *The Divine Comedy* he entered the lasting rest he had so loftily glorified in his masterpiece.

MY OWN LIFE

David Hume states, in a foreword first published in a posthumous edition of his *Essays: Moral, Political and Literary* (1777), that he never acknowledged his juvenile work, *A Treatise of Human Nature*. Moreover, he considers that work a failure. He asks his critics to direct their arguments not at what he wrote in *A Treatise of Human Nature*, but to the recast of it as found in *Essays: Moral, Political and Literary*, and *The Enquiry in Human Understanding*.

The edition of *Essays: Moral, Political and Literary* published during Hume's life had as a preface only Hume's short autobiography entitled "My Own Life." The additional foreword in the posthumous edition emphases statements about *A Treatise of Human Nature* also found in Hume's life narrative.

"My Own Life" provides a precise account of how *A Treatise of Human Nature* came about, why a recast was needed, and in which books its mature content can be found. One may suspect that a strong incentive for writing an autobiographical text had been Hume's desire to make clear the status of his juvenile work. He appears here regretful and apologetic for its too early publication.

This is not the only apology made in "My Own Life": Hume's first paragraph is an apology for autobiography. He finds that a lengthy autobiography easily impresses others of its author's vanity. Accordingly, one should make an autobiography as short as possible. Hume fears that even the very short history of himself—about eight pages—might be considered evidence of vain self-esteem. The only appropriate reason for writing his life he finds in presenting it as the history of his writings.

Posterity owes thanks to the historian in Hume who deemed it proper to fill in some historical data on the subject matter as well. Thus, on the first page Hume narrates when and where he was born, his descent from an aristocratic family, and about his brother, his sister, his economic status, and his education. He decides to conclude the last page "historically," with a description of his own character. He portrays himself as self-controlled and of a mild disposition, "of an open, social, and cheerful humour, capable of attachment, but little susceptible of enmity, and of great moderation," and so on.

Though in Rousseau's lengthy *Confessions* the author appears unconcerned to be considered an indulger in vainglory, both Rousseau and Hume find it appropriate to show their characters to be as virtuous as possible; indeed, as blameless. However, Hume remains uneasy about the moral excellence he ascribes to himself. The last paragraph of "My Own Life" is as apologetic as the first: "I cannot say there is no vanity in making this funeral oration of myself, but I hope it is not a misplaced one; and this is a matter of fact which is easily cleared and ascertained."

In-between the personal opening and closing statements Hume describes his intellectual career and what contributed to it. As a young man he developed an aversion to everything except philosophy and general learning, but his "slender fortune" did not allow him to comfortably satisfy his intellectual desires. Instead of exclusively studying Cicero, Virgil, and other classical writers, he had to engage in an additional trade.

With recommendations from some influential merchants he tried to make a living in Bristol, but he soon found "that scene totally unsuitable." This failure was followed by a retreat to France, where he composed *A Treatise of Human Nature*. Hume writes about the publication of this treatise: "It fell *dead-born from the press*, without reaching such distinction, as even to excite a murmur among the zealots." He overcame this disappointment by publishing a second book, the first part of the *Essays*.

In spite of Hume's apparent meager resources, he had the good fortune of making eminent friends, such as the Marquis of Annandale, General St. Clair, the Earl of Hertford, General Conway, and others, who looked after his welfare or found him suitable positions. Through these influential friends he became aide-de-camp to General Grant, librarian to the faculty of advocates, secretary to the British embassy in Paris, and at last he received an invitation to become Britain's undersecretary of state after his return to Edinburgh in 1767. Within thirty-five years his "slender fortune" grew into a small fortune, and into wealth; he describes himself as having become "very opulent" in 1769.

Though Hume explicitly states he was inspired to write his *History of England* by the mere fact that as a librarian he had a large library for his use, there are no details about what precisely inspired him to write his philosophy books. About his philosophical writings he only expresses regret that those who criticize him continue to do so on the basis of his juvenile work. However, he takes these criticisms in a positive spirit; he decides never to reply to them.

Hume intended in his self-narrative to remain within a history of his writings, and from these he only mentions the most important ones by name. This leaves the reader with the impression that Hume indeed sought to present himself in all humility and strove sincerely to avoid the vainglory he apparently so disliked.

KAHLIL GIBRAN: A SELF-PORTRAIT

This self-portrait consists of some of Gibran's letters, which were edited, translated, and introduced by Anthony R. Ferkis.[11] Plato, Simone Weil, and Erasmus projected their autobiographic endeavors into a single epistle; the self-portrayal of the Lebanese poet, painter, and philosopher comes about in forty-eight letters, addressed mainly to Mikhail Naimy (a leading literary figure in Lebanon during Gibran's days) and to May Zaideh (a Lebanese writer), and some additional letters to friends and family.

The letters Sartre wrote as his "wartime diaries" were written with the intention of publication at a future date. It is uncertain if a similar intention existed with Gibran when he wrote the letters framed as *A Self-Portrait*. However, the fact that Gibran wrote an autobiographical novel, *The Broken Wings*, seems to suggest that he had no objections to autobiographical acts. Moreover, he considered *The Broken Wings* the best book he ever wrote.

Most of the letters in *A Self-Portrait* were written to friends in Lebanon or elsewhere in the world during Gibran's long exile in the United States. The letters are authentic autobiographical texts, yet the mosaic-like self-portrait could not exist without the editor's restoration, as it were, through the introduction at the beginning of the book and in the comments accompanying each letter.

It seems right to question not only the nature of this self-portrait, but also Gibran's place among philosophers and literati. Although more than 9 million copies of *The Prophet* have been sold as poetry and wisdom literature (and Gibran's other works are also selling well), from a rigorously academic point of view the philosophical and literary value of Gibran's work is not obvious to all. There are enormous differences in opinion about Gibran's work. Robert Irwin finds Gibran the "favorite poet of those who don't like poetry," while Liesl Schillinger describes *The Prophet* as "ecstatically embraced by scarf-swathed disciples of Isadora Duncan and Madame Blavatsky, hash-brownie-munching beatniks, herbal tea-drinking New Agers and, evidently, by quite a lot of ordinary people as well."[12]

However, no matter how critically one may look at Gibran's creations, at least within the genre of New Age philosophy Gibran's opus must be considered a pearl of extraordinary worth. And these days, New Age philosophy seems the only kind of philosophy still speaking to the masses.

The letters in *A Self-Portrait* are drenched in an exile rhetoric, expressing a great yearning for Gibran's native Lebanon. Some letters contain advice to, and character analyses of, the friends he writes to.

Characteristic of many of these letters is also a sense of unfulfillment, even to the extent that he denies being an artist and a poet. Gibran is tortured by "a hunger" to produce great and profound works of art, and at the same time, he questions his talents: "Will Gibran ever be able to deflect the people's eyes from the skulls and thorns towards the light and the truth? Or will Gibran be like so many others who returned from this world to Eternity without leaving behind any reminders of their existence? I don't know."

An example of one of Gibran's inner struggles is the following. In 1908, when Gibran had already published some of his popular works, he intended to publish a philosophy book, *Religion and Religiousness*, of which he expected much. Unfortunately he never finished or published this book.

Gibran was highly critical of his own work. Not only the philosophy book, but the "many volummes" of poetry and prose he wrote as a youth were never published. He was also aware of "a deep abyss" between himself and other writers, whom he considered in bondage to "superficial literary words" and lacking in spiritual freedom. He considered a good critical ability to originate in an ability to write, not vice versa. He writes to Mikhail Naimy, "You are a poet and a thinker before everything else, and your unique power of criticism is the outcome of your keen poetic thinking and feeling." One may conclude that Gibran's self-criticism might also have been based on his artistic expertise.

Gibran metaphorically compared his life, and life in general, to the seasons of the year. The spring is his childhood and years of youth in the mountain village of Bsharré. Gibran observes that the things he loved as a child remain important throughout his life; he sees himself as a prisoner of time and circumstances. He submits to his destiny. Yet in spite of this deterministic self-understanding, he commends Mikhail Naimy for having interpreted his work "with hope," with a look toward Gibran's future and not his past. Gibran considers his past to have consisted "only of threads, not woven. It has also been stones of various sizes and shapes, but not a structure."

He describes his stay in Paris to Ameen Guraieb, and encourages him to visit the "City of Knowledge and Arts." Whereas Gibran developed an antagonistic bond with the city of New York (and U.S. city life in general), perhaps an old cultural–colonial bond between the French and the Lebanese gave him a sense of being at home in the French capital. In Paris the museums, the opera, and other cultural monuments inspired him; he was particularly impressed with Victor Hugo, Rousseau, Chateaubriand, Renan, Raphael, Michelangelo, Da Vinci, Beethoven, Wagner, Mozart, and Rossini. These (although not all of them are French) were "great men who love great deeds, and this is the light which causes us—the sons of knowledge—to walk proudly upon the path of life."

A Self-Portrait gives insight into the lifelong relationship Gibran had with May Ziadeh. According to Jamil Jabre, "It is difficult to imagine a man and a woman falling in love without having known or met one another except by correspondence. . . . This was the case of the great Lebanese woman writer, May Ziadeh and Kahlil Gibran." Whatever the relationship between Kahlil and May might have been, the letters in *A Self-Portrait* mainly reveal their literary ties. Ziadeh reviewed all of Gibran's books and Gibran replies to these reviews elegantly. For example, he distances himself from her interpretation of the main figure in *The Madman*, and claims that the words of the madman do not represent his own feelings and thoughts. Yet in another letter to Ziadeh he states, "The Soul, May, does not see anything in life save that which is in the soul itself. It does not believe except in its own private event, and when it experiences something, the outcome becomes a part of it." It is obvious from this statement, and from Gibran's words to Mikhail Naimy, that although the type of madness expressed in *The Madman* was not his own, he too confesses to having an intimate knowledge of it: "I say that madness is the first step towards unselfishness. Be mad, Meesha [Mikhail]. Be mad and tell us what is behind the veil of 'sanity.' The purpose of life is to bring us closer to these secrets, and madness is the only means. . . . Your mad brother."

In 1922 Gibran's doctor advised him to stay away from all cities. To prevent a further deterioration of his generally weak health, Gibran moved to Boston and there rented a small cottage near the sea with his sister. His heart condition improved, but this period of recovery caused a one-year break in his work schedule and postponed the publication of other works for several years. He observes that his sister's manner of orderly living was a hindrance to his creativity and he longs to return to his own "hermitage" in New York. Chaotic living sharpened his imagination.

In spite of the good medical care, his health remained miserable. In 1928 Gibran observed that he found pleasure in being ill. The tranquility he found through it brought him closer to abstract things. Furthermore, thoughts of death came to his mind. He writes to May Ziadeh, "Whenever I think of the Departure which the people call Death, I find pleasure in such thinking and great longing for such departure." But there was "the word" that he had not yet spoken, and until then cessation of his work seemed "more bitter than gall." Gibran lived on creatively for some more years. The last letters of *A Self-Portrait* are mainly accounts of his illness. He kept on longing to return to Lebanon, where at last he was welcomed in his coffin and awarded a burial place and memorial.

SPIRITUAL AUTOBIOGRAPHY

As an introduction to the autobiographies of Simone Weil and Hazel Barnes, I think it appropriate to insert some paragraphs on the very few women philosophers who wrote autobiographical texts (letters, journals, essays, novels, and autobiography "proper"). Among these exceptional females we find Lou Andreas-Salomé, Hazel E. Barnes, Simone de Beauvoir, Sissela Bok, Mary Daly, Mary Hays, Elizabeth Hamilton, Mary Harris Jones, Rosa Luxemburg, Ayn Rand, Abigail L. Rosenthal, Anna Maria van Schurman, Susan Sontag, Gertrude Stein, Edith Stein, Mary Warnock, and Simone Weil.

Though in the twentieth century women obtained greater possibilities in this region of intellectual life, the male still predominated among the philosophical autobiographers. Hagiographies on women and autobiographies by women saints were not uncommon throughout the Middle Ages and even after; however, these saintly lives are not necessarily concerned with philosophy. In *A History of Women in the West*, one is confronted with the many limitations imposed on women in the past: "Roles for which women were destined were silent ones: motherhood and homemaking, tasks relegated to the obscurity of a domesticity that did not count and was not considered worth recounting. Did women so much as have a history?"[13]

This question answers to a great extent the question of whether women had autobiographies. Yet the general editors of *A History of Women in the West* were able to include in each volume a section named "The Woman's Voice," which contains some of the rare early texts. Until the Renaissance and Enlightenment women were in general excluded from being taught letters or writing. During the Middle Ages the "earliest personal writings by women were clearly the work of women of letters whose social and economical status was well-defined. The sources are fragmentary, but the works of the best-known figures, such as Eloise and Hildegard, allow us to enter into the more private parts of the self and to learn something about their inner development."[14]

In "Witnessing Philosophers," Amélie Oksenberg Rorty asks why there are so few woman philosophers. She suggests that women perhaps "lack the self-confidence that sustains most original male authors."[15] It appears as if females with philosophical inclinations were encouraged by their respected male colleagues to overcome this assumed "lack of self-confidence" only in their personal dialogues and correspondence. Oksenberg Rorty refers to philosophers' patronesses such as Queen Christiana, the Comtesse de Boufflers, and Mme de Chatelet, and some famous correspondence partners were Descartes and Princess Elisabeth of Bohemia, Leibniz and Lady Masham, Hume and la Comtesse de Boufflers, Rousseau and Sophie Volland, Mill and

Harriet Taylor, and Peirce and Christine Ladd Franklin. These letters show that women are not less talented in questioning, presupposing, and implying philosophical issues.

The earliest female philosopher to write an autobiography seems to have been Anna Maria van Schurman. Although she was from a Dutch background, she was born in Cologne in 1607. Her family returned to Utrecht, where van Schurman developed into a well-known scholar. She associated with Voetius, and took an active part in the Utrecht Circle. Her liberal assumption that piety and science coincide became the subject of her own criticism, and after a deep religious crisis she left the Voetians and joined the puritan movement of the Labadists. She then became one of the Frisian leaders of this revivalist group. In her autobiography, *Eucleria*, she describes her life: her childhood, her intellectual development, her intellectual and spiritual crisis, her "choosing of the best part" (in Greek, *eucleria*), and her becoming a part of the true church.[16] A model for her remarkable narrative seems to have been Augustine's *Confessions*, from which she freely quotes.

SIMONE WEIL'S SPIRITUAL AUTOBIOGRAPHY

Simone Weil draws extensively from a universal philosophical heritage in her apology for her particular way in Judeo–Christianity, yet she calls her synopsis of life a spiritual, not a philosophical, autobiography. This life narrative is one of six letters appearing, together with nine of her essays, in *Waiting for God*.[17] All texts in this book contain philosophical and autobiographical reflections on Weil's brand of religiousness, but it is in "Spiritual Autobiography" that she explicates the development of and reasons for her view.

The letter is written as a farewell to a close friend, the Catholic priest Father Perrin. Weil maintains that it is not due to Perrin that she acquired her particular beliefs, although this relationship caused her to question anew matters of faith, dogma, and sacraments. She feels for Perrin as for a father and brother: feelings of "affection, gratitude and admiration." Her friendship with Perrin would have been impossible if she had not already received much of his "message" before they had ever met. This message, she claims, she could not have received through any human influence.

During her adolescent years she had made the resolution that the problem of God had to be left alone, though, in spite of her Jewish upbringing, she "always adopted the Christian attitude as the only possible one." When she was fourteen she underwent a great despair, which she interprets as the result of feeling extremely inferior in comparison to her genius brother. After months of inner affliction she suddenly felt "the everlasting conviction that any human being, even though practically devoid of natural faculties, can penetrate to the kingdom of truth reserved for genius, if only he longs for truth and perpetually concentrates all his attention upon its attainment." She discovered only years later—when she read for the first time the New Testament—the analogy between that insight and the Gospel statement that those asking for bread will not receive stones.

From her early childhood on she remembered having associated the idea of justice with that of love for one's neighbor. Reading Marcus Aurelius convinced her of the Stoic concept of *amor fati*: "The duty of acceptance in all that concerns the will of God."

At sixteen she went through a typical teenage phase of emotional disquiet. When she contemplated a mountain landscape the idea of purity brought her inner tranquility. She recognized this meditative event as another Christian formation in her personal development. She had always felt as if she had been born into the Christian community, so there was no need to enter it, except perhaps in a dogmatic sense. Since she considered church dogma problematic, she was "prevented by a sort of shame from going into churches," though she liked being in them.

She describes her way forward into a nondogmatic spirituality as marked by three important contacts with Catholicism, "contacts . . . that really counted." From her narrative in the "Spiritual Autobiography" these three "contacts" seem to relate to her experience as a factory worker, her visit to Assisi, and her study of the New Testament in the Greek language.

The first contact was initiated by the affliction and brutality she encounted while working for ideological reasons in a car factory; she wanted firsthand experience of the effects of heavy industrial labor on its workers. She found that the affliction of others there entered her flesh and soul: "There I received forever the mark of a slave. . . . Since then I have always regarded myself as a slave." An event relating to receiving this mark was her unexpected encounter with a procession in a small Portuguese fishing village. The festivities in honor of the village's patron saint gave Weil the strong conviction that "Christianity is pre-eminently the religion of slaves, that slaves cannot help belonging to it, and I among others."

Another formative encounter was her visit to Assisi. In the chapel of Santa Maria degli Angeli—where St. Francis used to pray—she felt for the first time in her life compelled to go down on her knees. This led to an invitation, the following year, to visit Solesmes, where she followed the whole liturgy for Easter (1938). There she met a young English Catholic who introduced her to seventeenth-century British metaphysical poets. George Herbert's poem "Love" became particularly important to her. She recited this poem like a mantric prayer and, during one such recitation, found herself suddenly in a mystical presence. In Weil's words, "Christ himself came down and took possession of me." This was in spite of her skepticism until then of apparitions and the like.

Nevertheless, this experience did not convert her into a dogmatic Catholic. Instead, she started to understand Plato as a mystic, and Dionysus and Osiris were in a certain sense Christ as well. Her reading of the Bhagavad-Gita in 1940 was part of her spiritual progress; it strengthened her universal beliefs concerning non-Christian religions and Judaism.

During all these years, Pascal's words on prayer had, as it were, instilled in her a fear of his method; that is, prayer as the way to religious self-persuasion. She rejected Pascal's method as the worst form of attaining faith. Her spiritual development up until then was marked by the absence of any form of prayer. Yet her next significant encounter was when she decided, together with a study companion in New Testament Greek, to learn by heart the prayer known as the "Our Father." She became, as it were, enchanted by its words and began to use it in a daily and meditative manner. This new habit led her into clearer and greater mystical experiences.

Though the last event seems to me her third contact that "really counted," her story does not clearly indicate what particular "contacts" she had in mind. Perhaps one could exchange the event of studying the New Testament in Greek with the importance of her friendship with Father Perrin, since the three important contacts in her spiritual development were said to have been within Catholicism. She does admit the great importance of this friendship in her letter to Perrin: "You have provided me with a source of the most compelling and pure inspiration that is to be found among human things. For nothing among human things has such power to keep our gaze fixed ever more intensely upon God, than friendship for the friends of God."

The narrative of her spiritual road is followed by an apology for not joining the Catholic, or any other, church, in spite of her "genuine vocation." Her main objective is what she perceives as the lack of a harmonious solution to the relationship between the individual and the collective in Christianity, a harmony she understands in a Pythagorean manner as the just balance of contraries. Weil contents that only when intelligence is given a central position, and can function in total liberty, can the harmony she aims at be reached. She finds it impossible to cross the church's threshold, since she perpetually locates the intellect outside the church.

Weil discerns between a collective and an individual spirituality and language. The individual language is God's secret language. Weil identifies this kind of talk, for example, in Master Eckhart's thinking. She explains the discrepancies between the collective language of the church and the intimate "secret" language of God as the difference between the language of the marketplace and that of the nuptial chamber. She accuses the church of a rough sort of totalitarianism because of its collective oppressiveness of individual truth. Her own spiritual lineage is traced back to all heretical "friends of God," to Eckhart, and even to St. John, the beloved disciple of Christ.

Weil's "Spiritual Autobiography" leaves it beyond doubt where she personally, as a philosopher and intellectual, stands in relation to Christianity. She leaves the church a spiritual testament in which she argues for change: To be taken seriously the church would have to reject all forms of abuse of power.

THE STORY I TELL MYSELF: A VENTURE IN EXISTENTIAL AUTOBIOGRAPHY

Unlike most of the autobiographical texts I discuss in this chapter, Hazel E. Barnes's *The Story I Tell Myself: A Venture in Existential Autobiography* is not a short story nor a small volume, but an extensive yet captivating account of her life. Barnes became well-known as a scholar and philosopher through her introduction of Existentialism to the Anglo-Saxon world with her translation of Jean-Paul Sartre's *Being and Nothingness*.

Barnes encountered Existential philosophy at thirty-four, yet she finds Existentialism the essential fabric of all of her being and life. Looking back at eighty, her life unfolded to her in trains of Sartrean concepts and terminology.

Barnes questions her reasons and justifications for her autobiographical project. The question, "Does consistency with my basic intellectual orientation require that I attempt here an existential self-psychoanalysis?" (meaning existential psychoanalysis as a particular Sartrean type of auto/biographical writing; see more on this topic in the next chapter), she answers with "no" and "yes." She rejects the idea that her life narrative is as it were a case study that proves Sartre's philosophy of psychoanalysis as correct, but, simultaneously, she rejects other types of psychoanalysis, such as Freud's, Jung's, and Lacan's. However, since she characterizes her inner life by a series of conversions and epiphanies, she admits that "some degree of [Sartrean] self-analysis is inevitable."

Apart from Barnes's prominence as a Sartre scholar, she also practiced Sartre's thought by adopting and adapting his theory of consciousness, ego, and self. She does not elaborate much on Sartre's philosophy, but we do receive an account of how Sartre, and a few other philosophers, influenced her life. In comparison to the paradigmatic autobiographies of Sartre and Simone de Beauvoir, Barnes aims at finding her own medial between these works: "a path somewhere in between Beauvoir's diachronic approach and Sartre's synchronic one. A chronological order is appropriate for the years of formation [childhood, education, graduation, first teaching job]. . . . Writing of the rest of my adult existence seems to require a horizontal rather than a vertical progression." But like Sartre, Barnes finds her autobiographic act "perforce a novel," in which "words distort even as they reveal." However, the picture she portrays is said to be a true reflection of how she reflectively sees herself.

In "Who Is the Subject of Autobiography," an essay published a year after the autobiography, Barnes looks back on her finished project and defines the writing of an autobiography as "an extension of what we do inwardly each day of our lives; that is, we construct an ego/self that is an object for others as well as for ourselves in our every encounter. An autobiography is a visual map of what has been our network of ends and means." She discovers that the I subject she created in her life narrative actually exists out of two "I's." The "I" described in the section on her childhood is different from the "I" in the section on aging: "Frequently the 'I' of the later writer passes judgment on that earlier 'I.'"[18]

Though her self-analysis in *The Story I Tell Myself: A Venture in Existential Autobiography* is profoundly Sartrean, she cannot rephrase her life into a fundamental project "formula" such as Sartre inferred for himself, Baudelaire, Genet, and Flaubert. Moreso, Barnes values the actual life narrative over auto/biographers' critical abstractions. I suggest that Barnes's hesitation to fully embrace the Existential psychoanalysis objective—that is, to uncover the fundamental project—might be related to a disappointment with the fundamentalist project of her childhood. Immersing into this project afresh would possibly involve a confrontation or inner conflict caused by a strict religious upbringing. Though Barnes explicitly chose for atheism during her college years, integrating the new conviction in her life was characterized by avoiding conflicts with her family and surroundings. The classical ideals of inner and outer harmony seem to have had a greater sway over Barnes's preferences than the revolutionary ethos of the twentieth century.

Much in the fashion of the ancient Skeptics, who found tranquility accidently by giving up their search for peace of mind, Barnes considers that she might after all have uncovered her fundamental project. In declining to present a distinct character for her life she finds, "I fly in the face of my overcultivated tendency perpetually to hunt for networks of meaning and unifying motifs in what I have been and to pass judgement on myself. Suddenly I wonder: is *THAT* my fundamental project?" Though Barnes remains questioning what her precise fundamental project may have been, she seems to come close to it when describing her father's influence on her life. He envisioned Hazel—and her brother and sister—as high-soaring eagles. Her father encouraged her to study; his message was, "You don't have to be an ordinary woman." In addition, Hazel's aunts were significant others for presenting her with an alternative female role model: These aunts were teachers, and unmarried.

Barnes recognizes as another basic difference between her own and Sartre's philosophy her foregoing of the radical socialist commitment that Sartre maintained most of his life. Whereas Sartre in his writings and through his way of life aimed at confronting bourgeois culture, Barnes felt comfortable in the quite conventional role of a university professor. It is only at the end of her active teaching career that she discovered a sense of alienation: "Gradually, passing time has led me to wonder whether I have moved from the status of full citizen to that of resident alien in this world that used to be mine."

Barnes's actual life narrative begins with the chapter "Being a Child," in which she traces her parents' backgrounds, describes the Barnes family in breadth and depth, and narrates her elementary school years. Although her family belonged to an old-fashioned type of Free Methodists (Barnes takes care to point out the difference between the church of her childhood days and its present evolution), her father was not the typical Free Methodist church attender. Her father's admiration for William James seemed to her at odds with his fundamentalist beliefs. One of Barnes's first close encounters with philosophy derived from her father's zeal to have his two teenaged daughters, Hazel and her five years younger sister Jean, memorize and recite each day sections from the venerated philosopher's work.

Barnes summarizes her childhood environment as "nurturing, protective, and, partly because of its inherent contradictions, conducive to personal growth. But it could not have been idyllic. . . . I thought of myself as basically unhappy. And when I was about ten years old, I found it necessary to adopt a strategic retreat." She diagnoses herself as having suffered from a temporary childhood neurosis. Several times there were stomach and intestinal upsets, which were followed by fuguelike retreats from school and her surroundings. She finds it meaningful that her "specific complaint was of nausea," signifying, as she much later recognized, a revulsion against the way she lived. Through reading, for example, Sartre's *Nausea* and *Being and Nothingness*, she discovered that the nausea described there is a feeling akin to the nausea she suffered from as a child.

Barnes not only understood these few neurotic episodes in Sartrean terms, but refers as well to Laing's *Politics of Experience*. Laing considers a "fugue" (although his example of a fugue concerns a patient suffering from a severe psychosis, which is not at all comparable with Barnes's childhood retreats) equivalent to "a period of self-discovery, of renewal, a rebirth." Barnes reports that by the summer of 1929 she was completely and lastingly cured from her neurosis. She confirms with this anecdote Laing's observation and description of self-recreating processes.

Later, at college, Barnes decided to major in classics, and her dissertation topic was "Philosophy as Catharsis in the Enneades of Plotinus." Barnes confesses to a lasting fascination for Plotinus's melding of rationalism and mysticism, yet she never became a follower of Plotinus. This she attributes to her early exposure to Free Methodism. Barnes embarked during her college years on a "process of total deconversion." A climax to this process seems to have been her undefinable experience of a "nothingness" comparable to that described by Plotinus. Yet she considers that the apocalyptic moment of consciously rejecting belief in God came to her through reading Howard Smith's *Kamongo.* She also credits William James's view on religious experiences as a significant influence. His writings convinced Barnes that there are no claims to ultimate truth.

After Liberal Arts College and graduate studies at Yale, she worked three years in Greece as an instructor in English. On her return to the United States she started on a thirty-eight year academic career. Barnes describes these years mainly in Chapters 5 to 7 of her autobiography, and she summarizes these as "engagements with Existentialism and with feminism, inward conversations, recollections and observations drawn from my formidable number of years as a teacher and scholar, and other commentaries on events, times, and places." Barnes explores the possibility that in spite of having undergone decisive changes during these years as well, she seemed to have established a core personality by then. She experienced continuity within herself. This makes her conclude "that the history of my fundamental project is closer to that which Sartre attributes to Flaubert than to that of the tumultuous Sartre."[19]

I will focus now on Chapters 5 to 7 of *The Story I Tell Myself: A Venture in Existential Autobiography*, though mainly on what relates in it to philosophizing.[20]

Barnes became incidentally engaged with Existentialism through a question of one of her students. Through studying the Existentialist movement, she discovered that it spoke to her condition: Existentialism provided "a philosophical theory that gave foundational support to convictions that I held without being able to justify them except in the way one subjectively takes certain values to be self-evident."

Sartre's thought appealed to her strong individualism and sense of self-determination. Like Sartre, Barnes never perceived a self that could be discovered inside by digging it up as if it were a buried treasure. She found particular significance in Sartre's insistence that people must individually create an ethics. She heard in Sartre "the plea for the need to develop collectively an ethics appropriate to all of humanity that would not violate individuals' freedom to establish their own value systems." Her attempt to answer this quest found expression in her book *An Existentialist Ethics*. Barnes found most meaningful of Sartre's ontology the assumption of "absolute equality of all self-making individuals." Sartre's insistence that social rules and traditional values are mere human interventions seemed to open up a new future that would transform the status of women and other victims of discrimination.

Barnes understood Simone de Beauvoir's *The Second Sex* as a logical consequence of *Being and Nothingness*. She found herself largely in agreement with Beauvoir's feminism, but she realized that changes in society make the relevance of *The Second Sex* for the twenty-first century slightly different. I skip here much of the interesting section in which Barnes compares her own ideas on feminism with those of Betty Friedan, Camille Paglia, Nel Noddings, and other contemporary feminists. It is sufficient to say that Barnes finds herself "moving back and forth between what are generally considered respectively the more conservative and the more radical sides of the [feminist] controversies."

Apart from Barnes's active involvement with feminism, she translated in addition to *Being and Nothingness*, *Search for a Method*, the prefatory essay of Sartre's *Critique of Dialectical Reason*. Other major publications by Barnes on Existentialism are *The Literature of Possibility*, *Sartre*, and *Sartre and Flaubert*. In spite of being a prolific writer, she considers herself first and foremost a teacher.

Whereas Chapters 5 to 7 are mainly concerned with Barnes's professional life, Chapter 8, "Living in the Rockies," and Chapter 9, "Making an Ending," are comparable to the first four chapters of the book in which a private-life narrative is presented. In these last two chapters Barnes describes the Barnes–Schwalbe home at Boulder, and her relationship with her life companion Doris Schwalbe. A cornerstone in this relationship was a shared enthusiasm for philosophy. Unlike the agreement-based Sartre–de Beauvoir family structure of "essential and contingent loves," Barnes and Schwalbe did not set out rules for their household:

> As Doris and I worked out a lifestyle, we literally had no models; at least they were not ready at hand, and we did not search for them. At no time did we ever fall into the pattern of dominance and submission which had been accepted as the normal structure for marital and parent–child relations and which has often been built into that of other dual associations, whether based on sexual attraction or long-lasting friendship.

It seems that despite a sense of alienation and old age, Barnes's account of her life as a senior citizen still reveals an harmonious being and an openness for new inquiries and insights.

CONFESSIONS OF A MEDICINE MAN

In Alfred Tauber's *Confessions of a Medicine Man*, an M.D. and professor of philosophy describes his life and career: his development from a young medical prince, empowered with technological and scientific knowledge, into a wise and empathetic witness of human suffering.[21]

Tauber sees his confessions as an autobiographical and philosophical essay in which he, as the son of a doctor, compares the medical world in which he grew up with that in which his own children are growing up.

The exemplary life of Dr. Tauber senior seems to have been a major guiding light in the clinical practice that his son advocates. The father was confronted with exceptional moral dilemmas during the Hitler era in Europe, when he felt morally obliged to give the best medical treatment not only to those close to him, his Jewish friends, family, and community members, but also to the Nazis who would persecute and kill them.

In his book, Tauber Jr. describes his own initiation into the American medical bureaucracy, where he too had to confront grave moral dilemmas and deal with policies that contradicted the humanistic and charitable ideals impressed on him in childhood. To resolve the conflicts between caregivers, patients, and involved third parties—those who see medicine mainly in terms of big business—Tauber's radical reorientation offers a return to old-fashioned basics: "I am a physician, not a health care manager, nor a politician. My interests concern serving the patient. Medicine is a calling based on a special social relationship." In short, he advocates a relational philosophy that supersedes the scientific and technical ideology pervading clinical practice today.

Confessions of a Medicine Man differs from the usual autobiographical essay. About twenty autobiographical anecdotes, each about one page in length and not necessarily in chronological order, powerfully illuminate the author's arguments by portraying particular problematic situations he encountered in his clinical work. However, the author's critical and philosophical reflections also draw abundantly on his personal and professional development.

In his search for a new ethics Tauber first explores the growing public awareness that science cannot be the sole basis for clinical care. The perception of self, in particular one's perception of oneself as healthy or sick, is seen as contributing to physical well-being. An essential part of the book is devoted to understanding the modern person's concept of the self from a historical philosophical perspective.

Essential in relating philosophical concepts of self to medical practice is that it demonstrates the consequences of "understanding who we are" within the physician–patient relationship. Tauber strongly favors ideas of intersubjectivity and is critical of present-day medical ethics conferring on the patient almost absolute autonomy. He traces the idea of autonomy back to Descartes, Locke, Newton, and Kant, but the notion of the autonomous self was considered to have become superfluous in the Romantic era, when "the self, no longer set, established, or structured, was now an organic process of experience. . . . Relation has replaced entity."

From Tauber's perspective patient autonomy is a farce, since by the very fact of becoming ill people become dependent on medical care. The illustrative example for this is Tauber himself: While suffering severely from a kidney stone, and after several emergency-room visits and hospitalizations, he had to decide alone to "pass" the stone with an operation or without. Though a physician, he was unable to decide. Only after his sixth emergency-room visit did his colleagues make the needed decision for him.

Tauber contends that the doctor–patient relationship would be more realistic and more ethically informed by recognizing the patient's loss of autonomy and adopting, instead, absolute respect and loving care for the patient. In a previous era Savonarola expressed this task as follows: "The physician that bringeth love and charity to the sick, if he be good and kind and learned and skillful, none can be better than he. Love teacheth him everything."

For practical use in this age, Tauber looks to Levinas's ideas on recognition of the infinite in the face of the other. But as Tauber also points out, the inequality in the doctor–patient relationship (caused by the assumed loss of autonomy) does not agree very well with Levinas's thought.

Nietzsche's idea of "the eternal return" is also relevant in the new ethics, since it teaches the physician true responsibility in clinical care. Tauber's greatest achievement is in his having shown through this autobiographical essay the need for physicians to become practicing philosophers themselves instead of relying heavily on professional advice from medical ethicists.

CONCLUSION

The endless constructs of possible content and styles in philosophical autobiographic texts are beyond the chronological and psychological limits often found in biographies. Most biographers present their subjects' lives from a historical and psychological perspective, which is a biographical approach approved of by the general public. In the philosophical autobiographies presented so far none of the philosophers presented their lives through the so-called objective style and seemingly all-inclusiveness of the biographer.

Characteristic for philosophical autobiographic texts are particular intentions for life-writing: justifying a certain philosophy of life, reasons for changing one's thoughts, accounts of how thoughts developed in particular life situations, and so on. To write a biography guided by such specific philosophical intentions is not common in biography in general, not even in philosophical biography. Nevertheless, the intentions expressed in a philosophical autobiography may influence a biographer; at least some philosophers expressed the hope that their self-narratives would influence posterity to receive the views they held about themselves or their work (e.g., Plato, Erasmus, Hume). The testimony of a philosopher is often a testament as well. As Cardinal John Henry Newman words it in *Apologia pro Vita Sua*, "My friends may, upon first reading what I have written, consider much in it irrelevant to my purpose; yet I cannot help thinking that, viewed as a whole, it will effect what I wish it to do."[22]

It seems that the subjective account of the philosopher's intellectual development, and the philosophical self-justification or meaning of his or her life, often remains underdeveloped in the art of most biography while it remains at the center of many philosophical self-narratives. That these philosophical intentions are often neglected in biography might originate in a distrust of the voice of self-narration among contemporary biographers and theorists. Instead, the voice of biography is preferred as more objective, truthful, and authoritative, although there are also scholars minimizing the differences between biography and autobiography.

Most philosophical autobiographies have not been written with any kind of psychoanalytic intention, and neither are all philosophical life-narratives appropriate detailed texts to be used in such analyses. This should not lead anyone to conclude that philosophers suffer from a lack of self-knowledge or self-understanding. The fact that relatively few philosophers have produced texts extensively describing and analyzing their own self-development—similar to that of a successful psychoanalysis—only shows that most philosophers do not give expression to their personal self-understandings in a descriptive, narrative form. In general, philosophers articulate their self-understandings and self-knowledge in critical essays and theories of the self.

I have chosen the autobiographies of Augustine, Rousseau, and Sartre as case studies in philosophical psychoanalysis because of these philosophers' detailed stories of childhood and the way they related their first years to their further development. The fact that these three philosophers lived in completely different times and areas and subscribed to completely different philosophies was an additional factor in my choice. Indeed, I could have chosen as alternative case studies the tantamount or perhaps even more interesting self-narratives of Kierkegaard,

Mill, or Russell. To do at least some justice to these last-mentioned eminent philosophic–psychoanalytic documents, I will touch on these works in the epilogue of this book.

NOTES

1. Plato, *Epistles*, trans. by R. G. Bury, Loeb Classical Library, vol. 9 (London: Heinemann, 1929), 463–565.

2. Marcus Aurelius, *The Essential Works of Stoicism* (New York: Bantam, 1965), 110, 136.

3. Peter Abélard, *The Story of Abélard's Adversities*, trans. J. T. Muckle (Toronto: Pontifical Institute of Medieval Studies, 1964).

4. Boethius, *The Consolation of Philosophy* (Oxford: Oxford University Press, 2000).

5. Charles F. Horne, ed., *The Sacred Books and Early Literature of the East*, vol. 6 (New York: Parke, Austin, and Lipscomb, 1917), 99–133. See also the Internet Medieval Sourcebook, available at: <http://www.fordham.edu/halsall/basis/1100ghazali-truth.html> (last accessed June 2002).

6. *Encyclopedia Judaica*, 1971 ed., s.v. "Ghazali, Abu Hamid Muhammad Ibn Muhammad Al-Tusi Al-."

7. Desiderius Erasmus, *The Correspondence of Erasmus*, vol. 4 of *The Collected Works of Erasmus*, trans. R.A.B. Mynors and D.F.S. Thomson (Toronto: University of Toronto Press, 1977), 220–238, 403–410.

8. Dante Alighieri, *Vita Nuova*, trans. and intro. M. Musa (Oxford: Oxford University Press, 1999), 5, 6, 19, 53, 54, 70, 82, 85, 86, 90, 93.

9. This quote is, according to D. H. Higgins, from a letter of Dante to Can Grande. Dante Alighieri, *The Divine Comedy*, trans. C. H. Sisson, intro. D. H. Higgins (Oxford: Oxford University Press, 1998), 21.

10. David Hume, "My Own Life" in *Essays: Moral, Political, and Literary* (London: Longmans, Green, 1889), 2, 7–8.

11. Kahlil Gibran, *A Self-Portrait*, trans. and intro. A. R. Ferkis (London: Heineman, 1972), 28, 31, 36, 50, 56, 62, 78, 85.

12. Stefan Kanfer, "But Is It Not Strange That Elephants Will Yield—and That *The Prophet* Is Still Popular?" *New York Times on the Web*, June 25, 1972, available at: <http://www.nytimes.com/books/98/12/13/specials/gibran-elephants.html> (last accessed January 2001); Liesl Schillinger, "Pioner of the New Age" *New York Times on the Web*, December 13, 1998, available at: <http://www.nytimes.com/books/98/12/13/reviews/981213.13schillt.html> (last accessed January 2001); Robert Irwin, "I Am a False Alarm" *London Review of Books Online*, September 3, 1998, available at: <http://www.lrb.co.uk/v20n17/irwi2017.htm> (last accessed January 2001).

13. George Duby and Michelle Perrot, "Writing the History of Women," in *A History of Women in the West*, vol. 1., ed. P. Schmitt Pantel, trans. A. Goldhammer (Cambridge: Harvard University Press, 1992), ix.

14. Danielle Regnier-Bohler, "Literary and Mystical Voices," in *A History of Women in the West*, vol. 2., ed. C. Klapish-Zuber (Cambridge: Harvard University Press, 1992), 443.

15. Amélie Oksenberg Rorty, "Witnessing Philosophers," *Philosophy and Literature* 22, 2 (1998): 309–327. A resource book for some of the texts mentioned by Oksenberg Rorty is *Women Philosophers of the Early Modern Period*, ed. Margaret Atherton (Amherst: Hackett, 1994).

16. Anna Maria van Schurman, *Eucleria, of uitkiezing van Het Beste Deel*, intro. S. van der Linde (Leeuwarden: De Tille, 1978).

17. Simone Weil, *Waiting for God* (New York: Harper and Row, 1973), 62, 64, 65, 66, 67, 69, 71, 74, 77, 79.

18. Hazel E. Barnes, "Who Is the Subject of Autobiography," *Sartre Studies International* 4, 2 (1998): 25, 29.

19. Ibid., 29–30.

20. Hazel E. Barnes, *The Story I Tell Myself: A Venture in Existential Autobiography* (Chicago: University of Chicago Press, 1997), xvi, xviii, xix, 320, 190, 39, 41, 45, 295, 146, 147, 201, 273.

21. Alfred I. Tauber, *Confessions of a Medicine Man: An Essay in Popular Philosophy* (Cambridge: MIT Press, 1999).

22. John Henry Cardinal Newman, *Apologia Pro Vita Sua* (New York: Doubleday, 1956), 125.

CHAPTER 3

Philosophical Psychoanalysis and Qualitative Research

> What psychoanalysis calls the resolution or dissolution of the Oedipus complex is a complete joke, it's precisely the way an endless debt is inherited, the analysis never ends, Oedipus infects everyone, passed on from father to child. It's crazy how much nonsense has been spawned by the Oedipus complex, particularly in relation to children.
>
> Gilles Deleuze and Félix Guattari, "On Anti-Oedipus"

PHILOSOPHICAL PSYCHOANALYSIS

In this chapter I propose ideas for an alternative form of psychoanalysis that I call philosophical psychoanalysis. Philosophy "in itself" can be used as an approach for such a different kind of psychoanalysis: the analysis of the self and its development from a solely philosophical perspective. The purpose of the new approach I advocate is not psychotherapeutic; it is merely a suggestion for how to understand persons as subjects. Further on in this chapter I show the philosophical origins of qualitative research, its relationship to psychoanalysis, and how the qualitative approach can attribute a research status to philosophical psychoanalysis comparable to that of Freudian psychoanalysis.

From the 1950s onward there have been several types of psychoanalyses that were philosophically informed. Outstanding among these is Ronald D. Laing's antipsychiatric method. Laing persisted in being a psychoanalyst, and the organization he founded, the Philadelphia

Association (PA), is a psychoanalytic society. Typical for Laing and for most contemporary PA members is that they "moved away from the classical Freudian frame of reference, but this is not to be equated with becoming unpsychoanalytical."[1] In the introduction to *Thresholds between Philosophy and Psychoanalysis*, Chris Oakley observes that "the prevalent tradition within psychoanalytic orthodoxy has been one of resistance towards philosophy. There has been a tendency within Anglo-American psychoanalysis to relegate philosophical concerns to the status of defence."[2] As an exception to this policy, Oakley names W. R. Bion's psychoanalytic application of the philosophies of Plato and Kant.

As Laing did, PA analysts place philosophy in the midst of analysis. They deem that "to repress philosophy is merely to enable implicit assumptions to dominate, often accompanied by vestiges of dogmatism, and without being seriously interrogated."[3] The PA school of psychoanalysis seems to be the only faction left from the early days of philosophical psychoanalysis; these analysts continue to practice a critical, radical, subversive, and open-minded psychoanalysis.

In addition to Laing and fellow travelers, there were other philosophical psychoanalysts, such as Erich Fromm, Herbert Marcuse, Karl Jaspers, Jean-Paul Sartre, and Gilles Deleuze and Félix Guattari. Traditional psychoanalysts generally consider these analyst-philosophers "Freud bashers."

It was only toward the end of the last century that philosophy became fashionable for Freudian psychoanalysts and philosophers were drawn to Freudianism. For example, in *The Analytic Freud* we find a collection of articles by philosophers emphasizing the importance of Freudian thought for philosophy, particularly for analytic philosophy.[4] The philosopher John Cottingham presents a similar argument in *Philosophy and the Good Life*.[5] He contends that if philosophers want to attain insight into how emotions and reason link, they will need a (Freudian) psychoanalytic theory. Another eminent inquirer into the new Freudian philosophy is Marcia Cavell.[6] In *The Psychoanalytic Mind* Cavell describes her theory of mind as commencing in Ludwig Wittgenstein and Donald Davidson. She presents a philosophical antisubjectivist position as congenial to Freud and the neo-Freudians.[7]

Among contemporary feminist theorists the trend also seems to be to remain close to Freud. For example, Chris Weedon describes the importance of psychoanalysis (Freudian and Lacanian) for feminism as offering a challenge "to discourses which assume the unified, self-present subject of rationality, and to theories of innate biologically determined sexual identity. The concept of an unconscious and the separation of the psychic structures of femininity and masculinity from direct biological determination are both important."[8] Weedon seems to echo in her observation the view presented by Juliet Mitchell in *Psychoanalysis and Feminism*.[9] In comparing the relevance of Freud, Reich, Laing, and "neofeminists" (i.e., Beauvoir, Friedan, Figes, Greer, and Firestone) for feminism, Mitchell claims Freud's views on femininity as preferable and correct. She finds that the neofeminists have too much in common with Laing and Reich, particularly in that they rejected the concept of the unconscious.

In *Psychoanalytic Criticism: Theory and Practice*, Elizabeth Wright finds that feminists embrace Freud and Lacan somewhat coolly. Wright considers Jane Gallop's *Reading Lacan* the "first full-length literary project which sets out to challenge and subvert the psychoanalytic discourse from within its own feminist ranks, trying to create an intercourse between Lacanian psychoanalysis and feminism whereby each challenges the other's essentialism."[10]

Other contemporaries exploring the interface between philosophy and psychoanalysis are Richard Wollheim and Jonathan Lear. These scholars also use philosophy in defense of Freud, and in the continuation of this chapter I will render their contribution to philosophical psychoanalysis.

David Snelling considers that after "decades of philosophical preoccupation with the scientific status of psychoanalysis, we have seen in recent years the emergence of a new approach to the topic, from within the philosophy of mind."[11] Indeed, philosophers' critique concerning the credentials of psychoanalysis seems to have been replaced by inquiry, by a "fruitful dialogue" between the two disciplines. This might well be the consequence of the recognition that classical psychoanalysis and its neo-isms cannot be transformed by philosophical criticism, no matter how true and scientific the critique might be. Neither Adolf Grünbaum nor thinkers such as Karl Popper, Frederic Crews, or Jean-Paul Sartre had much chance to change the conceptual world of the majority of psychoanalysts. Philosophical arguments against the Freudian belief system are understood and interpreted within the framework of the particular belief system, and not in the context of the critic's logical underpinnings. After all that has been said against psychoanalysis, it might be wisdom to engage now in new strategies of action to provide useful alternative psychoanalytic approaches.

The alternative approach of psychoanalysis that I suggest is the sincere and serious philosophical attempt of individuals to freely understand and analyze themselves or others profoundly. This type of analysis is not constrained to the psychiatrist's couch, but may occur in various settings and life situations. I use in my private practice as a philosophical analyst such an approach, although that approach differs from how I analyze the autobiographies of Augustine, Rousseau, and Sartre; in these last instances I apply a methodological framework.[12] Nonetheless, the methodological paradigm I present in this book could also be used in the practice of a philosophical psychoanalyst.

Jonathan Lear, psychoanalyst and philosopher, proposes a new kind of "post-Freudian" philosophical psychoanalysis.[13] Although Lear presents in *Open Minded: Working Out the Logic of the Soul* a fascinating defense of psychoanalysis, it is doubtful if his aim of rescuing and reviving Freud impresses the critics of his trade. He includes and aims to transcend the arguments of "Freud-bashers," and thus to create a nondogmatic psychoanalysis. Yet Lear simply disqualifies the arguments of the critics of psychoanalysis by maintaining in typical psychoanalytic fashion that these criticisms were directed against Freud, and not against Freudian theory. This is analogous to what often happens in psychoanalytic sessions: The patient's criticism is interpreted as hostility toward the analyst. Nevertheless, Lear believes that he has denounced the narrow-minded dogmatism of professional philosophy and psychoanalysis by requestioning the dynamics of the unconscious. Elementary in this search is an attempt to justify the unconscious as the only reasonable explanation for human irrational behavior. Lear uses Plato, Wittgenstein, and other philosophers to explore obscure meanings in human consciousness, but none of these philosophers seems to be able to reach the profoundness of Freud. In spite of all the philosophical arguments and knowledge displayed by Lear, his conceptualizing might turn out in the eyes of the critics of psychoanalysis to be merely the latest transparent fashion for the aged emperor. It seems to me that a real dialogue between the Freudians and others has to advance considerably differently.

In *Love and Its Place in Nature: A Philosophical Interpretation of Freudian Psychoanalysis*, Lear presents his views as a "radical evaluation" of psychoanalysis. He deems that it is only "because psychoanalysis was founded in the treatment of illness and philosophy tends to focus on health that they look like different disciplines. As psychoanalysis and philosophy turn their attention to the growth and development of the individual, their boundaries should fade."[14] The philosophy that Socrates invented and practiced was actually his own particular type of psychoanalysis. In *Happiness, Death and the Remainder of Life*, Lear extends his hypothesis on Socratic psychoanalysis.[15] For Socrates, Aristotle, and all of us there is a remainder of life, "a beyond." In Freud's theory "the beyond" is discovered by considering the aim of all life. Whereas the manifest content of life may remain as conceived by Aristotle, Darwin, and others as a positive striving for goodness, health, growth, and survival, in *Beyond the Pleasure Principle* Freud claims that at a deeper level "*the aim of all life is death.*"[16] However, Lear considers Freud mistaken when he introduces death as an enigmatic signifier to explain the mind's self-disruptions and compulsive repetitions. Lear finds that beyond the pleasure principle there is merely a lack of principle. Yet Freud's mistake opened the door to new possibilities in human self-understanding; it disclosed that "mind by its very nature works under pressure and that there is an overall tendency in the system towards discharge."

Unlike the critical but positive accounts of Freud's and Aristotle's psychoanalytic understandings, Lear describes the Socratic–Platonian method of psychoanalysis as a dangerous fallacy. Without any irony he considers that only a lucky "bugger" like Socrates may attain the Platonian beyond of absolute knowledge and happiness. We are reminded that what we know of Socrates through Plato is merely the latter's fantasies about his mentor. Lear finds a basic difference between Freud's and Plato's methods in their conception of the control of aggression: "The *latent* content of the metaphor of the cave is that human aggression could be contained within an overall framework of good. One of the fundamental moments in the development of psychoanalysis comes with Freud's recognition that this is not possible."

Lear's approach differs greatly from Socrates and what I propose, because he maintains that the unconscious and its mechanisms is the exclusive source for deriving meaning when persons are confronted with all-to-human irrationality and other puzzling actions. Lear finds that human beings are not transparent to themselves. However, why should this necessarily lead to the conclusion that humans have a depth consisting of "complex psychological organisms who generate layers of meaning which lie beneath the surface of their own understanding?" Why would it in principle be impossible for individuals to attain a deep self-understanding and profundity by serious self-reflection, when apparently some individuals succeeded in attaining an in-depth self-knowledge without psychoanalytic intervention or faith in an unconscious? Philosophical psychoanalysis as I propose it can confer meaning on irrationality, on the obscure and paradoxical, on wishes and fantasies, and on vices and virtues by a careful philosophical investigation in these issues.

Among the people I spoke with in my private philosophy practice are those who have received psychoanalytically oriented psychotherapy and have felt that the Freudian method did not address their specific problems or what they considered the background of their problems. People often feel the need to relate their present problems to their past, but not necessarily through a Freudian or other clinical developmental theory. If one looks for nonclinical developmental understandings of the self one can find numerous philosophers who aimed at analyzing and describing the development of the self, the soul, the emotions, or memory.

Charles Taylor's *Sources of the Self* is a comprehensive historical account of what philosophers thought about the self. Janet Coleman's *Ancient and Medieval Memories: Studies in Reconstruction of the Past* is an impressive account of philosophical theories concerned with memory. Plato, Aristotle, Cicero, Pliny, Plotinus, Augustine, Gregory the Great, Abelard, Averroes, Aquinas, Scotus, Ockham, and many others all had their own alternating views on memory. Coleman presents an overview of the legacy of the "via antiqua" and the "via moderna," while comparing these with modern theories of mind and remembering. Coleman also included Wollheim's psychoanalytic understandings in the history of philosophies of memory.[17]

In "Keeping Time," Marcia Cavell shows Freudian remembering as a psychological act. However, she finds that "Freud, and psychoanalytical theory after him, took an unfortunate turn . . . in minimizing the importance of the external world, *reality*, in *psychic* reality." Cavell's regret is also expressed in her quotation of Hans-Georg Gadamer: "It is time to rescue the phenomenon of memory from being regarded merely as a psychological faculty and to see it as an essential element of the finite historical being of a person."[18]

Philosophers' understandings of the self can be conservative in nature and correspond to Freudian conceptions. Others are revolutionary, such as Plato's or Rousseau's. Of course, some might consider the opposite: Freud is the revolutionary, and not Plato or Rousseau. In practice sessions I compare the client's description of the past with work done by philosophers in their autobiographies. The common element is conferring meaning to the past, the present, or the future according to a person's own philosophical insights.

I differentiate between two tendencies in analyzing the self and life (i.e., between a conservative and a radical tendency). Two contemporary conservative theories on self are those of Alasdair C. MacIntyre and Richard Wollheim. I aim to describe here the "vices" of these two philosophical understandings versus the "virtues" of a radical approach.

Geoffrey Hartman coined the word "kakangelic" as characteristic of the nature of the Freudian approach: "Freud brings bad (*kaka*) news about the psyche, and offers no cure except through the very activity—analysis—which reveals this news."[19] Most conservative perspectives on the self and life are equally kakangelic. Nevertheless, it seems over-optimistic to claim that the radical paradigms I make explicit in Augustine's, Rousseau's, and Sartre's autobiographies are necessarily good news to all.

My psychoanalytic approach shares in Sartre's method of Existential psychoanalysis in that I do not adhere to the Oedipal or other unconscious complexes as necessary stages in persons' psychological development. For that reason, I explain further on some of the basic assumptions of Existential psychoanalysis.

THE MACINTYRE–WOLLHEIM NARRATIVE-SELF AND PHILOSOPHICAL PSYCHOANALYSIS

As an introduction to MacIntyre's narrative-self it may be best to become acquainted with the intellectual development of MacIntyre. Although MacIntyre is a well-known philosopher and probably not in need of an introduction, I nevertheless insert here a brief evaluation of his work. The MacIntyre epic began with a critique of Freudian psychoanalysis and a book on Marxism and Christianity. Although the early MacIntyre and Sartre shared interests in psychoanalysis and Marxism, they remained philosophical opponents. At that moment in time they also shared the belief that a scientific account of human behavior cannot explain to us the specifically human. Sartre and MacIntyre both find that to understand the specifically human we need "a different account, the kind of portrayal that the novelist rather than the scientist gives us."[20] At the age of twenty-three MacIntyre aspired to practice two of the great belief systems of the twentieth century; namely, Marxism and Christianity. MacIntyre became skeptical of both, and about twenty years later he wrote in his foreword to the 1971 edition of *Marxism and Christianity*, "I am able to assert less because I know more."[21]

MacIntyre wrote many papers and book reviews after his two early works, and only in 1966 did he start a new project by writing *A Short History of Ethics*. In 1981 he continued his project in ethics by showing himself totally disenchanted with modernity in *After Virtue: A Study in Moral Theory*. This book, which contains MacIntyre's thought on the narrative-self, brought him international fame. It was followed by two other substantial works on ethics. In these two works MacIntyre offers a reply to those who understood *After Virtue* as a defense of relativism.[22] However, *After Virtue* is clearly in favor of an orthodox understanding of the Aristotelian–Christian tradition; hence, conceiving MacIntyre as a relativist seems to me indeed ungrounded. MacIntyre finds that phenomenology and analytic philosophy fail to reveal deficiencies in moral thinking and practice because of their detachment from an historical understanding of ethics. Moreover, since history and the history of ideas are an academic, value-neutral enterprise, they cannot reveal or acknowledge the need for a living tradition of ethics. With *After Virtue* MacIntyre aims to reconstruct a narration of ethical traditions that is not value free. Aristotle's and Aquinas's ethics are chosen as core concepts to save the postmodern world from total moral disintegration.

MacIntyre opposes the modern liberal conception of self; it is objected to because it lacks Aristotelian *telos*, an intrinsic moral goal for all people leading to the good life. In MacIntyre's account the virtues are made manifest in practices such as chess, painting, chemistry, and history, and one could add philosophical psychoanalysis and psychotherapy. Philosophical psychoanalysis, for example, has internal and external goods. External goods are achievements of excellence ensuring the technical skills of philosophy and psychoanalysis. Such excellence is manifested through university degrees, the scholarly paper, the academic book, the conference talk, scholarship, and so on. The internal goods share characteristics such as the competition to excel, but "their achievement is a good for the whole community" participating in the practice.[23] Accordingly, MacIntyre presents the following definition of a virtue: "A virtue is an acquired human quality the possession and exercise of which tends to enable us to achieve those goods which are internal to practices and the lack of which effectively prevent us from achieving any such goods."[24]

MacIntyre does not mention spontaneous virtues or animal virtues; that is, virtues obtained, so to speak, through grace or nature. Where are the narratives telling us about such surprising virtues, as found, for example, in Sartre's *The Respectable Prostitute*? How do these stories fit into MacIntyre's account of practices, institutions, and traditions as necessary conditions for the virtuous life? MacIntyre's account aims at being empirical and avoids considering living beings as specifically human or "animal."[25] That which he found wanting in the scientific account of human beings in his early investigation of Freud is in fact that which is lacking in his own account in *After Virtue*.

MacIntyre contrasts institutions and practices: Practices relate to individuals, to selves, but are in his view necessarily dependent on institutions, although this dependence might be harmful to the internal goods of the practices. Institutions are the social bearers of practices and the integrity of a practice depends on whether the virtues can be exercised in spite of the institutionalization of the practice. Traditions contain the established forms of society's institutions. MacIntyre considers his account of the virtues as a counterpart to Adam Ferguson's brand of sociology, which considers the institutions of modern commercial society as endangering certain virtues. MacIntyre's conceptual account of the virtues is supposed to be "a sociology which aspires to lay bare the empirical, causal connections between the virtues, practices and institutions. For this kind of conceptual account has strong empirical implications; it provides an explanatory scheme which can be tested in particular cases."[26]

I have no idea to which particular cases MacIntyre refers, but some particular cases came to my mind that demonstrate that his so-called empirical account is established on fables. Twentieth-century political facts show as erroneous MacIntyre's belief that social reality confirms in the most horrifying way his own and Hobbes's thesis. It is true that since the Reformation and the French Revolution there have been communist, fascist, and other totalitarian regimes trying to conquer modern social reality. However, these achieved their aims only for a relatively short time. MacIntyre's preference of slow developmental processes of change within established traditions rejects, just as Hobbes's philosophy did, any revolutionary, radical, or sudden change. And in Hobbes's absolutism civil disobedience is always identical with injustice. How does this all bear on contemporary social reality and the narrative-self?

Hobbes and MacIntyre are not the only philosophers tolerant of types of absolutism. J. H. Burns, in his essay "The Rights of Man since the Reformation," observes that with the exception of Theodore Beza, George Buchanan, John Locke, Jean-Jacques Rousseau, Tom Paine, and a few more, thinkers seem to have contributed more to scrutinizing and criticizing the concepts of individual liberty than actually contributing to it. Nevertheless, since the Reformation the state had lost "any position from which it could claim to exert a single, undivided, centralized control over society and the individual."[27] Luther's statement that one cannot go against conscience and that persons need to examine and judge their beliefs for themselves became not only the basic doctrine of Protestant individualism, but also that of universal conscientious objectors.[28]

The Universal Declaration of Human Rights, as approved by the General Assembly of the United Nations in Paris in 1948, declares a social reality analogous to the liberties envisioned by Luther and the Enlightenment and quite contrary to the worldviews of Hobbes and MacIntyre. For example, article 18 of the Universal Declaration of Human Rights states, "Everyone has the right to freedom of thought, conscience and religion; this right includes freedom to change his religion or belief, and freedom, either alone or in community with others and in public or in private, to manifest his religion or belief in teaching, practice, worship and observance."[29] Yet in spite of the general acceptance of the freedoms endorsed by the Enlightenment, even in countries strictly adhering to these rights there are some infringements on these freedoms from an unanticipated direction; namely, from government welfare and health departments. Similar to church authorities during the Middle Ages, these institutions often sacrifice the rights of particular individuals, such as the so-called mentally ill or minority groups, to advance their conceived standards of normality and mental health.

MacIntyre considers the Enlightenment a failed project; however, historians and philosophers find that the French Revolution gave radical social meaning to the ideas of the Enlightenment.[30] In reply to *After Virtue*, Richard Bernstein writes, "It makes no historical sense to suggest that the 'Enlightenment project was not only mistaken, but should never have been commenced in the first place' [*After Virtue*, p. 111]. . . . To oppose simply the failures of the 'moderns' with the wisdom of the 'ancients,' is to violate MacIntyre's own insistence that we cannot escape our historicity, our social identities, nor the traditions which inform our lives—including the Enlightenment itself."[31]

MacIntyre chooses Nietzsche and Trotsky as the outstanding antagonists of his type of conservatism, but a better choice would have been Martin Luther or Francis of Assisi (the last inspired the early Capuchins to a greater obedience to him than to the Pope). An exemplary opponent in our time would have been Jürgen Habermas. Habermas, in *Knowledge and Human Interest*, considers that the ideal dialogue can only take place in "an emancipated society which had realized the liberation of its citizens. . . . Only when philosophy discloses in the dialectical course of history the traces of the force which has distorted the constantly renewed efforts at dialogue . . . does it advance the process whose retardation it otherwise legitimates: the process of the human species towards emancipation."[32]

John Horton and Susan Mendus describe MacIntyre's narrative conception of self as dependent on the practices and history a person is born into: "The central question of our moral lives is not, as liberals maintain, about choices we have to make, but rather a question about how we are to understand who we are, independent of and antecedent to our choices."[33] According to MacIntyre, in order to attain self-realization one must recognize that the story of one's life "possesses a certain narrative structure in which what I am now is continuous with what I was in the past. Thus the search for what I am, and for what I ought to do, is indeed a search and not simply a set of decisions."[34] MacIntyre finds that the good, the virtuous life, materializes when a person lives out the unity of the narrative embodied in his or her life.[35] His conception of the narrative-self is quite similar to the psychoanalytical concept of self, which captures continuity as the basis for the healthy personality.

For example, the psychoanalytically oriented philosopher Richard Wollheim finds autobiographic writing or self-narration to be a person's struggle to get his or her life together. In *The Mind and Its Depths*, Wollheim envisions a partnership between the disciplines of philosophy and psychology, an alliance also accentuated in *The Thread of Life* and *On Emotions* and closely aligned to Freudian and Kleinian interpretations. In line with these concepts of self he considers that understanding the interaction between a person's past, present, and future is only properly done through understanding the interaction between the conscious, preconscious, and unconscious.

Wollheim finds self-narration a process of "working-through" similar to that aimed at in therapeutic sessions: "The person, finding out what it was about the past that incapacitated him from dealing with it, may now learn to deal with it. The memory will be restored to its proper function, and the past will eventually begin to exercise no more than due influence over the present" (i.e., the restoration of memory to its proper function).[36] In *The Thread of Life* Wollheim stresses that working-through can also occur outside the processes of psychoanalytic sessions. In the psychoanalytic process "an interpretation originates with the analyst and then is brought to bear by the patient upon, in that it informs a certain kind of experience of, that which exerts the tyranny of the past over him: notably a phantasy." But working-through is "something that patterns itself, strongly or weakly, over much of life, and there are two areas which are particularly propitious for it: creativity, and sexual experience."[37] One can obtain a limited freedom from past events; but this past that can be overcome is not the past known in historic narratives, but as it exists in archaic fantasies, in the unconscious.

I wonder if writing an autobiography is really so similar to Freudian working-through; at least such a correlation became not apparent in the in-depth research I did on the autobiographies of Augustine, Rousseau, and Sartre. I cannot find that any of these philosophers was concerned about "finding out what it was about the past that incapacitated him from dealing with it." It seems to me that therapeutic delving into the past as a "phantasy" or as a genuine memory was not the aim of Augustine, Rousseau, and Sartre. Though there were issues in their lives for which they sought healing, change, reconditioning, or transcendence, self-narrating was not considered the elementary tool to these transformations, but their philosophizing. Each of these philosophers remembered his childhood and recognized influences of that childhood on his life, but by philosophizing each radically transformed or even eradicated the influences of the past over the present.

My understanding of the good life considered through the criterion of continuity differs essentially from that of MacIntyre and Wollheim, and what is usually employed in psychoanalysis and psychotherapy. In most of these developmental theories thought has to be consistent with or only slightly different from former experiences, impressions, and ideas. Radical change and philosophical or religious "conversions" are considered a break with the past and a flight into a fantasy world. From a clinical perspective these are all symptoms of neurotic failure if not schizophrenic hallucinations. Most psychoanalytic and psychologistic interpretations relate consistency closely to continuity: The inner wholeness of a life depends on a healthy development that gives the past—the past in its historical and psychological meanings—its due influence over the present. When there is a lack of past influence, which may also be indicated, paradoxically, by an excessively dominating influence of past experiences, mental mechanisms such as transference and projection substitute for the connections that are missing in the patient's memory. The existence of the past in transferal metaphors forms a pathological continuity in which the patient establishes a fallacious consistency with his or her real self. However, in some alternative psychotherapeutic treatments, rebiographing is used to help patients to write their pasts differently by letting them invent narratives of their pasts that interpret matters in a novel way; this is the extreme antidote to endorsing "due influence" of the past over the present.

Instead of searching for continuity and unity of self through due influence of the past over the present, as is the case in MacIntyre's and Wollheim's concepts of self, I propose that continuity and consistency are obtained through philosophical reflection. To verify the way continuity and consistency are arrived at I analyze the philosophers' life-narratives aided by parameters appropriated from Dewey's philosophizing. From a Deweyian perspective one can observe in persons two kinds of mental activities: one that is slavish and one that is free. The dialectical interaction and the difference between the two activities depends on "the presence of reason or intelligence as an instrumental force."[38] Although I use Dewey's differentiation of the two types of activity to facilitate understanding the lives in the autobiographies, I use no other implications of his philosophy in this context.

Slavish mental activity consists of the following:

1. Thoughts, and the influence of those thoughts, of which a person is not entirely aware. For example, one brought up in a sexist or racist environment might not be aware of the sexist or racist content of his or her thoughts.
2. External philosophical influence a person cannot oppose due to lack of intellectual discernment or vitality. For example, a person exposed to continuous political or ideological brainwashing may not wish to condone the ideology, but not having the philosophical skills that enable the individual to understand what is wrong with it, he or she will not be able to reject it rationally. To a certain extent, therefore, he or she will condone the ideology.

Free mental activity consists of philosophy used consciously as an instrumental force to change thought and action. For example, one who identifies rational behavior as moral behavior will change his or her thoughts and actions into rational thoughts and rational actions.

The narrative-self I propose is not characterized by an ideal narrative structure in which the person can only be a little different in the present, or in the future, from what he or she was in the past. From my perspective the search for the good life may direct persons to make drastic changes from their past being, as is made explicit through accentuating philosophical continuity and consistency in the lives of Augustine, Rousseau, and Sartre. When perceived through the two types of mental activity, one discovers the influence of philosophical assumptions held by the family and the community the child-philosopher is born into or grows up in, or ways of life based on particular philosophical assumptions the philosopher is aware of only by looking at his or her life retrospectively. But slavish mental activity is not—at least not always—decisive for the rest of the person's life. An example of free mental activity that negates or transforms the meaningless type of activity is the philosophical conversion, the radical change of mind. In his philosophical autobiography the psychiatrist–philosopher Jaspers described his conversion to "philosophical faith": "Increasingly . . . genuine philosophy showed itself to me" and "it does bring the basis of consciousness into clear focus which alone gives limit and meaning to the results of science and the possibility of planned creativity."[39]

Psychoanalytic and psychologistic interpretations of autobiographies mainly consider important what Dewey termed the slavish and meaningless facets of thought and activity. These interpretations view philosophical thought and its realization in life as expressions of sub- or unconscious causal processes that originate in childhood. The idea of mental activity as an "instrumental force to radical change" is merely an illusion in the mind of a person who has not undergone analysis and who is accordingly led astray by the superego's defense mechanisms.

Philosophers defending and encouraging such standard psychoanalytic views are Ben-Ami Scharfstein and E. A. Burtt. They recognize philosophical activity as flowing from childhood events, and do not regard philosophical thought as an autonomous force. Scharfstein claims that "it is a fact that attitudes towards existence as a whole, whatever it may be and whether or not it is clearly conceivable, are based on or strongly influenced by our experiences. This is . . . most true of our experiences as small children."[40] E. A. Burtt came to the extreme yet psychoanalytically consistent conclusion that only the psychoanalyzed philosopher can think as he should; having freed himself of unconscious motives he will detect the unconscious suppositions in philosophical texts.[41]

Another type of psychologistic interpretations can be recognized in the contemporary fashion of asking "who's philosophy" instead of "what philosophy." Brenda Almond criticizes the "who's philosophy" trend for pinpointing philosophy, and particularly morality, in certain traditions or ways of life; there is white male, black, feminist, gay, lesbian, ethnic, linguistic, sociopolitic, or religious philosophy.[42] In such "lonely provincialism" there is no need "to pursue the humanistic ideal of a common intellectual tradition based on a common reason."[43] Almond traces "holistic" theorizing—that is, philosophy that claims its source and meaning in biography—to Wittgenstein's doctrine of forms of life, Quine's web of belief, and Davidson's conceptual schemes.

The interpretation I propose aims to provide evidence countering holistic theorizing and standard psychoanalytical and psychologistic understandings of philosophical autobiographies. Augustine, Rousseau, and Sartre not only described their awareness of slavish aspect of mental activity, but also described an autonomous philosophizing and how free philosophical activity changed their very being and life.

Philosophical psychoanalysis, therefore, is not concerned with justifying various Freudian psychoanalytic and psychologistic explanations of the lives of philosophers, their philosophies, and their autobiographies. I mention psychoanalytic and psychologistic explanations for the purpose of demonstrating the great differences (and in some instances also the similarities) between these and the way Augustine, Rousseau, and Sartre understood and described their lives; that is, as a combination of two kinds of philosophical activity, as a complex pattern of movement in the world of ideas.

It is neither my interest nor my aim to defend or to combat Freudian types of interpretation of philosophical lives and philosophical texts. After all, those believing in Freudian psychoanalysis cannot be reached through a voice other than their own; my voice, uttering the views of a Freudian nonbeliever, cannot be convincing. But a radically different interpretation of philosophical autobiographies can demonstrate to non-Freudians the validity of their beliefs.

Others, those who have not yet determined their position, might be encouraged to do so. There is still hope that they may be convinced by what I present as data for an alternative psychoanalytic understanding of philosophical autobiographies; that is, the disclosure of patterns of philosophical activity as essential for the understanding of these autobiographies. These data are mainly validated through the autobiographical narratives. Not only do the experiences of life shape the mind; the mind can also receive or create new thoughts. And, in turn, such autonomous activity of the mind can transform the philosopher's life.

EXISTENTIAL PSYCHOANALYSIS AND PHILOSOPHICAL PSYCHOANALYSIS

Sartre's philosophical approach to understanding human beings is evident in his early writings, *The Psychology of Imagination* and *Being and Nothingness*. Sartre considered experimental psychology the only true type of psychology, whereas he considered nonexperimental attempts to explain human behavior as pseudoscientific or philosophy.

In *Being and Nothingness* he describes desire as "anything but the consciousness of . . . objects as desirable."[44] His view of desire is different from that of the empirical psychologist, who considers "desire as being *in* man by virtue of being 'contained' by his consciousness, and [who] believes that the meaning of the desire is inherent in the desire itself."

This difference in the understanding of desire makes all the difference in Sartre's view of human beings as the subject of philosophical investigation: "Fundamentally man is *the desire to be*, and the existence of this desire is not to be established by an empirical induction." Instead of considering human beings defined by desires originating in a Freudian libido—drives and tendencies that are claimed to exist empirically—he considers persons defined by the conscious pursuit of particular ends; that is, the "original project" that is determined by "original choices." Sartre called the investigation and classification of these ends Existential psychoanalysis. What Existential psychoanalysis has in common with empirical psychoanalysis (by which Sartre means Freudian types of psychoanalysis) is that the fundamental attitude of a person (i.e., respectively the "original choice" and "the complex") is not "expressed by simple, logical definitions because it is prior to all logic. . . . [It] requires reconstruction according to laws of specific synthesis." In contradistinction to the Freudian complex that is explained through the libido apparatus, in Existential psychoanalysis it is sufficient to reveal the original project by a (phenomenological) description of past events. Illuminating events by the light of knowledge will reveal the original choices "each time as evidently irreducible." Sartre differentiates between consciousness and knowledge; though all we can know is in the realm of our consciousness, we might not know all there is to know.

Nevertheless, the reconstruction of the fundamental attitude of a person, in Freudian as well as in Sartrean analysis, seems best described in the narrative of a case study. Accordingly, Sartre wrote very little on Existential psychoanalytic theory, but practiced his type of psychoanalysis by writing case studies in the literary form of biographical novels. His theory of psychoanalysis is found mainly in Part 4 of *Being and Nothingness*, particularly in the second chapter and the conclusion.

Since for Sartre consciousness is in principle consciousness *of* something (i.e., unconscious issues are nonexistent), he rejects Freudian psychoanalysis as a form of self-deception. In our computer-oriented age, Sartrean consciousness can best be compared to software, which always contains (is) a program. Without the program software, the "life," the functioning of the computer hardware, is nonexistent.

In contradistinction to my description of Existential psychoanalysis, most commentators on Sartrean psychoanalysis prefer to emphasize some superficial issues they believe Sartre shares with Freud, Lacan, and other psychoanalysts or therapists. To them, Sartre, against his will and achievements, is Freudian, or neo-Freudian, just as some interpreters consider Sartre a Marxist. To this end these commentators disregard Sartre's dominant antipsychology and anti-Freudian argumentation, which totally undermines these so-called similarities.

I need to accentuate here that Sartre saw the ideal relationship between analyst and analysand in Existential psychoanalysis and similar analytic situations as one of positive reciprocity. For example, in the essay "Psychoanalytic Dialogue" Sartre writes, referring to Laing and other antipsychiatrists, "A new generation of psychiatrists are seeking to establish a bond of reciprocity between themselves and those they are treating. . . . I do not see why conventional psychoanalysis should not join them one day."[45]

Hazel Barnes researched psychoanalytical approaches similar to Sartre's. She mentions the work of Erich Fromm, Karen Horney, and the Dutch phenomenological psychiatrist J. H. Van Den Berg. She concludes that phenomenological psychiatry is close to Existential psychoanalysis, and that Van Den Berg's research has significance for Sartrean practices. "If Van Den Berg's presentation of the phenomenological—and existential—approach is (as surely we must assure it is) the result of comparing the case histories and reports of the psychiatrists whom he mentions, then we are justified, I believe, in saying that there is clinical evidence to support at least some of the claims of existential psychoanalysis."[46] Though it is possible to find Sartrean influences in my type of philosophical psychoanalysis, my method essentially differs from Sartre's. For example, I do not aim to disclose fundamental projects, but to make explicit the dialectical patterns of slavish and free mental activity, and to show how this dialectic process contributes to consistency and continuity in the analysand's thinking and living.

PHILOSOPHICAL PSYCHOANALYSIS AS QUALITATIVE RESEARCH

Qualitative research originated in phenomenology, yet nowadays mainly social scientists practice it. Qualitative researchers from diverse disciplines publish yearly hundreds of papers and books using or explaining qualitative methods, yet the general public and most professionals remain ignorant about this flourishing alternate way of obtaining and using knowledge. I will not present here a substantive introduction to qualitative research, but it seems appropriate to present a framework of references showing the affinity of qualitative research with philosophy and psychoanalysis.[47]

If one considers data analysis as the heart of qualitative research, one should add to it that the in-depth and subjective understanding of data makes the qualitative difference. In addition, qualitative research is based in dialogue or interview with an individual or group. Pamela Maykut and Richard Morehouse refer to Mikhail Baktin as presenting the heart of qualitative research. Baktin finds of paramount importance "the connection between the knower and the known. . . . If a person (or subject as he says) is to be understood as a person and not as a thing, then the relationship between the researcher and the other person must be a dynamic and a mutual relationship, what he calls a dialogue. He sees the researcher and the subject of research connected as in a dialogue or interchange with one affecting the other." Maykut and Morehouse describe the elementary posture for the qualitative researcher as empathy. They relate this qualitative posture to Michael Polanyi's *Knowing and Being*, where Polanyi uses the concepts of "in-dwelling" and "extent knowing" in relation to empathic being.[48]

Larry VandeCreek, Hilary Bender, and Merle R. Jordan find that qualitative research "invites us to call upon those empathic listening skills of an *I–Thou* relationship in order to listen to the lived experience of those whom we ask to participate with us as co-researchers in a qualitative research venture."[49]

It is common that qualitative researchers refer to philosophers such as Schleiermacher, Dilthey, Husserl, Heidegger, Gadamer, Habermas, Buber, Giorgi, and Polinghorne as originators of their method, yet a comprehensive historical–philosophical survey of qualitative research seems at present unobtainable. André J. J. de Koning considers Brentano to be a progenitor as well:

> Brentano expressed his concern about an overemphasis upon method in the field of psychology as early as 1874, in his "Psychology from an Empirical Standpoint." He was interested in investigating the presuppositions underlying empirical psychology, as well as investigating by means of experimental, qualitative procedures. Psychological research, like any scientific investigation . . . should not limit itself to questions which can only be dealt with through statistic procedures.[50]

Qualitative research claims for itself a scientific stance, but different from the objective, statistic inquiry into data. It is said that "While quantitative surveys are an outstanding medium for gathering a breadth of information regarding 'How many?' and 'How much?,' qualitative research is the best research method for discovering underlying motivations, feelings, values, attitudes and perceptions."[51] Where quantitative research is associated with observable facts and Auguste Comte's positivism, qualitative research refers to the meaning of events and is associated with phenomenology.

Maykut and Morehouse include Freud and Piaget in their wide spectrum of qualitative researchers. They observe that Freud's case studies contribute partly to psychoanalytic theory formation; at the other side, Freudian theory is not based on statistic data analysis. Freud composed his theory against the background of his medical and literary knowledge.[52]

Marcia Cavell quotes Jonathan Lear and Roy Schafer to show qualitative listening aspects in Freud; a loving, empathetic, listening analyst makes for a striking difference with the common picture of Freud as the detached scientific analyst. To Cavell the psychoanalyst is more like a sensitive art critic than a scientist:

> Like the critic, the analyst too gathers up the patient's behavior into themes, or styles, or repetitive patterns; the critic points out, for example, how often the characters in a painting by Manet aren't looking at each other, seem somehow estranged; the analyst tells her patient that he seems often to cast people in the role of an authority which he then tries to evade. This may not be something he *intends* to do in the narrow sense, but more a matter of habit and style.[53]

Steinar Kvale presents psychoanalytic therapy as the qualitative research method per excellence. He contends that in the training and practice of the average psychoanalyst the techniques of psychoanalysis are accentuated, while psychoanalytic methodology is neglected and misunderstood. Most psychoanalysts suffer from a methodological blindspot that can briefly be formulated as "taking the nature of scientific method in psychology as given and rejecting any knowledge not acquired by the traditional scientific methods."[54] However, according to Kvale, Freud's method in psychoanalysis is one of research and treatment advancing together. The psychoanalyst's intensive case studies of individual patients are akin to the interviews of the qualitative researcher; both use an in-depth and empathetic listening in their work with human beings: "Qualitatively regarded, the intensive studies of individuals give the therapist a broad context for interpreting the meaning of the patient's behavior. The therapist obtains a unique and penetrating knowledge of the relation of the patient's behavior to his present life situation and to his past history." During the treatment the analyst's observations have to be descriptive, and only when the treatment is concluded can the case be interpreted scientifically.

Kvale describes another qualitative characteristic as follows: "The psychoanalytic interpretation of meaning is open to multiple meanings and layers of meaning of an act. It involves hypothesis generation and hypothesis testing, and raises the issue of validity of interpretation." The tendency to overstep the descriptive stage in research may lead to an "interpretation mania." In qualitative therapy Kvale's focus is on the internal logic of the analysand's development and on a reciprocal personal involvement between therapist and patient. Kvale finds that in psychology crises and suffering are often neglected as sources for a profound understanding of human behavior, but "in dialectics, conflicts and radical changes are the important loci of acquiring knowledge, where new tendencies, superceding the old, are breaking through to realization." In spite of the fact that Kvale's arguments are based in a profound psychoanalytic literacy, the image of Freud that he presents still needs to be discovered by the majority of psychoanalysts.

There are also narrative approaches that share characteristics with the qualitative research method. In *Retelling a Life: Narration and Dialogue in Psychoanalysis*, Roy Schafer's perception of the self is "anti-essentialist"; it is always in flux and grounded in a narrative construct. He finds that psychoanalysis "emerges as an array of master narratives that dictate specific and incommensurable storylines for the interpretive work of analysts."[55] Frederick Wyatt considers Schafer's and likewise Donald Space's accentuation of narrative in psychoanalysis a new advent:

> The idea that psychoanalysis draws from the narrative . . . was not voiced in the earlier writings on psychoanalysis. Instead it is conventional for psychoanalysts to speak of the "materials" of psychoanalysis—a fatal term when one acknowledges its lifeless and impersonal sound. Materials are produced or mined, then they are worked upon, and product is made of them. With such a conception there is little room for interaction.[56]

Jens Brockmeier relates, in an outstanding article, "Autobiography, Narrative, and the Freudian Concept of Life History," to Paul Ricoeur's phenomenological hermeneutics as having been vital to the development of the new narrative understandings in psychoanalysis. However, Ricoeurian hermeneutics differ from these approaches in that "the traditional identity question 'who am I' is not an empty one, but ultimately leads . . . to the 'very invariant condition of a hermeneutic existence.' Thus for Ricoeur, the fundamental function of narrative is to 'construct the durable properties of a character,' what he calls 'narrative identity.'"[57]

Although not concerned with psychoanalysis, it seems to me fitting to mention here Theodore R. Sarbin's conception of a narrative psychology. Sarbin briefly formulates his approach in an autobiographic essay as "the recognition that life is storied, that a narratory principle guides both the interpretation of human events and the performance of human actions. . . . The narrative approach is more like history and biography than it is like chemistry and physics, the models for traditional psychology."[58]

I will not elaborate further on the various and many qualitative and narrative approaches used at present in the social sciences. One may conclude that qualitative and narrative approaches are suitable to use in humanistic branches of research, in particular because these approaches originated and are comparable to methods belonging to humanistic departments.

The proposition I present in this chapter as philosophical psychoanalysis has common aspects with the qualitative approaches mentioned. I examine in the following chapters particular issues in the context of the lives of Augustine, Rousseau, and Sartre: the patterns of slavish and free mental activity, and matters about consistency and continuity. This examination one may compare to a qualitative interview inquiry concerning specific matters in the life of an interviewee. The results of these inquiries I compare in the epilogue; however, this is done without reaching final conclusions concerning necessary consequences of philosophical psychoanalysis in other instances of autobiography. Research and the comprehension of the subject go hand in hand.

NOTES

1. Chris Oakley, "Introducing an Incomplete Project," in *Thresholds between Philosophy and Psychoanalysis*, ed. R. Cooper (London: Free Association Books, 1989), 5.
2. Ibid., 6.
3. Ibid., 7.
4. Michael P. Levine, ed., *The Analytic Freud: Philosophy and Psychoanalysis* (London: Routledge, 2000).
5. John Cottingham, *Philosophy and the Good Life: Reason and the Passions in Greek, Cartesian and Psychoanalytic Ethics* (Cambridge: Cambridge University Press, 1998).
6. One should not confuse the work of Marcia Cavell with that of Stanley Cavell. Stanley Cavell is a well-known philosopher who only in his later works has given explicit expression of his psychoanalytic worldview. See more on the psychoanalytic inclinations of Stanley Cavell in Stephen Mulhall, *Stanley Cavell: Philosophy's Recounting of the Ordinary* (Oxford: Clarendon Press, 1998), 207–222.
7. Marcia Cavell, *The Psychoanalytic Mind: From Freud to Philosophy* (Cambridge: Harvard University Press, 1993).
8. Chris Weedon, *Feminist Practice and Poststructuralist Theory* (Oxford: Basil Blackwell, 1988), 71.
9. Juliet Mitchell, *Psychoanalysis and Feminism* (New York: Vintage, 1975).
10. Elizabeth Wright, *Psychoanalytic Criticism: Theory and Practice* (London: Routledge, 1991), 198.
11. David Snelling, "Subject, Object, World," in Levine, *The Analytic Freud*, 101.
12. For details on the approach I use in the private practice of philosophy, see Gerd B. Achenbach, *Philosophische Praxis* (Cologne: Jürgen Dinter, 1984);

Gerd B. Achenbach and Thomas Macho, *Das Prinzip Heilung* (Cologne: Jürgen Dinter, 1985); Shlomit C. Schuster, "Philosophical Counselling," *Journal of Applied Philosophy* 8, 2 (1991): 219–223; Shlomit C. Schuster, *Philosophy Practice: An Alternative to Counseling and Psychotherapy* (Westport, Conn.: Praeger, 1999). For more literature on philosophical counseling, see Shlomit C. Schuster (1989, creation and copyright date), *The Philosophical Counseling Website*, available at: <http://www.geocities.com/centersophon> (last accessed April 2001).

13. Jonathan Lear, *Open Minded: Working Out the Logic of the Soul* (Cambridge: Harvard University Press, 1998).

14. Jonathan Lear, *Love and Its Place in Nature: A Philosophical Interpretation of Freudian Psychoanalysis* (New Haven, Conn.: Yale University Press, 1998), 183.

15. Jonathan Lear, *Happiness, Death, and the Remainder of Life* (Cambridge: Harvard University Press, 2000), 83, 84, 85, 164, 16–32.

16. Sigmund Freud, *Beyond the Pleasure Principle*, quoted in *Happiness, Death, and the Remainder of Life*, 83 (emphasis Jonathan Lear).

17. Charles Taylor, *Sources of the Self: The Making of the Modern Identity* (Cambridge: Harvard University Press, 1989); Janet Coleman, *Ancient and Medieval Memories: Studies in Reconstruction of the Past* (Cambridge: Cambridge University Press, 1992), xiv.

18. Marcia Cavell, "Keeping Time," in Levine, *The Analytic Freud*, 85, 87.

19. Geoffrey H. Hartman, *Easy Pieces* (New York: Columbia University Press, 1988), 143.

20. Alasdair C. MacIntyre, *The Unconscious: A Conceptual Analysis* (London: Routledge and Kegan, 1962), 98.

21. Alasdair C. MacIntyre, *Marxism and Christianity* (Middlesex: Penguin Books, 1971).

22. John Horton and Susan Mendus, "Alasdair MacIntyre: *After Virtue* and After," in *After MacIntyre: Critical Perspectives on the Work of Alasdair MacIntyre*, ed. John Horton and Susan Mendus (Oxford: Polity Press, 1994), 12.

23. Alasdair C. MacIntyre, *After Virtue: A Study in Moral Theory* (London: Duckworth, 1981), 190.

24. Ibid., 191. Although this is a suave and articulated definition, I prefer the *New Webster Dictionary* on the subject. Virtue is any praiseworthy quality or trait, merit, or inherent power to produce effects. In contrast to MacIntyre's definition, the Webster definition attributes virtue to the so-called primitive, the less privileged, and those not in positions to acquire external goods (note that according to MacIntyre the internal goods are inherent in the external goods). Since I am unable to disregard narratives about good dogs who through a particular instinctive virtue rescued children from burning houses (or abandoned babies being raised by wolves and monkeys), it seems to me proper to include animals in any listing of beings in which virtue is manifest. Some animals are said to be more virtuous than human beings with regard to friendship, faithfulness, and gratitude. Richard Sorabji's research revealed that to different degrees ancient philosophers credited animals with exercising justice, with possessing a sense of justice and injustice. The standard example of storks that feed their aged parents appears in Philo, Plutarch, Porphyry, Cicero, and others. Richard Sorabji, *Animal Minds and Human Morals: The Origins of the Western Debate* (Ithaca, N.Y.: Cornell University Press, 1993), 119–121.

25. MacIntyre began comparing human and animal intelligence in his latest book and through this comparison draws conclusions concerning "our treatment of the disabled." However, this is a continuation of his Aristotelian conception of virtues. See Alasdair C. MacIntyre, *Dependent Rational Animals: Why Human Beings Need the Virtues* (La Salle, Ill.: Open Court, 1999).

26. MacIntyre, *After Virtue*, 196.

27. J. H. Burns, "The Rights of Man since the Reformation: An Historical Survey," in *An Introduction to the Study of Human Rights*, ed. Francis Vallat (London: Europa, 1972), 19.

28. Roland H. Baiton, *The Reformation and the Sixteenth Century* (Boston: Beacon Press, 1956), 61.

29. Francis Vallat, ed., *An Introduction to the Study of Human Rights*, (London: Europa, 1972), 121.

30. Emmet Kennedy, *A Cultural History of the French Revolution* (New Haven: Yale University Press, 1989); Tony Judt, "You Say You Had a Revolution," *Tikkun: A Bimonthly Jewish Critique of Politics, Culture and Society* 4 (1989): 115–117.

31. Richard J. Bernstein, *Philosophical Profiles: Essays in a Pragmatic Mode* (Cambridge: Polity Press, 1986), 139–140.

32. Rüdiger Bubner, *Modern German Philosophy* (Cambridge: Cambridge University Press, 1981), 185–186.

33. Horton and Mendus, "Alasdair MacIntyre: *After Virtue* and After," 9.

34. Ibid.

35. MacIntyre, *After Virtue*, 203.

36. Richard Wollheim, "On Persons and their Lives," in *Explaining Emotions*, ed. A. Oksenberg Rorty (Berkeley and Los Angeles: University of California Press, 1980), 315.

37. Richard Wollheim, *The Thread of Life* (Cambridge: Cambridge University Press, 1986), 234, 235.

38. John E. Smith, *Purpose and Thought: The Meaning of Pragmatism* (Chicago: University of Chicago Press, 1978), 158.

39. Paul A. Schilpp, ed., *The Philosophy of Karl Jaspers* (New York: Tudor, 1957), 79.

40. Ben-Ami Scharfstein, *The Philosophers: Their Lives and the Nature of Their Thought* (New York: Oxford University Press, 1980), 122.

41. E. A. Burtt, "My Path to Philosophy," *Philosophy East and West* 22, (1972): 429–440.

42. Brenda Almond, "Philosophy and the Cult of Irrationalism," in *The Impulse to Philosophise*, ed. A. Phillips Griffiths (Cambridge: Cambridge University Press, 1992).

43. Ibid., 205.

44. Jean-Paul Sartre, *Being and Nothingness* (New York: Washington Square Press, 1966), 682, 692, 698, 701, 62.

45. Jean-Paul Sartre, *Between Existentialism and Marxism* (New York: Pantheon Books, 1975), 204, 205.

46. Hazel E. Barnes, "Humanistic Existentialism and Contemporary Psychoanalysis," in *Sartre: A Collection of Critical Essays*, ed. E. Kern (Englewood Cliffs, N.J.: Prentice-Hall, 1962), 160.

47. Good introductions to qualitative research are Pamela Maykut and Richard Morehouse, *Beginning Qualitative Research: A Philosophic and Practical Guide* (London: Falmer Press, 1999); Larry VandeCreek, Hilary Bender, and Merle R. Jordan, *Research in Pastoral Care and Counseling: Quantitative and Qualitative Approaches* (Decatur, Ga.: Journal of Pastoral Care, 1994).

48. Maykut and Morehouse, *Beginning Qualitative Research,* 37, 25.

49. VandeCreek, Bender, and Jordan, *Research in Pastoral Care and Counseling,* 71, 73.

50. Peter D. Ashworth, Amedeo Giorgi, and André J. J. de Koning, eds., *Qualitative Research in Psychology* (Pittsburgh, Pa.: Duquesne University Press, 1986), viii.

51. Professionalism Committee of the Qualitative Research Consultants Association, *FAQs Regarding Qualitative Research,* available at: <http://www.qual.com/faq.html> (last accessed April 2001).

52. Maykut and Morehouse, *Beginning Qualitative Research,* 8.

53. Cavell, *The Psychoanalytic Mind,* 97, 98, 100, 101.

54. Steinar Kvale, "Psychoanalytic Therapy as Qualitative Research," in Ashworth, Giorgi, and de Koning, *Qualitative Research in Psychology,* 156, 157, 159, 179.

55. Roy Schafer, *Retelling a Life: Narration and Dialogue in Psychoanalysis* (New York: Basic Books, 1992), xvii.

56. Frederick Wyatt, "The Narrative in Psychoanalysis: Psychoanalytic Notes on Storytelling, Listening, and Interpreting," in *Narrative Psychology: The Storied Nature of Human Conduct,* ed. T. R. Sarbin (New York: Praeger, 1986), 195.

57. Jens Brockmeier, "Autobiography, Narrative, and the Freudian Concept of Life History," *Philosophy, Psychiatry & Psychology* 4, 3 (1997): 181; Paul Ricoeur, "Narrative Identity," in *On Paul Ricoeur: Narrative and Interpretation,* ed. D. Wood (London: Routledge, 1991), 195, 197.

58. Theodore R. Sarbin, "Steps to the Narratory Principle: An Autobiographical Essay," in *Life and Story: Autobiographies for a Narrative Psychology,* ed. D. J. Lee (Westport, Conn.: Praeger, 1994), 7.

CHAPTER 4

The Philosopher Reborn

> I repeatedly asseverated that to me no fortune seemed favorable unless it afforded leisure to apply oneself to philosophy; that no life was a happy one except insofar as it was lived in philosophy.
>
> Augustine, *Answer to Skeptics*

PHILOSOPHICAL CONFESSIONS

Augustine's *Confessions* is more than an intellectual autobiography. It is a philosophical autobiography: In it Augustine describes his philosophical development in the context of his life's history. The text was written with the aim of justifying a particular way of life, showing the usefulness of philosophy in finding practical wisdom. *The Confessions* is about faith, sin, and praise: Faith and even sin are ultimately reasons for worship. Augustine's autobiography is also an introduction to all of his philosophical–theological writings. His act of praise can be explained as a vindication of his philosophical understanding of the Catholic way of life.

John Burnaby finds that Augustine wrote *The Retractationes* (written toward the end of his life, about 426–427 C.E.) not so much to justify himself as to defend what he had written against misinterpretation or misapplication.[1] But in *The Confessions* Augustine already embarks on an apologia to clarify his attitude toward non-Christian philosophies.

Because of the tension between classic and Christian culture (e.g., the Carthage council in 398 C.E. prohibited the reading of pagan books by its church members) an apologia for philosophy was urgently needed in the African Catholic Church. Among the African Christians philosophy was not an accepted tradition as it was in the churches of Rome and Milan. Two centuries before Augustine, Clement of Alexandria defended Greek philosophy against the attacks of Tertullian of Carthage, who declared philosophy to be "the mother of all heresy." But Clement's defense of philosophy was ambivalent and obscure: He thought that pagan philosophy was a "harlot" to be avoided, yet he also compared philosophy to the divinely inspired Hebrew Scriptures, even finding it to be a preparation for understanding the New Testament.

Augustine wrote *The Confessions* during the years 397 to 401 C.E., some ten years after his conversion to Catholicism. Augustine's self-narrative leads up to a garden scene, in which he hears a mysterious voice saying, "Take up, and read." The continuation of the story can be summarized as a penitent Augustine searching for truth by way of the Catholic tradition; his conversion is central in his life story.

Questions can be raised about Augustine's reasons for writing the autobiography, and more than one answer can be given to each question. In *The Retractationes* Augustine refers to *The Confessions* as an act of worship, although "what others think about them is a matter for them to decide."[2] Augustine writes that he worked on two themes in *The Confessions*: himself (books 1–10) and Scripture (books 11–13).[3] These two themes describe a personal and universal philosophical journey to what he considered ultimate truth. There are just two statements in *The Confessions* that he reconsidered at the end of his life (i.e., a "trifling" pronouncement and an "obscurity" in explanation). In *The Retractationes* Augustine does not change any substantial issue as it appeared in his autobiography.

Augustine wrote his life narrative at the beginning of his career as a bishop. As bishop he was confronted with the responsibilities of his profession and had to undergo a further inner transformation to face up to his new position. Whereas the period of his priesthood had still been a period of reflection and study (the philosopher's life), as a bishop Augustine became a public figure with religious responsibilities for his community. This change from a *vita contemplativa* to a *vita activa* may have caused an even more drastic metamorphosis in Augustine's life than his conversion experience.

In the months just after his conversion there was apparently no reason for reflecting on continuity in his life; he did not experience the need for writing down a "thread of life." Although some of the so-called Cassiciacum dialogues, which Augustine wrote in the time between his conversion and baptism, are of autobiographic content, these early writings are not an attempt to reach any comprehensive understanding of his "whole" life. Ten years later, however, as a bishop, it seems that Augustine did have reasons to reflect on continuity in his life.

Peter Brown considers that *The Confessions* were written out of an inner need and as therapy. And with more diagnostic exactness, James O'Donnell believes that *The Confessions* were the cure for Augustine's writer's block, since after *The Confessions* "began the torrent of his great works, including, significantly, a series of works re-beginning and then completing triumphantly projects that had come to nothing in the years before *The Confessions*." Without claiming that this self-narrative was indeed the cure for a writer's block, it seems to me that Augustine, after having defended his reasons for philosophizing, could now with a good conscience and a free pen express all his philosophical thoughts. John O'Meara and other scholars maintain that Augustine had been asked by Paulinus, Bishop of Nola, to write an account of his own life, which resulted in *The Confessions*.[4]

As a bishop, Augustine's principal occupation was the interpretation of Scripture: in sermons, pastoral work, and disputations with heretics. The course of philosophical dialogue on the Christian faith, which he began in Cassiciacum and at Ostia, appears to have come to an end. Accordingly, Augustine the philosopher had to question why and how he could continue his philosophical life as a bishop. Answers to these questions are found in *The Confessions*.

Augustine begins answering these questions by showing that it was through his reading of Cicero's *Hortensius* that he was inflamed with "that love of wisdom [which] is in Greek called Philosophy." This love of wisdom left him "free to love, and seek, and obtain, and hold, and embrace Wisdom itself, whatever it was."[5] With the reading of Cicero's exhortation, the first step was taken on Augustine's way to life as a philosopher. This first metamorphosis had a lasting influence on his life. Augustine's conversion to philosophy logically resulted in searching for a philosophy of his own.

Cicero's *Hortensius* persuaded Augustine to live the examined life. By examining his self he found a need for his lost childhood faith. But the Catholic faith as he had known it in Thagaste, his home town, did not blend with his philosophy-converted soul. He then turned to the Manichaeans, who claimed to have rationally obtained knowledge of divine truth as found in the Scriptures. After having become a member of this anti-Catholic sect, Augustine nevertheless continued his reading in philosophy.

In this period he wrote a treatise, *On the Beautiful and the Fitting*. Since this first text was already lost during his lifetime, we can only guess at its contents; as he described it in *The Confessions*, it contained a mixture of his literary and philosophical education and Manichaean ideas. After awhile Augustine found the Manichaeans less rational than they claimed to be. When he started to compare "the books of secular philosophy" with "the fables of the Manichaeans," a third philosophical change occurred in his life.

The Manichaeans referred Augustine, with his problematic questions, to their Bishop Faustus, who—so they believed—had all the answers. When he finally met Faustus and had a private discussion with him, Augustine became disappointed with Faustus's ignorance of the philosophers' "reasonable explanation by calculations, the order of times, and the visible testimonies of the stars."[6] After nine years of Manichaeanism, Augustine decided to make a new start in Rome, continuing his search for "Wisdom itself, whatever it was," although despairing of ever finding it.

O'Meara maintains that in some sense Augustine continued to be a Manichaean. He considers that Augustine had only a "mood of Skepticism" and never was a convinced academic.[7] Although Augustine explicitly mentions in *The Retractationes* that even after his conversion he had to write a book against the arguments of the Academics for personal reasons as well as to help others who had despaired of finding truth. It is apparent that Augustine's third stage of philosophical development was skepticism: In Rome, Augustine was of the opinion that "those philosophers which they call Academics, should be wiser than the rest, for that they held men ought to make a doubt upon everything, and decreed that no truth can be comprehended by man."[8]

After a year of teaching rhetoric in Rome, he was promoted to a better teaching job in Milan, where he came under the Neoplatonic influence of Bishop Ambrose. Although it is generally agreed that Augustine had no knowledge of Neoplatonism before he came to Milan, this can be questioned: For example, Brown suggests that Augustine may well have read Plotinus's *On Beauty*.[9] Brown, however, does not seem to have considered the possibility that Augustine might have read this work seven years before his Neoplatonian period, and that he was inspired by it to write his first philosophical work *De Pulchro et Apto* (*On the Beautiful and the Fitting*). I imagine that in *De Pulchro et Apto* Augustine might have presented a view about beauty opposing that of Plotinus. Whereas Augustine in his Manichean period could have been taught by the Manichaeans some Neoplatonism to demonstrate the superiority of their own type of gnosticism, it was only after he was freed from Manichaeanism that he could begin to appreciate it. Moreover, the particular combination of belief in Catholicism and the teachings of Plotinus roused in him a positive interest in his childhood faith.

His recently adopted skepticism, however, prevented him from embracing new promises of truth. How could he know that it was not another deception? Although this Catholic–Neoplatonism, as a further philosophical intervention, helped him reconcile many contradictions in his reading of the Scriptures, the disappointed Augustine needed some "strong" proofs before he could come to terms with religion.

This fourth stage of philosophical development, becoming acquainted with Catholic–Neoplatonism, Augustine describes as a period of recovering from skepticism. He ceased to have doubts about the God of his new Neoplatonist friends. He hoped that through a spiritual (i.e., Neoplatonian) reading of the apostle Paul he would find a true philosophical way of life, not just another view of the perfected life. He wanted a philosophy that could enable him to live an exemplary life. This pragmatic insight, that truth can be known through its results, brought about an inner crisis. Augustine reached the point of "inversion."

In contrast to my view on Augustine's conversion as an inversion of his principle of "reason guiding to belief," O'Meara considers Augustine's conversion to have been in two parts: first the conversion of the intellect caused by his study of the Platonists and the Scriptures, and second the conversion of the will through Christian submission.[10]

The word "inversion" that I use to characterize the inner change that Augustine experienced in his conversion coincidentally has a reference in psychoanalytic theory. Traces of psychoanalytic "inversion" ("similar to, but in many ways different from, 'homosexuality'") are ascribed to Augustine in a work O'Donnell considers to be a more worthy psychoanalytic study of Augustine: "Die Deutung Augustins" by W. Achelis.[11]

Where up to Augustine's conversion philosophical understanding had guided him to believe, now faith became a prerequisite for philosophical understanding of truth: Augustine first needed to have a divine revelation of what to do and when he faithfully obeyed this revelation he was instantly enlightened on a matter that had troubled him for many years; that is, his weakness in overcoming sexual desire. When he heard a mysterious voice telling him to read the Scriptures, he became convinced that at that very moment, rather than in an eternal tomorrow, he could overcome his doubts and weakness.

After Augustine's conversion he found that human intelligence could not obtain absolute truth unless assisted by divine grace. Though Neoplatonian concepts are almost equal to the Scriptures, without following the teachings of Christ the Platonists cannot understand divine truth and will not be able to live the life of beatitude. Augustine, the convert, believed that without divine assistance or grace, philosophy may even be harmful to persons searching for truth. For example, the Platonists' books may deflect a person from Christian piety or may show Platonism and Christianity as both ways leading to the same truth.[12] Nevertheless, divine predestination can use philosophy as a tool for its purposes as well.

Thus, Augustine reaches the fifth and last stage of a Christian pragmatic philosophy. Etienne Gilson confirms the essence of Augustine's philosophy as pragmatic: "He was in search, not of a theory alone, but of a practice as well. The wisdom he sought was a rule of life: adhering to it meant practicing it."[13]

From the former stages of his philosophical development Augustine retained rhetorical tools, logical analysis, the dialectic method of argumentation and synthesizing, and a history of philosophy leading up to a Christian wisdom. However, philosophical tools are constructive only through grace. Grace (or mercy, loving kindness) is a spiritual, virtuous, divine influence a person may accept or reject. In Augustine's view it is necessary to welcome this influence, for it is only by this power that a human being can know absolute truth.

Yet in the tenth book of *The Confessions* Augustine maintains that in addition to grace one can only attain philosophy in its purified essence by a process of expiation. The process of confession, prayers, and contemplation is summarized by Augustine in the following sentence: "Thou knowest both my unskillfulness and my infirmity: oh, teach me, and heal me."[14]

By describing the five stages of his philosophical development, Augustine justified his reasons for continuing the philosopher's life in his episcopal vocation. Although Max Wundt states that three conversions (stages of development) in Augustine's life (i.e., the *Hortensius*, Neoplatonism, and the religious experience) are generally recognized, he argues for a fourth conversion that took place in 391 C.E. when Augustine was ordained as a priest. With this fourth conversion, Wundt thinks that philosophy became only a matter for the justification of religion.[15]

In contradistinction to Jerome, Ambrose, and others, Augustine used his life experiences as a proof of the goodness of philosophy. Jerome had rejected philosophy as harmful and Ambrose had come to believe that "Julian the Apostate had lapsed from Christianity when he had 'given himself over to philosophy.'"[16] B.M.G. Reardon describes Augustine's new appreciation of philosophy as follows: "For faith and reason are not . . . two formally contrasted, still less antithetic, principles. He cannot conceive of faith without reason; and he is certain that reason, in its upward flight, approaches faith."[17] Augustine compares the Israelites despoiling the Egyptian treasuries as described in the book of Exodus with his own use of Greek and Roman philosophy.

Augustine apparently also knew the arguments about the contradiction between his early "philosophical" and later "theological" works (i.e., the Cassiciacum dialogues in comparison to his mature writings, such as *On the Trinity*), and wrote against them. There was no essential change in his Christian philosophy, his writings simply expressed progress in philosophical faith.[18] Similar evidence for continuity is found in Augustine's desire to use philosophy in his episcopal life; he described his search for a philosophical exegesis in the second part of *The Confessions*.

The first ten books of *The Confessions* discuss why there must be philosophy: Augustine's life teaches the necessity of philosophy as a way of life. The last three books of *The Confessions* are about the Scriptures and are a demonstration of the use of philosophical hermeneutics and a description of philosophy's practicality for the Biblical expounder. Augustine's philosophical–spiritual exegesis is a continuum of his philosophical development.

The question has often been raised as to whether the last three or four books of *The Confessions* are a fitting conclusion; indeed, if they belong to the work at all, since the autobiographic part seems to end with book nine or ten. Nevertheless, the assumption that only the first section is autobiographical has been rejected by several scholars, among others Robert Crouse: "Thus the last three books of *The Confessions*, far from being merely an appendix to the biography, provide the necessary logical conclusion of the whole work." Different and opposing opinions about the unity of *The Confessions* are described by O'Meara. According to O'Meara, *The Confessions* are not even a partial autobiography: "It is the use of Augustine's life and confession of faith in God as an illustration of his theory of man."[19]

For Augustine, the "autobiographic" sections on Genesis relate to his life's narrative through the theme of praise. And from other narrative perspectives as well, the two parts are interrelated: The first part contains Augustine's personal history, and the second is about the beginning and the end of universal history according to Scripture. The Scriptures had become for Augustine "all prophetic, all inspired, all authoritative, all has a reference beyond itself to the future, a significance within the total pattern of redemptive history."[20] Augustine's autobiography is a God-inspired knowledge of his personal history and for that reason it is a sacred and prophetic history.

Augustine's analogy between personal and universal history resembles the soul's journey in Neoplatonic philosophy from and to the Divine, and the generation of the Divine emanations. Autobiographical and universal history are related through the author's self-knowledge. Memory and a faculty that transcends knowledge of the temporary (i.e., "truth that dwells in the innermost house of thought") make known to the self its final, redemptive, and eternal history. Augustine's eternal history starts with knowledge of the Creation and ends with a prayer for rest in the Creator on "the Sabbath of life everlasting."[21] Not only is repetition as a rhetorical design used in the theme of personal and eternal history, but in the eighth book of *The Confessions* Augustine repeats conversion stories. The conversion story of St. Anthony is repeated in that of the two friends, and again in Augustine's and Alypius's conversion story.

The story of Augustine's conversion and the conversion of the two friends have eight major elements in common: "[They] go out in the garden together; one reads and/or thinks about the life of St. Anthony; the reader undergoes a conversion . . . ; the reader tells his companion . . . ; the companion responds . . . converts with his friend; both tell their friends . . . ; the friends marvel at the story; the converts break off their engagements."[22]

Besides these rhetorical designs within the narrative, philosophical themes and aims unite the segmented structure of *The Confessions*. A philosophical theme that unites the two parts, recognized by John Cooper, is the philosophical question, "What is existence?" in Book 1, Chapter 2 and Book 13, Chapter 1. Eugene Vance sees the continuation of narrative into the didactic. He considers Augustine's major purpose in the last three books as the development of an ontological theory based on language: "For Augustine, the end of self, the self in language, the self as language, is Genesis."[23]

The two last books of *The Confessions* had such a great influence on Augustine's era that one may attribute historical importance to them. The Pelagian controversy was triggered by a paragraph from the last section of *The Confessions*: "Grant what thou dost command, and command what thou wilt," proved to be a sentence so laden with controversial philosophical–theological meaning that it resulted in nine more essays by Augustine against Pelagius's interpretations.

The philosophical nature of these last chapters (reflections on human nature, memory, language, and creation) is obvious, but how philosophy is used in the exegesis of Scripture has to be explicated. Augustine turned to the book of Genesis not only as a professional expounder. Scripture had now taken the place of secular philosophy. Augustine's new book of philosophy had to be studied spiritually and philosophically. To do this, he used logic and rhetoric as philosophical tools, dialogue and prayer and meditation, respectively, as Platonic and Neoplatonic methods of inquiry. Further, Augustine's hermeneutics is a return to the lessons learned from his experiences, as described in the earlier chapters of *The Confessions*.

My view of Augustine's allegorical and epistemological method of interpretation is from the perspective of the earlier chapters of *The Confessions*: Ambrose's admonition that "the letter killeth, but the spirit giveth life" encouraged Augustine to cease understanding Scripture literally and rather to look for a spiritual meaning by divesting it of "the veil of mystery." By reading "books of the Platonists," Augustine began to understand the mysteries of Scripture metaphorically: "I came to get a sight of these invisible things of thine, which are understood by those things which are made."[24] Allen Gilmore discusses Augustine's allegoric technique, however, without mentioning its Neoplatonic origins.[25]

Through the analogy (or allegory) with material existence Augustine began to understand spiritual issues. The allegorical reading of Scripture now reconciled contradictions in the text; moreover it allowed for a pluralistic reading. Augustine explained this as follows: "For I know a thing to be manifoldly signified by corporeal expressions, which the mind understands all one way: and another thing again understood many ways in the mind, which is signified but one way by corporeal expression."[26]

May one conclude that in postmodern fashion Augustine was doing away with the Biblical text as intended by its divine "Author"? On the contrary, Augustine believed that God's foreknowledge allows for different but specific readings of truth. The aptness of an allegoric reading has to be confirmed by "truth dwelling in the innermost house of thought."

Gilson described Augustine's understanding of truth as follows: "When we arrive at truths, we arrive at something contained within our reason which cannot be explained from the point of view of reason and which compels us to transcend reason and to affirm the existence of the light that illumines it, i.e. subsistent, eternal and unchangeable Truth, i.e. God." [27] To know truth is a spiritual gift and a mystical privilege that Augustine explains as follows: "I am here put in mind still to say, truly the things of God knoweth no man, but the Spirit of God . . . those things which we know by His Spirit, even so no man knoweth them, but the Spirit of God."[28] This absolute spiritual realm we encountered earlier in Augustine's mystical experience at Ostia, which he described as "making contact with that eternal wisdom which abides above all things."

May it not be more than fortuitous that soon after Ostia the first narrative draws to a close? The narrative climax is not Monica's death, but the moment both Monica and Augustine received "first fruits of the spirit." The terminology "first fruits of the spirit" seems to relate to a mystic event described in the New Testament as the manifestation of the Holy Spirit to the followers of Jesus during the feast of first fruits; that is, Shavuot or Pentecost. The Ostia experience, comparable to other mystical and spiritual experiences, was the epistemological cornerstone for Augustine's philosophical–spiritual hermeneutics.[29]

So far we have observed in Augustine's autobiography that he became a true Christian through his longing for wisdom. His philosophical odyssey led him to accept the teachings of the Catholic Church as representing supreme wisdom. All his philosophical development is there to be praised; all is well with philosophy, by God's grace. *The Confessions* are an apologia for Augustine's own philosophical life and for the philosophical life in general. However, he warns that philosophers are incapable of finding the ultimate truth and wisdom without a spiritual understanding of the Christian faith. Augustine was aware that his pursuit of wisdom had caused him to embrace a religion in which he could realize his philosophical ideals. We will now see how Augustine articulated these ideals in some of his eminent writings.

PHILOSOPHICAL REFLECTIONS, THEOLOGY, AND AUTOBIOGRAPHY

Agostino Trapè presents a comprehensive list of Augustine's writings in which he arranges these works in ten categories: autobiographical, philosophical, apologetic, dogmatic, moral and pastoral, monastic, exegetic, polemical, letters, and treatises and sermons.[30] Augustine himself had his works—in his library and in *The Retractationes*—divided into three sections: his books proper, his letters, and his sermons. I divide Augustine's works into the following three categories: polemical and apologetic works, writings on philosophical–theological subjects, and exegetic works.

In each of these sections, however, one can find certain characteristics of the other two, and some of these works also contain additional autobiographic elements; for example, *The Academics*, *On the Blessed Life*, *On Order*, *The Retractationes*, and *Sermons* 355 and 356. Augustine's autobiography proper, *The Confessions*, likewise contains characteristics of these three categories. All his writings are characterized by recurring themes and topics.

In *The Retractationes* Augustine separates his early and later works by the date on which he became a bishop, which is about the time he wrote *The Confessions* (397–401 C.E.). I divide his early and later works the way he did. In each of the three categories I adopted I will discuss one work that was written before and another that was written after *The Confessions*.

Polemical and Apologetic Works

Outstanding in his polemical and apologetic works are *The Academics* and *The City of God*. Augustine's development can be regarded not only as representing progress in philosophical faith but also as representing progress in quantity and quality of writing. His first work, *On the Beautiful and the Fitting*, a polemic work written seven years before his conversion, has been lost. His first work after his conversion is a polemic against philosophical skepticism called *Against the Academics* or *The Academics* (386 C.E.). Augustine, the ex-Manichaean, finds it important to explain why he did not continue in the secular and Skeptic philosophies that opened his eyes to Mani's myths. Twelve years after his conversion Augustine began to work on his magnum opus, *The City of God* (413–427 C.E.), in which he combines the polemic and apologetic styles. Through the years apologetic writings outnumbered polemic works. In the polemics Augustine attacks the arguments of his opponents, while in the apologetics he defends his Christian beliefs by explaining them and showing them to be superior to the beliefs of his opponents. In *The Academics* and *The City of God* there are themes similar to those found in *The Confessions*: defeating skepticism and knowledge of destiny.

According to O'Meara, *The Academics,* written about fifteen years before *The Confessions,* is both in opposition to and in support of the Platonists.[31] In *The Retractationes* Augustine writes that he wrote against or about the Academics "to remove from my mind—because they were disturbing me—their arguments which in many men instill a despair of finding truth." Heil argues that "it is not so much the content of skeptical discourse which disturbs Augustine, but the effects of such discourse on the minds of men."[32] Though Augustine indeed seemed disturbed by some of their philosophical arguments, he supported the Skeptics' search for the happy life and wisdom.

The Academics was written in Cassiciacum and is one of the four so-called early dialogues. In comparison with other Cassiciacum dialogues, the references to classical authors are bountiful. *The Academics* is addressed to Romanianus, and is an exhortation to study philosophy. Romanianus had been a life-long friend of Augustine, a follower of the Manichaeans and then a Skeptic. Augustine's attempt to win Romanianus over to his newfound, true philosophy is described as dependent on the guidance of Fortune itself. Augustine gives several examples from his own life to persuade Romanianus that it was through divine providence that he at last found the wisdom he had always been seeking. He narrates that through the writings of the apostle Paul he had found true philosophy.[33] Romanianus is admonished to turn to the Scriptures, as did Augustine. If Romanianus would only seek, he would find truth.

In the book to Romanianus Augustine recaptures the gatherings of his friends and family for the purpose of discussing a philosophical subject. The definition of wisdom Augustine gives to the partners in dialogue is the same as found in Cicero's *De Officiis* 2.2.5: "Wisdom is a knowledge of divine and of human things." This definition contradicts the definition of wisdom held by the Skeptics to the effect that the happiness of the wise is obtained by the search for truth; it does not depend on finding truth.

Augustine refutes the Skeptic definition of wisdom while his fellow debaters seem to accept the Skeptic proposition of "the truth-like." Augustine explains why the Skeptics do not go beyond the "truth-like." Their search for truth and knowledge seldom becomes wisdom for several reasons: life's turmoil, a lack of intelligence, a lack of perseverance in the search for truth, or the false certainty of having already found it.

Augustine contends that unless a man is convinced that he will find truth, he will not dare to embark on the search. This statement he justifies by showing that even the Skeptics believed in the possibility of finding truth. However, the Skeptics thought that only an elite was worthy of finding it, and they concealed the truth. The reason for the Skeptic esoteric doctrine was to protect themselves from the materialistic philosophy of the Stoics. According to John Mourant the notion that the Skeptics were crypto-Platonist is not well-grounded. Nevertheless Mourant quotes Sextus Empiricus, who taught that the "Academics' skepticism was merely a means of testing the fitness of their pupils for admittance to their mysteries."[34]

Augustine did not exactly know the content of this esoteric doctrine—which was only revealed to a person if he had been a Skeptic until his old age—but he expected it to be Plato's theory. Augustine supported the Skeptics' faith in Platonic truth, for he could not find in Platonic doctrine anything that opposed Scripture. Mourant finds that the function of Neoplatonism in this dialogue is in part a "negative one, of destroying the errors of Stoicism and Epicureanism, [and] of maintaining more positively certain truths, e.g. a spiritual reality." O'Meara finds Augustine in disagreement with the Platonists only in one aspect: "their failure to see that Christ was the way of authority."[35]

Augustine holds it against the Skeptics that they misled the majority of the people by discouraging them from seeking. In order to inspire people to seek knowledge, a twofold force is needed: the force of authority and that of reason. The force of authority—which was lacking among the Skeptics—is found in Christ's commandment, "Seek and you will find." Nevertheless, Brown maintains that the principal lesson of the Cassiciacum dialogues is Augustine's demand for discipline: "To answer metaphysical questions and to contemplate 'such a God,' the mind must receive a proper training, an eruditio."[36]

It can be concluded that Augustine's exhortation to Romanianus to search for a true philosophy is a recommendation to accept a twofold authority: that of the Christian faith and that of reason (i.e., philosophy). Augustine's admonishments are the logical conclusions of the experiences he describes in *The Confessions.*

Augustine wrote *The City of God* between 413 and 420 C.E. Before he concluded this lengthy work he had already written many treatises against Julian, the Manichaeans, Donatists, Pelagians, Arianism, and other heretical doctrines. This might explain why in *The City of God* Augustine mainly directed his polemic against "pagan" worship and the ancient philosophers; only sporadic mention is made of the Manichaeans and heretics in general.

The City of God contains twenty-two books and is divided into two sections. In the first ten books Augustine rewrites the history of Rome from a Christian vantage point, methodically refuting the arguments of traditional interpreters of Roman history. His method is to teach "truth as it is," and his truth has historical, literary, philosophical, and theological content. Like Augustine's personal narrative in *The Confessions*, the historical narrative of the city of Rome is metaphysical. In *The City of God* Augustine "carried the general thought of Plato into his own general thought. . . . The appeal away from the illusion of things seen to the reality that belongs to God alone, the slight store set by him on institutions of time and place, in a word, the philosophical idealism that underlies and colors all Augustine's utterances on doctrinal and even practical questions."[37] There is little explicit discussion of Plato's philosophy in *The City of God*. The explicit use of Plato's thought is merely a tool in the hands of an apologist, an appreciation and devaluation when it serves Augustine's argument in favor of Christianity. Robert Russell considers that it was incumbent upon Augustine to show only where Platonism had failed and not so much where it had succeeded.[38]

As in *The Confessions*, the Platonists are praised and criticized. Augustine treats the Platonists as the most worthy philosophers "because they could conceive that the reasonable immortal soul of man could never be blessed but in participation of the light of God the world's Creator."

Augustine rejected Stoic and fatalistic historical approaches. In refuting fatalistic, astrological arguments he pointed out the diversity of conditions and qualities as found in the story of Esau and Jacob: According to astrology, the twin brothers would have to share in an identical fate, but "one of them bound himself to serve for wages, the other served not at all: the one was loved by his mother, so was not the other: the one lost his honor and inheritance . . . and the other obtained it."[39] Fate, then, does not depend upon the position of the stars or upon oracles, but upon the will of God. The Stoics, and especially Cicero, thought that freedom of will and fate were interrelated, but they denied the existence of divine foreknowledge. Augustine rejects this position: God's rule of human history does not contradict either free will or divine foreknowledge.

In the second part of *The City of God* the history of the two cities is analyzed, using the criteria of two kinds of love: the love of self and the love of God. Augustine explains the origin of the divine and the mundane city with a reference to the book of Genesis. Here and throughout *The City of God* his interpretation of Scripture is blended with metaphysics and revelation. For example, he answers the question about creation, "Who made it, how, and when?" with "God by His word, because He is good." Augustine, however, does not know if he has reached this understanding through a direct revelation or through some Scriptural verses.

He finds the Trinity reflected in all of creation. Similarly, he finds a triune division in philosophy; there is natural, rational, and moral philosophy. These three all lead to a beatitude: "The natural for nature, the rational for doctrine, the moral for use."[40]

Starting with the book of Genesis, two lines of destiny, the "good" and the "evil," are traced throughout all the books of Scripture. The arrival of the Christ did not destroy the evil of the mundane city. On the contrary, the good heavenly city is persecuted by the evil of the earthly city. But the final persecution afflicted on the divine city will end in victory for those who worship the true God. The last three books of *The City of God* are books on judgment; Augustine examines the rewards and punishments of God for the two opposing destinies. In this context he discusses perfect goodness according to the philosophers and according to the morality of the heavenly city.

Philosophers' predictions about ultimate goodness are considered vain, because they find goodness in temporary issues such as desires and virtues. The nature of earthly life is antithetical to strength, beauty, health, and vigor; man is subject to sin and corruption. Philosophers belonging to the earthly city cannot acknowledge that there is a conflict between the temporary and the eternal, between the earthly and the spiritual. The perpetual struggle of "flesh" against "spirit," of evil against good, and the continuous human failure to attain moral perfection explain why the philosophers only have a partial understanding of goodness. The final absolute good—that is, peace—can only be comprehended in life after death.

Augustine's articulation of his own human vulnerability and his hope for perfection such as he described in *The Confessions* in a hereafter resembles his confession of universal human weakness in *The City of God*. Augustine argues that Plato and Porphyry were wrong in their theories of reincarnation and of the purged soul liberated from the body. Although Augustine claims to have a clear understanding of the reasons and contents of God's judgments, he is careful not to have these judgments implemented by potential future citizens of the heavenly city while they are on Earth. According to Robert O'Connell, the distinction on earth between the two cities is kept "suitably vague and flexible; the mystery is vast, and our minds are so small."[41] Augustine's philosophical faith does not predict a happy ending for all, but at least *The City of God*, like *The Confessions*, ends by celebrating the perpetual Sabbath of eternal life. Like Augustine's own history in *The Confes-*

sions, the history of the two cities is hidden and can only be understood through Augustine's metaphysical method.

Philosophical–Theological Subjects

Outstanding as philosophical–theological subjects are *The Happy Life* and *On the Trinity*. Among Augustine's philosophical–theological works are many themes germane to everyday life, such as order, music, freedom of will, teaching, marriage, celibacy, widowhood, and even a handbook on life (*The Enchiridion*).

The Happy Life (or *The Blessed Life*) was written in 386 C.E., shortly after his conversion. In this, as in the other early dialogues, Augustine treats concrete and practical issues in a philosophical–theological framework. Augustine started to work on *On the Trinity* only four years after completing *The Happy Life*, while he was still writing *The Confessions*. In spite of this, *On the Trinity* was not completed until the year 416 C.E. It contains a theological and dogmatic discussion of the Christian triune God, and a trinitarian philosophical anthropology. *The Happy Life* and *On the Trinity* are both relevant for a better understanding of the philosophical meaning of Augustine's conversion account in *The Confessions*.

Augustine wrote *The Happy Life* in preparation for his baptism, about fifteen years before *The Confessions*. Like *The Academics*, *The Happy Life* was written while he was at a retreat at Cassiciacum, an *otium*, the traditional leisure during which the Roman aristocracy usually found cultural resurgence. R. J. Halliburton finds Augustine in his Cassiciacum period influenced by the examples of the life of St. Anthony, the Egyptian monasteries, the monastery of Milan, and others. During Augustine's retreats at Cassiciacum an experimental community came into being spontaneously. Brown considers that "the Otium Liberale" appealed to Augustine because "life had, recently, been far too complicated." However, Charles Brockwell pointed out that the desire to establish a common household in pursuit of philosophy already existed in Augustine at the age of twenty. Such communal life—guided by *charitas*—only became possible after his conversion.[42]

While at Cassiciacum, Augustine followed the habit of the ancient philosophers, whose enthusiastic, lively discourses dealt with practical questions as well as moral and political problems. The discussion about the happy life should be understood as perpetuating the tradition of ancient philosophy, and not as symptomatic of a psychological drive or a personal problem; it is not a wish for unattainable happiness, as assumed in Oscar Salinas's psychological analysis. Salinas contends that Augustine's childhood was a rather unhealthy experience that left him with a core of unhappiness for the rest of his life: Augustine's "obsession with happiness led to another compounding problem, that of the lack of substance in relationships."[43]

Augustine presents philosophy as the gateway to the happy life. He envisions himself as a sailor in search of a happy land. His journey began by reading Cicero's *Hortensius*, but then "for quite awhile [he] . . . was led astray," by the Manichaeans. When he abandoned them, "for a long while the Academics steered" his course. Other obstacles along Augustine's way to his fixed goal were the charms of women and the lure of honor. Finally, Plato's philosophy and many advisers guided him to his desired objective. However, he was not yet certain, metaphorically speaking, where, on dry land, the happy land was located. The dialogue has to clarify this.

Augustine's mother, Monica, has a central place in the dialogue. He praises her as having gained "the mastery of the very stronghold of philosophy"; she is in possession of "the kernel of philosophy."[44] Monica's definition of the happy person as one who wishes for and possesses good things is similar to Cicero's definition. The person who does not possess what he or she wants is considered miserable. If God is one's eternal desire, Augustine and his partners in dialogue conclude that whoever possesses God must be happy. The academics are depicted as forever searching for that "which they cannot find"; they are not only unhappy and foolish, but are diagnosed by Monica as suffering from intellectual "epilepsy." Through Monica's questions and manner of speech it is clear that she has not enjoyed the "liberal education" of the other participants in the retreat. Nevertheless, she is exemplary for her intuitive and logical understanding of God and life, which Augustine contributes to her devout Christianity. Monica is designated as "our mother."[45]

The Catholic Church, in *The Happy Life*, is symbolized by Monica's spirituality: Augustine depicts Catholic spirituality as the way to the "happy land" he had set out for at the beginning of the dialogue. Possibly through listening to Ambrose, or even to her own son, Monica seems to have received a broader, more philosophical faith then she had when she was still in the African town of Tagaste (or can one assume that Monica always had possessed such mature spirituality and during Augustine's childhood had implanted not only a love for God in her son but perhaps a love for wisdom as well?). In Monica's wisdom Augustine finds parallels with Roman and Greek philosophy; however, Augustine considers her spiritual wisdom as surpassing theirs.

As in *The Confessions*, Monica's genuine faith enables her to share the ultimate wisdom and truth with the philosophically educated Augustine. The five stations along Augustine's journey in *The Happy Life* are the same five stages of philosophical development he described in *The Confessions*.

Augustine's book *On the Trinity*, written some thirteen years after *The Confessions*, epitomizes metaphysical speculative thought. According to John Cavadini, *On the Trinity* appears in most contemporary research as "an intractable mass of speculation floating oddly aloof from foundation in any particular context." However, Cavadini's position on *On the Trinity*, a position I agree with, is that in it Augustine reiterates earlier philosophical dialogues refuting Neoplatonic views of salvation and certain Platonized Christian views.[46]

Augustine wrote this treatise as a polemic against the misuse of reason; that is, "a crude and perverse love of reason" that creates a concept of God that is corporeal instead of spiritual. His arguments in *On the Trinity* are similar to his arguments against the Manichaeans and the Skeptics in *The Confessions*.

The Holy Trinity is understood as an "equality"; it encompasses three manifestations of God, and these are one and the same. They are differently related, but there is no difference in their nature. Although "God the Son" is diminished because he was sent, and the same holds true for "God the Spirit," they are no less God in their nature than "God the Father" because He sent them.

Knowledge of God must be sought from God and from the Scriptures, and not through the teachings of those who try to understand the mystery of the Trinity through ordinary logic. Augustine criticizes philosophers and scientists. His argument against the philosophers is that if they had truly possessed knowledge, they would have foreknown future events. Although the philosophers "have understood as much as they could the eternity of the Creator," they were not able to foresee the bodily resurrection of the dead. Augustine differentiates between the intellectual cognizance of eternal things and the rational cognizance of temporal things.

Against the teachings of Pythagoras and Plato on the reminiscence of truth, Augustine proposes an intellectual perception of truth: "We ought rather to believe, that the intellectual mind is so formed in its nature as to see those things, which by the disposition of the Creator are subjoined to things intelligible in a natural order, by a sort of incorporeal light of a unique kind; as the eye of the flesh sees things adjacent to itself in this bodily light, of which light is made to be receptive, and adapted to it."[47]

On the Trinity contains more then one connotation pertaining to Augustine's theory of illumination; for example, "Truth itself is the light of the mind," or "unshaken and stable truth . . . sheds in an immovable eternity . . . the light of incorruptible and most sound reason."[48] Rational cognizance of ultimate truth is fruitless because of the weakness of the human mind when marred by sin and error. The process of clear understanding in *On the Trinity* resembles the process of repentance and supplication described in *The Confessions* as the way of obtaining wisdom.

O'Connel points out that to Augustine the human mind is so fashioned that in spite of its weakness it can never entirely suppress the memory of having been created in the image of the divine. The wayward, debased mind has some recollections of the lucid knowledge of the Creator. The mind is naturally directed to God, as has been foretold by the Psalmist: "All the ends of the earth shall be reminded and shall be converted to God."[49]

Augustine describes human nature as a "human trinity," consisting of memory, understanding, and will. The bond between the Holy Trinity and a human trinity is the charity of God. God is charity and Scripture is the divine speech of love. Through hearing God speak, words are committed to the mind's memory. Consequently, the divine word or Logos—God the Son—then exists in the human mind. This divine word, the true inner word, antecedes all language.

Gerard Watson showed that the philosophical background for Augustine's inner word is found in Stoic and Neoplatonic philosophy: "The theory of the inner word was not, then, simply an ad hoc construction by Augustine, a theory of human mind and language which he was forced to invent in *De Trinitate*. . . . [It] derived from Neoplatonism . . . and [was] coherent with a theory of meaning which he had put forward in an earlier work [i.e., *De Dialectica*]." Ordinary language is only semiotic, its purpose being communication between human beings. The mind's eye, or intellectual vision, is enlightened through contemplation of the divine speech. Remembering and contemplating the divine Logos is the source of human willpower and action. Consciousness renewed by the inner word approaches its true godlike self as "memoria Dei, intellectus Dei and amor Dei."[50]

In *The Confessions*, Augustine's own conversion story and those of others are evidence of how this theory works in reality: God spoke and Augustine and other converts underwent metamorphoses because they heard the inner word. Augustine's description of the function of memory, understanding, and will in *On the Trinity* is similar to and explains the function of memory, understanding, and will in *The Confessions*.

Exegetic Works

Outstanding in the exegetic works are *The Lord's Sermon on the Mount* and *The Tractatus on the First Epistle of John*. In his exegesis of Scripture Ambrose was influenced by philosophy as taught at the Alexandrian school. For Ambrose, and likewise for Augustine, interpreting was a spiritual and allegorical art. Nevertheless, Augustine established his own criteria for interpretation in *The Doctrina Christiana*. He rejected the concept that Scripture can be understood only by divine grace, without human assistance. The "science of reasoning" is knowledge instituted by God to be used in the interpretation of the Scriptures. For him, grammar, natural science, and other classic studies were necessary tools in the understanding of Scripture. Nevertheless, an exegesis that is not inspired by the love of God and of one's neighbor is not exegesis, no matter how correctly the human tools are utilized. God's charity is the touchstone for understanding the Scriptures.[51]

In this section on exegesis the books chosen are *The Lord's Sermon on the Mount*, which contains a synthesis of Augustine's moral doctrine, and *The Tractatus* or *The Homilies on the First Epistle of John*, for Augustine's famous dicta "Love, and do what you will." Both these works strongly resemble *The Confessions*, in that spirituality is seen as a pilgrimage. True spirituality is a development consisting of many stages, in which philosophy as well as cultivation of the emotions is necessary.

The Lord's Sermon on the Mount (or *The Lord's Sermon*) was written during the first years of Augustine's priesthood, between 393 and 396 C.E., about five years before *The Confessions*. It is an ethical treatise and offers solutions for problems encountered in the Christian way of life: "The lesson contained in *The Sermon on the Mount* was a way of life for all the followers of Christ."[52]

According to Luc Verheijen, there is a resemblance between Augustine's analyses of anger and hatred in *The Lord's Sermon* and Cicero's treatment of these in *The Tusculan Disputations*. The biography of the Stoic Zeno in Diogenes Laertius's *Vitae philosophorum* also contains the idea that "anger is the desire to punish someone who seems to have harmed us unjustly . . . [while] hatred is an inveterate anger."[53]

The Lord's Sermon is structured on the number seven: "St. Augustine makes the Beatitudes correspond to the Gifts of the Holy Ghost and regards both of them as seven stages of grace."[54] Seven beatitudes, seven gifts of the Holy Spirit, and seven petitions are found in the prayer taught by Christ (i.e., the Our Father). Augustine's reference for seven prophetic gifts is Isaiah 11:2–3. In *The Lord's Sermon* for the first time Augustine interprets the ascension of the soul in seven stages, an idea that is repeated in his later works.[55] Thus, the beatitude of humility, "Blessed are the poor in spirit," relates to the gift of God fearing. The beatitude of meekness relates to godliness, sorrow to knowledge, justice to fortitude, mercy to counsel, and purity to understanding. "Blessed are the peace makers" is the seventh and most elevated beatitude in the stages of grace and relates peace to wisdom.

In Neoplatonism, the Hypostases, or spheres of the divine being, might range from three to six or more. For example, such multiplications of Hypostases is found in the metaphysics of Iamblichus and his followers. It is not too far-fetched to recognize in these additional stages of purification and blessedness the Neoplatonic idea of purification and transformation through a hierarchy of emanations. The stages in

The Lord's Sermon resemble the stages of ascent of "the Hasid," Isaac the Blind, a thirteenth-century Spanish Kabbalist. His contemplative mysticism, inspired by Neoplatonism, is an instruction "on detailed meditations associated with basic prayers, according to the concept of the 'Sefirot' as stages in the hidden life of God."[56]

Another Neoplatonic characteristic of *The Lord's Sermon* is Augustine's preference for the contemplation of truth over acts of righteousness. The powers of evil would even deceive those who believe in Christ. Accordingly, he finds it of paramount importance that the "eye be clear and single-visioned for the finding of the way to wisdom, whose voice so great a host of errors and deceptions of wicked and perverse men tries to drown out, and the avoidance of all of which constitutes the surest peace and the imperturbable security of wisdom!" Right intention is of paramount importance: "All our works are clean and pleasing in the sight of God if they are done with a single heart, that is, with that supernal intention whose end is love; for love is the fulfilling of the law."[57] The way to attain this is mainly by prayer and contemplation. The seventh, highest stage is realized by the avoidance of sin, and in this the use of reason is crucial.

Augustine analyzed three steps in the "process" of temptation and sin: suggestion, pleasure, and consent. To illustrate this he used the example of fasting. Appetite is aroused by the sight of food or the memory of food. If these sensations bring pleasure, one will be tempted to break one's fast, but the pleasurable sensation can also be controlled through reason.

These reflections on gradual transformation and purification resemble the conversion account in *The Confessions*. When Augustine understood that through divine grace St. Anthony and others could control their desires by not yielding to them, he concluded that he too could live differently. He believed that yielding to one's desire, as well as the rational rejection of "forbidden fruits" is a matter of free choice. Yielding to temptation leads to sin, which when constantly repeated becomes a habit.

Augustine admits that overcoming sinful habits is extremely difficult, so much so that he compares the strength needed to overcome them with the power at work through Christ when he resurrected Lazarus. From his conversion experience and life thereafter Augustine seems to have become aware that through perseverance and divine assistance it is possible to overcome temptation and change habits.

When the soul, or as Augustine calls it, the "eye of the heart" or the "eye," with the aid of rational discernment has been made "single," that is, made one with its desire for God, "it will be fit and capable of beholding its own interior light."[58] As in *The Confessions*, here too rationality is considered essential for spiritual progress. Whereas the five stages of development in *The Confessions* are a historical description of an individual's development, the seven stages described in *The Lord's Sermon* are a prescriptive account for spiritual progress.

In *The Tractatus on the First Epistle of John* (or *The Tractatus*), written some fifteen years after *The Confessions*, Augustine addresses the conflict between the Catholic Church and the Donatist sect. In the way he treats this issue it is possible to differentiate between Augustine the preacher and Augustine the political rhetorician. The Donatists had caused a schism in the African Catholic Church by their demands for puritanical clergymen and saintly church members. Because of their militant ways of fighting for a "pure faith," Augustine sanctioned their persecution and forced conversion in 405 C.E.

In *The Tractatus* Augustine offers his flock not only a spiritual explanation based on the Scriptures, but also practical instruction and an apology for the Catholic Church's policy toward enemies, who included all heretics, but in particular the Donatists. Augustine finds that most of the heretical movements differ with the Catholic Church in their understanding of sin. Pelagius and his followers believed Christians had only to choose between good and evil. For Augustine the issue was more complex. Sin was part of human nature and only a Christian death could bring the final redemption or, in Brown's words, "the Christian life as seen by Augustine, could only be a long process of healing." Julian rejected Augustine's teaching about sin as Manichaean. From his point of view Augustine depicts people as if they were created by a devil and not by a just and loving God. A just God would not allow the "punishment of others for the sin of their father, the condemnation of helpless babies, the passing of sentences on men who had been unable to act otherwise."[59]

Gerald Bonner portrays Julian as the only philosophically equipped campaigner on the Pelagian side, though his campaign started too late: Pelagianism had already been condemned by the Pope and the emperor, and the polemics of Jerome and Augustine had made a considerable contribution to that end.[60]

The remaining danger for the Catholic Church in Africa was the Donatists. For his rhetorical warfare against the Donatists in *The Tractatus on the First Epistle of John*, Augustine uses as strategic keynotes the concepts of "confession of sin" and "charity," concepts that are also vital elements in *The Confessions*. In the First Letter of John, in the Scriptures, Augustine finds the raw material for devising his weapons of persuasion and persecution. His prologue to *The Tractatus* clearly and simply states a solution to the conflict with the Donatists, who seem to lack charity and humility: "Where there is charity, there is peace: where there is humility, there is charity." In the homilies Augustine draws an analogy between God and light and man and darkness. People are trapped in darkness because of their sins, yet they can come to the light by confessing themselves sinners. God's essential charity is covering the lesser sins that Christians still might commit. Those persecuting fellow Christians for these lesser sins are considered as if persecuting Christ himself. According to these criteria, the militant Donatists are not the true church, but the true enemies of the church. Augustine contends that hatred and persecution are natural to antichrists, while the true Christians are recognized by charity and the indwelling of God, who safeguards the continuation of their pilgrimage to the Divine. To justify his harsh treatment of the Donatists, Augustine maintains that the dictates of charity can lead, when necessary, to cruel action: "Some actions seem harsh or savage, but are performed for our discipline at the dictate of charity. Thus a short and simple precept is given once for all: Love, and do what you will."[61]

Brook Manville finds that Augustine's conscience was not entirely quiet about persecuting the Donatists.[62] Nevertheless, Manville's assumption that *The Confessions* are a self-examination of guilt feelings caused by Augustine's drastic approach to the Donatists seems to me highly questionable. Whatever the case, even Augustine's remorse could hardly make his policies on heretics understandable or acceptable to the church or others today.

Augustine's autobiography clearly shows the continual need for confession of sin, independent of his argument with the Donatists or other dissenters. However, the solution to the Donatist problem in *The Tractatus on the First Epistle of John* repeats an essential message of *The Confessions*: self-humiliation.

PSYCHOANALYSIS INFORMED BY PHILOSOPHICAL REBIRTH

Augustine's *Confessions* is a highly self-aware documentation on how the ideas received from others or developed by himself transformed his life. The five stages of Augustine's philosophical development begin, as stated before, with his reading of the Hortensius, and leads to the rational theology and way of life of the Manichaeans. When he leaves this sect, he gives himself over to a gloomy skepticism. This skepticism helps him continue his search, which is now characterized by the restraint of a person who was once caught up in deception and refuses to be deceived again. It is Ambrose's exegetic system that strengthened Augustine's hope of finding the wisdom he sought when setting out on his philosophical journey.

Whereas in his former development Augustine had acted solely on specific rational, philosophical understandings, now, through a divine revelation, he is made to believe in the spiritual truth of Scripture.

This conversion experience, a philosophical–spiritual rebirth, is the beginning of a pragmatic Christian philosophy to which he remained faithful for the rest of his life. His description in *The Confessions* of his philosophical development and its consequences testifies that he was aware of the influence of philosophy in his life. Furthermore, Augustine practices philosophical psychoanalysis insofar as he evaluates philosophy in his personal search for absolute and divine truth for himself and for others; the writing of *The Confessions* is philosophical psychoanalysis marked by the themes of consistency and continuity (see Chapter 3).

How different are these themes and the Augustinian stages of personal and spiritual development from Freud's five stages (i.e., the oral, anal, phallic, latency, and genital stages)? Eminent Augustine scholar James O'Donnell finds that the Augustine most people know today is a Freudian Augustine. This is partly due to Brown and most others whose biographies are written, if not as openly Freudian, then as "closet psychobiographies." But O'Donnell also observes that "in an odd way, the Freudian readings of Augustine common in this century share with Augustine an emphasis on the selected emotional high points he chooses to narrate and so are hostage to his own storytelling."[63]

Though Augustine shows awareness in *The Confessions* of childhood sensual pleasures and sexuality, I could not find that he recalls these as negative. These memories neither seem to have had particular negative or even detrimental consequences for his emotional development. His childhood seems to have contributed to his search for wisdom and happiness in living.

The psychoanalyst Charles Kligerman could not be of a more different opinion. He describes in "A Psychoanalytic Study of *The Confessions* of St. Augustine" Augustine's childhood as characterized by a sibling conflict and a classical Oedipal sexual conflict. Monica is to blame for the last: "Normal identification was prevented by Monica's persistent undermining of the father." Because of her religious beliefs she is categorized as religious women "are": "Often frigid, but passively compliant, such women are extremely frustrating to their husbands." Although the father is "alright" for Kligerman, Augustine's "position was in effect an identification with the sadistic sexuality of his promiscuous father." Monica's tears for her son, and her prophetic dream about him, are evidence of her erotic wishes toward Augustine. Her love for Augustine is "an engulfing type of seductiveness." Augustine's conversion is resolving his guilty consciousness from the fear of not satisfying his mother's heart's desire (i.e., his conversion) before her death. Not skepticism or a lack of faith, but Augustine's dismay of celibacy made him reluctant to submit to Ambrose's type of Catholicism. The voice heard during Augustine's conversion experience in the Milan garden is explained as follows: "Probably it was his own voice projected and perceived in hallucinatory fashion. Since Augustine retreated from incestuous attachment to a mother identification, then redoubled his masculine strivings, during the height of his tension when the ego was especially weak, he resorted to projection and regression to a pregenital level. Thus it is the voice of a *boy or girl*—it does not matter."[64]

Andrés Niño, in "Restoration of the Self: A Therapeutic Paradigm from Augustine's *Confessions*," uses concepts of Kohut's self-psychology to analyze Augustine's narrative. Niño finds Augustine's experience "a living portrait of Kohut's *Tragic Man*, wounded by an anticipatory despair about the crushing of the self and the ultimate defeat of his aspirations." He contrast his view with the psychoanalytic studies of J. E. Dittes, C. Kligerman, and P. Pruyser, which aim at "the recognition of patterns, behaviors and responses which fit various psychoanalytic formulas such as the Oedipus complex, latent homosexuality, and narcissistic grandiosity." Unlike Kligerman's essentially negative interpretation of Augustine's life as unfulfilled and self-deceptive, within Kohut's perspective it is possible for persons to attain an adequate view of themselves outside the clinical situation. Particularly the soteriological aspect in Kohut's work—that is, religion is meaningful for "the maintenance of man's self"—is appropriate for understanding Augustine's self-narrative. Niño finds that the criteria for therapy, such as the attainment of cohesiveness of the self, were reached in Augustine's self-analysis. But instead of reaching self-cohesiveness through the empathetic responsiveness of a self-object, Augustine is said to have attained this in dialogue with God, "leading to a transformed and restored self."[65]

In the philosophical psychoanalysis I propose, I look for patterns of philosophical activity and how these contribute to or diminish consistency and continuity in the life described. In *The Lord's Sermon* Augustine interprets the ascension of the soul in seven stages: These stages are applicable in a universal sense; this is, the ideal way of the pilgrim's soul after conversion. Different from Freud's perception of necessary stages of development, in Augustine's approach each individual's life can be very differently "staged" before and after spiritual rebirth. Each individual life has a different destiny, and the destiny is unknown in advance.

Augustine's philosophical psychoanalysis is characterized by consistency of thought and the consistency of Augustine's thoughts with his life. This consistency, however, is not always founded in rational thought only, but in a philosophical–spiritual understanding of God and self.

Augustine's self-understanding is evoked by a philosophical meditation through which a person becomes "a Spiritual"; that is, a mature

Christian.[66] In *The Confessions* the description of the mystical experience at Ostia, in which Monica and Augustine are feted at a lavish spiritual banquet, is evidence of their spiritual maturity as Christians. Dependency on God for truth—expressed metaphorically in a daily quest for spiritual bread and for the spiritual source of life—is found throughout *The Confessions*, in *The Lord's Sermon*, and in Augustine's other writings.[67]

Augustine envisages God as the Truth and the Supreme Wisdom that cannot contradict itself. Although a person can become aware of a harmonious order in his or her personal life and in the world through philosophical education, especially through Neoplatonic philosophy, it is only through the instruction of the Divine Spirit that one can receive the final and ultimate vision (i.e., of God, the self, and the world in which all is consistent with all else and for all of which thanks and praise are given). In this view, the Divine Spirit is the ultimate source for psychoanalysis and the absolute psychoanalyst.

Many years before Augustine arrived at his final, elitist doctrine, in thought and actions he sought to attain harmony and perfection through philosophy. Augustine's reasons for living as he did evolved from philosophy, and throughout the five stages of his development his life is congruent with his thinking. After his conversion there was no change in his philosophical faith, but there was progress, as Augustine himself observed in *The Retractationes*.

Augustine was aided in his way of life by philosophy proper until his conversion. After his conversion he was not only helped by his knowledge acquired from the past, but he applied as a tool to the Scriptures and to his life a philosophical–spiritual hermeneutics. In a sense Augustine perpetuated his skeptical approach to the human mind that was not enlightened by divine intelligence. The lessons learned from his early rational search for truth were transcended and synthesized in his continual search for truth in the spiritual realm. He found his rational and spiritual worldviews consistent because of their common origin and goal in that they proceeded from and led to the divine.

Differences between rational and spiritual ideas exist only in the place they fill in the hierarchy of God's perfection. Rational wisdom attains completion by the acknowledgment that reason fails to grasp absolute truth. Only reason combined with faith and divine revelation advances into the spiritual realm of absolute truth.

Karl Jaspers and a few other scholars detected contradictions in Augustine's writings. Failing to recognize the hierarchic arrangement of concepts in Augustine's philosophy, these critics judge consistency only by rational standards, rather than judging the spiritual aspects of his thought by spiritual principles and the rational by rational standards. Augustine limited rational standards to the domain of rational knowledge. For example, one of the contradictions pointed out by Jaspers is Augustine's dualism in the area of God–world, the heavenly and the earthly cities, belief–nonbelief, sin–grace, and acceptance of the oneness of God (this in spite of Augustine's so-called dualism). It is obvious that if these topics are not seen from Augustine's spiritual worldview, "the contradiction is evident."[68] To Augustine the ultimate knowledge of truth is not rational: It is an inner experience that transcends reason; it is the mystical perception of truth.

Augustine's search for wisdom was a search for truth that would enable him to live a good and pleasant life. Inconsistent thought and the influence of such inconsistency on life were a major concern to him. Since consistency in thought and in living are congruent with the life of truth and wisdom, existing contradictions and inconsistencies must be resolved. Augustine's childhood experiences seem to have left him with a sensitivity to search for interior and exterior harmony.

Augustine received two different conceptions on how to live from his parents: the worldview of his pagan father versus that of his devout Christian mother. These two conflicting concerns seem to be archetypal in Augustine's view of the world. There are "two cities," and "two loves," and these had to be brought into harmony with each other. Unlike the psychological interpretations that interpret this conflict as an emotional or sexual (Oedipal) conflict that dominated Augustine's life, I find that the young Augustine began to find his way out of the conceptional conflicting influences of his upbringing by reading Cicero.

The idea of supreme wisdom, as described in Cicero's *Hortensius*, eventually became Augustine's ideal for education, providing him with a consistency that had been lacking in his parents' worldviews. From his father Augustine received a love for materialism and the classical world; his mother bequeathed him a love for spirituality and the Christian faith. But his parents agreed that a classical education would be the best guarantee for his future. Augustine might have felt cornered between those two opposing influences, since in his early education there is agreement on this one issue only, while on other issues his parents make conflicting demands of him.

Augustine's resolution of this conflict is through submission to a third party, the God of all wisdom. The result is a harmonious hierarchy of two types of love in which the love of God is superior to the love of the world. Worldly love is no longer in opposition to God, but at his service. Growing up in the teachings of the African Catholic Church did not give Augustine's inquiring mind the intellectual sustenance it longed for, but he also could find no interest in a life of material and cultural pleasures. His inner restlessness is interpreted in *The Confessions* as the call of the Creator, who created mankind for himself. Augustine's heart had to be restless until it found rest in God.

Reading *The Hortensius*, Augustine was encouraged to seek a wisdom that would overcome the contradictions inherited from his childhood, and from it he acquired the confidence that consistency in a philosophical way of life could be realized. Augustine gave expression to this new approach by looking for a consistent rational theology and lifestyle, which he believed he found with the Manichaeans.

In the first three stages of Augustine's development the reason for changing his thought and life emerges through the discovery of inconsistency. A change is made by looking for or adopting a better, more rationally consistent philosophy and way of life. Augustine's contact with Bishop Ambrose and his readings of the Platonists brought new light to his search for truth. His inner contradictions were slowly reconciled. The Manichaeans had demonstrated by their rational reading of Scripture that God can be reproached for many contradictions and immoral actions. The Neoplatonists showed Augustine that an allegorical, spiritual reading of Scripture does not create contradictions in the character and actions of God (or people). On the contrary, it reconciles apparent contradictions in the Scriptures themselves and between the Scriptures and scientific–philosophical theories.

Though it is gratifying for Augustine's consistency-bound soul to find that consistency is not only a matter of reason, this cannot eradicate his doubt in the ability of the human mind to find ultimate truth. He needs some stronger medicine to be cured of skepticism. The examples of the Christians who were able to believe and overcome passions and contradicting feelings within themselves created a crisis in Augustine. If it was possible to be at one with oneself, with wisdom, and with the Christian faith, then the step toward such divine consistency had to be taken in blind faith.

That Augustine could accept the superiority of revelation over reason only after a mystical experience shows how important rationality was for him and, somewhat modified, rationality remained important throughout his life. Though rationality was modified by revelation, reason remained necessary for receiving the divine vision.

The acceptance of the divine command made it possible to move beyond the inconsistencies Augustine had experienced in his worldview and sexual life. While Augustine was cultivating his new spiritual lifestyle, the old conflict flared up within the African Catholic Church: In 398 C.E. the bishops of the Catholic Church of Carthage prohibited the reading of philosophical books. The religious puritanism of the African Catholic Church had affronted Augustine in his youth, but now he was in a position to defend his own type of Catholicism by showing it to be consistent with the love of philosophy. Augustine analyzed his life as an authoritative argument against those Christians who considered philosophy a poison. *The Confessions* as the document of his conversion to and maturation in the Catholic faith shows that everything is through the grace of God; for everything, for philosophy too, thanks must be given to God.

In *The Confessions* Augustine combines the biblical account of creation and eschatology with his own past, present, and future. A total, everlasting consistency is achieved through the rational–spiritual truth of God. In Augustine's early and late writings there is the same rigid resolution of inconsistencies into a coherent whole. That consistency is important for Augustine until the very end of his life is evident from *The Retractationes*. In the context of his whole opus a final attempt is made to discover, confess, and retract everything that only in the continuity of life could be understood as inconsistent.

Another characteristic of Augustine's self-analysis and of his early and late writings is continuity. He understood his life and work as a development, as a journey to God. Brown emphasizes that through writing *The Retractationes* at the end of his life Augustine wanted to view his work as a whole. The chronological order in which Augustine criticized and explained his own writings is meaningful in that the reader is invited, as it were, to "appreciate the long journey which Augustine had taken to reach his present view."[69]

No great differences are found in the subjects, themes, and methods of Augustine's early and late works. However, there is an increase of apologetic–polemic and exegetic work and a decrease of philosophical–theological work after *The Confessions*.

Continuity is found in the content of his writings, which often originate in actual questions and problems: situations relating to his personal life, or for which his friends or community needed a solution. All three categories of Augustine's writings aim to expose and correct errors in thought and interpretation, and ultimately he addresses errors made in the course of everyday living. The continuum of life in his writings and, vice versa, writing as it influences everyday life, is documented by Augustine in *The Confessions* as follows: "The thirteen books of my confessions praise the just and good God for my evil and good acts, and lift up the understanding and affection of men to Him. At least, they had that effect on me while I was writing them and they continue to have it when I am reading them."[70]

Recurring and lasting themes in Augustine's life and work are the importance of love, friendship, philosophy, and religion. The theme of continuity itself is of crucial importance in Augustine's philosophy because nothing is without continuity. All has its origin in God and develops according to the divine will. Jaroslav Pelikan pointed out that in Augustine's autobiography there is "a sure, if unsteady, advance to an ultimate goal," while in Herodotus's classical historiography a series of repetitive patterns exist over which the spectator has no control. Georg Misch finds *The Confessions* strongly influenced by the Aristotelian concept of "genesis" or development.[71]

In *The Confessions* the thread of life is recognizable as a continuum only by seeing it from the divine perspective. Augustine became aware of this thread of divine continuity through awareness of "the memoria Dei." Augustine experienced continuity not by just remembering and understanding the past, present, and future through rational reflection, but through access to the "memoria Dei"; that is, the human memory recreated through hearing the divine word. Confessions and prayers are a continuous process of purification and healing, which begins the transformation of the human memory, understanding, and will into divine memory, understanding, and will.

Augustine's love of philosophy, the passionate years of his early manhood, and the rise and fall of the city of Rome all play a meaningful part in the divine scenario of redemption. From the divine perspective the thread of life is clear and meaningful. Augustine as seeker, sinner, and skeptic followed the invisible line of God's election, which became apparent to Augustine through his conversion to and maturation in the Christian faith. Individuals have access only to their own personal lines of continuity through attaining spiritual maturity and self-awareness.

Robert Elbaz maintains that after Augustine's conversion the biographical work had become meaningless for him and what remains is a metaphysical discourse.[72] Elbaz's considerations seem erroneous to me because they contradict the importance Augustine gives to autobiographical, biographical, and historical descriptions throughout his writings, especially in *The Confessions* and in *The City of God*. Elbaz fails to understand that it was precisely metaphysical discourse that made self-narration and history meaningful for Augustine, before and after his conversion. Factual data are significant for Augustine, as the literary meaning of the Scriptures remained significant in spite of the spiritual metaphysical content. The more important issue, however, is to understand the truth hidden behind the veil of factual data.

Augustine's "two cities" and "two selves," seen by eyes that have not experienced spiritual revelation, seem to exclude one another. Augustine's spiritual conception is that the city of God exists alongside the worldly city, but the heavenly city also exists in people who live like strangers in the worldly city. Likewise, the converted Augustine lives together with (inside) the old sinful Augustine. Or as Aquinas reformulated Augustine's doctrine on grace, "Grace does not abolish nature, but it completes it."[73] *The Confessions* is the description of two selves that are in harmony and at one: the completed "divine" or "new" self and the "natural" or "old" self that is in a continuous process of confessing the sins inherent in human nature.

Augustine's doctrine of self-transformation through grace contradicts the doctrine of the Manichaeans on the existence of two conflicting souls in an individual: a good soul and an evil one. Augustine attacked the Manichaean doctrine in *On the Two Souls*, while in *The Confessions* he illustrates his philosophy on the restoration of the self with his own personal case. Augustine's self prior to and following the revelation of the divine truth is continuously preparing for a divine destiny; his life before the conversion event and his religious–philosophical life thereafter were according to the unique divine blueprint.[74]

It was Augustine's opinion that until he accepted God's grace in its full measure he was subject to deception and compulsive behavior and to constrained slavish intellectual activity. Moreover, in *The Confessions* he maintains that only in life after death, in eternity, would he be able to completely comprehend the supreme divine vision and wisdom.

Nevertheless, he acknowledged that some non-Christian philosophies, such as Plato's, had brought him closer to true knowledge and wisdom. Augustine thus recognized that all people possess a measure of truth and intelligence through which they can distinguish falsehood from truth and earthly wisdom from divine.

Through following this personal inner light Augustine was led from confusion, deception, and emotional bondage to the true knowledge and superb harmony of God's wisdom, although in comparison with the divine mind, his mind had only weak intellectual powers of discernment. Augustine's autobiographical psychoanalysis demonstrates that by his own philosophical understandings and meditation he was able to transcend the influences of upbringing, the past, culture, and inadvertent enslavement to preconceptions. Within this philosophical psychoanalysis I have demonstrated Augustine's successful attainment of consistency and continuity, yet the attainment of this state is essentially different from the Freudian way to attain consistency and continuity.

NOTES

This chapter and the following two chapters are based on Chapters 2, 3, and 4 of my unpublished Ph.D. dissertation, "Philosophical Autobiography," which I submitted to the Senate of the Hebrew University of Jerusalem in 1997. These chapters have been extensively revised for publication in this book.

1. John Burnaby, "The 'Retractationes' of Saint Augustine: Self-criticism or Apologia?," *Augustinus Magister* 1 (1954): 86–92.

2. Augustine, *The Retractations*, trans. M. S. Bogan (Washington, D.C.: Catholic University of America Press, 1947), 130.

3. Augustine referred to the Christian and Hebrew Scriptures with the term "The Holy Scriptures," or in other words The Bible. I will use the term Scriptures when referring to these books.

4. Peter Brown, *Augustine of Hippo* (London: Faber and Faber, 1967), 165; James J. O'Donnell, *Augustine Confessions*, vol. 1 (Oxford: Clarendon Press, 1992), xliii–xliv, available at: <http://ccat.sas.upenn.edu/jod/> (last accessed March 2001); John J. O'Meara, *The Young Augustine* (Suffolk: Chaucer Press, 1980), 4.

5. Augustine, *The Confessions*, trans. W. Watts (Cambridge: Harvard University Press, 1950), vol. 1, 111–112.

6. Ibid., 217.

7. O'Meara, *The Young Augustine*, 110.

8. Augustine, *The Confessions*, vol. 1., 245.

9. Brown, *Augustine of Hippo*, 95.

10. O'Meara, *The Young Augustine*, 11.

11. O'Donnell, *Augustine Confessions*, vol. 1, xxxi.

12. Augustine, *The Confessions*, vol. 1, 395.

13. Etienne Gilson, *The Christian Philosophy of Saint Augustine* (London: Gollancz, 1961), 231.

14. Augustine, *The Confessions*, vol. 1, 205.

15. Max Wundt, "Ein Wendepunkt in Augustins Entwicklung," *Zeitschrift fur die Neutestamentliche Wissenschaft* 21 (1923): 53–64.

16. That Jerome rejected philosophy may be concluded from his letter to Eustochium (Ep. 22, 30). However, Jerome apparently never put into practice his oath against philosophy. Angelo Di Berardino, *Patrology*, vol. 4 (Westminster: Christian Classics, 1986), 215; Brown, *Augustine of Hippo*, 112.

17. Reardon, B.M.G., "The Relation of Philosophy to Faith in the Teaching of St. Augustine," *Studia Patristica* 2, 64 (1957): 288–294.

18. Augustine, *The Retractations*, 5; Augustine, *The Confessions*, vol. 2, 15.

19. Robert Crouse, "*Recurrens in te unum*: The Pattern of St. Augustine's *Confessions*." *Studia Patristica* 14 (1976): 389–392; O'Meara, *The Young Augustine*, 18.

20. Robert Austin Markus, *Saeculum: History and Society in the Theology of St. Augustine* (Cambridge: Cambridge University Press, 1970), 192.

21. Augustine, *The Confessions*, vol. 2, 473.

22. Donovan Johnson, "Story and Design in Book Eight of Augustine's Confessions," *Biography* 14, 1 (1991): 54.

23. John Cooper, "Why Did Augustine Write Books XI–XIII of *The Confessions*?" *Augustinian Studies* 2 (1971): 37–46; Eugene Vance, "Augustine's *Confessions* and the Grammar of Selfhood," *Genre* 6, 1 (1973): 1–28.

24. Augustine, *The Confessions*, vol. 1, 279, 393.

25. Allen A. Gilmore, "Augustine and the Critical Method," *Harvard Theological Review* 39 (1946): 141–163.

26. Augustine, *The Confessions*, vol. 2, 441.

27. Gilson, *The Christian Philosophy of Saint Augustine*, 18.

28. Augustine, *The Confessions*, vol. 2, 461.

29. Ibid., 49; Wilma Gundersdorf von Jess, "Augustine at Ostia: A Disputed Question," *Augustinian Studies* 3 (1973): 159–174.

30. Augustine, *The Retractations*, xv–xvi; Agostino Trapè, "Saint Augustine," in Di Berardino, *Patrology*, 343–403.

31. John J. O'Meara, "Introduction," in *St. Augustine: Against the Academics: Ancient Christian Writers*, ed. J. Quasten and J. Plumpe (Westminster, Md.: Newman Press, 1950), 16.

32. Augustine, *The Retractations*, 6; J. Heil, "Augustine's Attack on Skepticism: The *Contra Academicos*," *Harvard Theological Review* 65 (1972): 99.

33. Augustine, *Answer to Skeptics*, intro. D. J. Kavanagh (New York: Cima, 1948), 139.

34. John A. Mourant, "Augustine and the Academics," *Recherches Augustiniennes* 4 (1966): 93.

35. John A. Mourant, "The Emergence of a Christian Philosophy in the Dialogues of Augustine," *Augustinian Studies* 1 (1970): 71; John J. O'Meara, "Augustine and Neo-Platonism," *Recherches Augustiennes* 1 (1958): 102.

36. Brown, *Augustine of Hippo*, 121.

37. John J. O'Meara, *Charter of Christendom: The Significance of the City of God* (New York: Macmillan, 1961), 63–64.

38. Robert Russell, "The Role of Neoplatonism in St. Augustine's *De Civitate Dei*," in *Neoplatonism and Early Christian Thought*, ed. H. J. Blumenthal and R. A. Markus (London: Variorum, 1981), 160–179.

39. Augustine, *The City of God*, vol. 1, ed. R.V.G. Tasker (London: Dent and Sons, 1950), 146.

40. Ibid., 273, 332, 334.

41. Robert J. O'Connell, *The Origin of the Soul in St. Augustine's Later Works* (New York: Fordham University Press, 1987), 308.

42. Brown, *Augustine of Hippo*, 116; Charles W. Brockwell Jr., "Augustine's Ideal of Monastic Community: A Paradigm for His Doctrine of the Church," *Augustinian Studies* 8 (1977): 94; R. J. Halliburton, "The Inclination to Retirement: The Retreat of Cassiciacum and the 'Monastery' of Tagaste," *Studia Patristica* 5, 80 (1962): 330–331.

43. Oscar Salinas, "The Psychological Roots of Augustine's Theories of Good and Evil," *Biography* 15, 4 (1992): 350–352.

44. Augustine, *The Happy Life*, intro. L. Schopp (New York: Cima, 1948): 49, 67.

45. Ibid., 113, 99, 139 in the intro. to *The Happy Life*. Ludwig Schopp considers that "our mother" indicates that Monica, besides being the biological mother of Augustine and his brother Navigus, is also the spiritual mother of all present.

46. John C. Cavadini, "The Structure and Intention of Augustine's *De trinitate*," *Augustinian Studies* 23 (1992): 103.

47. Phillip Schaff, ed., *A Select Library of Nicene and Post-Nicene Fathers of the Christian Church*, vol. 3 (Edinburgh: T. and T. Clark, 1988), 81, 164.

48. Bruce S. Bubacz, "Augustine's Illumination Theory and Epistemic Structuring," *Augustinian Studies* 11 (1980): 44.

49. O'Connell, *The Origin of the Soul in St. Augustine's Later Works*, 267–268.

50. Gerard Watson, "St. Augustine and the Inner Word: The Philosophical Background," *Irish Theological Quarterly* 55 (1989): 87; Robert D. Crouse, "*In Multa Defluximus: Confessions* X, 29–43, and St. Augustine's Theory of Personality," in Blumenthal and Markus, *Neoplatonism and Early Christian Thought*, 184.

51. Gilmore, "Augustine and the Critical Method," 141–163; Christopher Kirwan, *Augustine* (London: Routledge, 1989), 6–13.

52. Augustine, *The Retractations*, 85.

53. Luc M. J. Verheijen, "The Straw, the Beam, the Tusculan Disputations and the Rule of Saint Augustine: On a Surprising Augustinian Exegesis," *Augustinian Studies* 2 (1971): 23–24.

54. Augustine, *The Lord's Sermon on the Mount*, trans. J. J. Jepson (New York: Newman Press, 1948), 8.

55. Frederick van Fleteren, "Per Speculum et Aenigmate: The Use of I Corinthians 13, 12 in the Writings of Augustine," *Augustinian Studies* 23 (1992): 79.

56. R. T. Wallis, *Neoplatonism* (London: Duckworth, 1972), 130; Gershom Scholem, *Kabbalah* (Jerusalem: Keter, 1974), 46.

57. Augustine, *The Lord's Sermon on the Mount*, 172, 132.

58. Ibid., 174.

59. Brown, *Augustine of Hippo*, 367, 392.

60. Gerald Bonner, "Pelagianism and Augustine," *Augustinian Studies* 23 (1992): 46–47.

61. John Burnaby, *Augustine: Later Works* (Philadelphia: Westminster Press, 1955), 259, 263, 326, 316.

62. Brook Manville, "Donatism and St. Augustine: The Confessions of a Fourth Century Bishop," *Augustinian Studies* 8 (1977): 126.

63. James J. O'Donnell, *Three Studies in Augustinian Biography*, Internet publication, 1999, available at: <http://ccat.sas.upenn.edu/jod/> (last accessed August 2000).

64. Charles Kligerman, "A Psychoanalytic Study of *The Confessions* of St. Augustine," *Journal of the American Psychoanalytic Association* 5 (1957): 470, 474, 478, 482.

65. Andrés G. Niño, "Restoration of the Self: A Therapeutic Paradigm from Augustine's *Confessions*," *Psychotherapy* 27, 1 (1990): 9, 10, 11, 17.

66. Roland Teske, "Spirituals and Spiritual Interpretation in Augustine," *Augustinian Studies* 15 (1984): 75.

67. Leo C. Ferrari, "The 'Food of Truth' in Augustine's *Confessions*," *Augustinian Studies* 9 (1978): 11.

68. Karl Jaspers, *Plato and Augustine* (New York: Harcourt, Brace, and World, 1957), 110.

69. Brown, *Augustine of Hippo*, 429.

70. Augustine, *The Retractations*, 130.

71. Jaroslav J. Pelikan, *The Mystery of Continuity, Time and History, Memory and Eternity in the Thought of Saint Augustine* (Charlottesville: University Press of Virginia, 1986), 144; Georg Misch, *A History of Autobiography in Antiquity*, vol. 1 (London: Routledge, 1949), 290.

72. Robert Elbaz, *The Changing Nature of the Self: A Critical Study of the Autobiographic Discourse* (London: Croom Helm, 1988), 26.

73. Pelikan, *The Mystery of Continuity, Time and History, Memory and Eternity in the Thought of Saint Augustine*, 147.

74. Peter I. Kaufman, "The Lesson of Conversion: A Note on the Question of Continuity in Augustine's Understanding of Grace and Human Will," *Augustinian Studies* 11 (1980): 64.

CHAPTER 5

The Philosopher True to Nature

> But these crises, although once quite frequent, were always short-lived, and now, when I am still not quite free of them, they are so brief and infrequent that they have not even the power to disturb my peace of mind. They are mere flickers of anxiety which have no more effect on my soul than a feather falling into the water can have on the course of a river.
>
> Jean-Jacques Rousseau, *Reveries of the Solitary Walker*

THE PHILOSOPHICAL SELF-PORTRAIT

Rousseau wrote three autobiographical works: *The Confessions of Jean-Jacques Rousseau; Rousseau, Judge of Jean-Jacques: Dialogues;* and *Reveries of the Solitary Walker*. In *The Confessions of Jean-Jacques Rousseau*, Rousseau presents a philosophical account of his emotional and intellectual development. These confessions are a narrative of his childhood, youth, and adulthood. He began to write the memoirs in 1764 and completed them in 1770. He considered *The Confessions* a self-portrait of human nature, of special and unique interest to philosophers.

Christopher Kelly indeed sees philosophical importance, or as he says, "necessity," in Rousseau's denial of the possibility of a history guided by standards of factual truth. Rousseau needed a philosophical standard of general principles about human nature as a guide for the writing of his own history. Kelly compares *The Confessions* with Hegel's *Phenomenology*, which he construes as a "philosophical biography."[1]

Some three years before Rousseau started to work on his confessions, he wrote in *The Preface to Narcissus: Or the Lover of Himself*, "This discourse will be, I admit, a very bitter satire, not on me, but on my century."[2] Rousseau's critics often fail to recognize the satirical aspect in *The Preface to Narcissus* and in all his other writings as well, even when it is quite obvious, as in the autobiographical dialogue *Rousseau, Judge of Jean-Jacques: Dialogues*. N.J.H. Dent is one of the few who recognizes that Rousseau wrote *The Confessions* "sometimes with wit."[3]

In *The Confessions* stories that may seem absurd on the surface make more sense when understood as satire. For example, Rousseau's account of the affirmation of his eternal salvation. He tosses a stone at the trunk of a tree. If the stone misses, he will be eternally damned, but if it hits the tree, Rousseau's eternal salvation is secured. Or the story of the mysterious disappearance and return three days later of one of his manuscripts.[4] These and other bizarre anecdotes are best understood as satirical hyperbole, although they do not lack a sarcastic core of bitter truth. Voltaire's influence on Rousseau is most apparent in such often unrecognized ridicule.

Rousseau's *Confessions* covers close to 700 pages, from which I emphasize only those issues that are of philosophical importance. Nevertheless, my analysis does not disregard the general larger context.

Rousseau's *Confessions* can be called the eighteenth-century version of Augustine's autobiography. Ann Hartle observes that "Rousseau's construction of his *Confessions* over and against the model of Augustine's *Confessions* suggest a parallelism of philosophical concern."[5] Through his autobiography Rousseau reflects on or attacks the philosophical and theological conflicts of his revolutionary century. Like Augustine, Rousseau aims not only to reveal his own true self, but to reveal human nature as a whole. Whereas Augustine believed himself to be successful in solving the mysteries of the soul in general, including his own, Rousseau claims to understand only his own soul, while the world around him remained a mystery because of a perceived lack of "transparency" in other people.

Religious confessions like Augustine's usually try to achieve a reconciliation between the confessor and a deity. Rousseau's *Confessions* have as their sole aim a person-to-person reconciliation. Convinced of his own purity of heart and good intentions, Rousseau tries to show that in spite of his many faults he was nevertheless the best of men.

Rousseau's aim is to describe "man in all truth of nature," that man being himself. An example of such a self-description is found in the following sentence: "I felt before I thought: this is the common lot of humanity."[6] He finds that he is different from other men, but his existence is comparable with theirs. He is different in that his great sensitivity makes him feel more intensely than others. In addition, Ronald

Grimsley observed that Rousseau "constantly stressed that his own personal philosophizing was much more fundamental and universal in its implications than the superficial and insincere reflection of philosophers obsessed with satisfying their own vanity."[7]

The Confessions of Jean-Jacques Rousseau start with an account of his childhood. Rousseau's mother died soon after she gave birth to him. Rousseau recalls having been a self-conscious child, who at the age of five, six, and seven read the novels that had belonged to his mother. He observes that by reading these books at such an early age he acquired an almost incurably romantic conception of human life and an unusual knowledge of emotional life. His childhood reading shaped his self in a particular manner, it left him with "confused emotions . . . odd and romantic notions of the human life, of which experience and reflection have never been able wholly to cure."

From his seventh to eleventh years Rousseau educated himself by reading the books he found in the library of his grandfather, who had been a Protestant minister with philosophical interests. Rousseau read Bossuet, Ovid, and Molière, but his favorite book was Plutarch's *Lives of Famous Men*. He traces the origin of what he characterizes as his free republican spirit, which could not endure slavery or servitude, to the influence of these intellectual readings. He identified completely with the individuals he read about: "I believed myself a Greek or a Roman, I lost my identity in that of the individual whose life I was reading."

He lived with his father, nurse, and aunt until he was twelve years old, but his family was less real to him than the fantasy world created by his reading. Nevertheless, Rousseau attributes his love of music to the influence of his aunt, who often regaled him with cheerful songs. The period of self-education ended when he was sent, together with his cousin, to the Protestant minister Lambercier to learn Latin and "all the sorry trash which is included under the name of education." But Rousseau praises Pastor Lambercier for not demanding to much of him. He was cognizant of his tutor's strong influence on his personality: "If it had lasted longer it would have completely decided my character."

Another influence evoked a powerful upheaval in his emotional life, especially in the areas of love and sex. Rousseau describes how the kindness and the disciplinary methods of the Pastor's sister, Mademoiselle Lambercier, shaped his tastes, desires, and passions, and his own self, for the rest of his life, "and that in a manner exactly contrary to that which should have been the natural result." The sensual pleasures he derived at puberty from the corporal punishment he received from Mademoiselle Lambercier were the cause for his "idle longings": "I spent my life in idle longing, without saying a word, in the presence of those whom I loved most." He found his self composed of elements that sometimes appear incompatible and yet coalesced into a uniform whole, while elements he considered compatible crystallized into a conflicting conglomeration. For example, this was his analysis of the development of his sensuality: "One of the most powerful movements of my soul was tempered in the same spring from which a stream of sensuality and effeminacy has entered my blood."

Rousseau's hatred of injustice was awakened not only by Plutarch, but by an unfortunate incident in which he was falsely accused by his tutors of having broken a comb. He found that this incident brought his childhood to an end. The Lamberciers had suddenly become human beings rather than gods who could read into peoples' hearts. The respect, intimacy, and confidence that had previously existed between the pupils and their tutors had disappeared. Rousseau and his cousin were now more afraid of being accused of wrongdoing than of actually doing wrong. A few months after the comb incident Rousseau was back in Geneva, where he stayed with his uncle for three years.

He wanted to become a Protestant minister, but due to lack of finances he was sent to learn the profession of engraver with M. Ducommun, a watchmaker. Rousseau dates the beginning of his love for solitude and his flights of fancy to the time of his apprenticeship with Ducommun. Solitude gave him a chance to concentrate on the interesting situations he found in the books he read: "I became one of the persons who filled my imagination. . . . Finally, the fictitious state in which I succeeded in putting myself made me forget my actual state with which I was so dissatisfied." This escape into an imaginary world continued until the age of sixteen, when he decided to leave Geneva.

On his wanderings he met a Catholic curé, a parish priest, who sent Rousseau to Madame de Warens, a convert to Catholicism. Instantly a mother–child relation developed between Rousseau and de Warens, whom Rousseau calls Maman. Nevertheless, before accepting him into her household, de Warens sent him away to convert to Catholicism.

After Rousseau's disappearance from Geneva his father made some attempts to bring him back home, attempts Rousseau felt were not very serious. The son drew an important moral lesson from his father's behavior: "to avoid those situations of life which bring our duties in conflict with our interests, and which show us our advantages in the misfortunes of others." This principle, which made a profound impression on Rousseau, he calls "the true philosophy, the only philosophy which is really suited for the human heart."

It might have been because of this principle of "true philosophy" that Rousseau accused a servant girl of stealing a ribbon when he himself had stolen it. After this incident he must have felt the need to make some adjustments in his early principles. Through conversations with M. Gaime soon after this incident he discovered outlines for new moral boundaries. Until he wrote *The Confessions* he never revealed his "shameful" theft and false accusation. The desire to free himself of those guilt feelings was an important incentive for him to write *The Confessions*.

Rousseau attributes significant influence on his life and thought to the young Savoyard Abbé, M. Gaime, who taught him morality and practical wisdom: "He put before me a true picture of human life, of which I had only false ideas; he showed me how, in the midst of contrary fortune, the wise man can always strive after happiness . . . ; that there is no true happiness without prudence." M. Gaime also was the source of Rousseau's conviction that lofty virtues are rare in society. From Gaime's point of view, people achieved happiness and honor through the performance of ordinary duties rather than through the competitive struggle to climb ever higher on the social ladder.

Rousseau even considered following in Gaime's professional footsteps, but after a futile attempt to enter the priesthood he returned to Madame de Warens. He ascribes this failure to destiny: "I was destined to be the rejected of all professions." Because of his interest in music Madame de Warens introduced Rousseau to the composer Le Maitre. With this teacher, whom Rousseau regarded highly, he embarked on a music career. Then Le Maitre had to leave town precipitately and Rousseau had to accompany him, but he abandoned his teacher on the street when the latter had an attack of epilepsy. This is his third and last confession: He denounces his forsaking Le Maitre as shameful behavior. His first confession was about his falsely accusing the servant girl, and the second was about being caught in an act of exhibitionism.

During a visit to Mademoiselle du Châtelet, a friend of de Warens, Rousseau experienced that an "interesting and intelligent conversation with a woman of education and character are better calculated to form the understanding of a young man than all the pedantic philosophy that can be acquired from books." Rousseau observed in du Châtelet a tendency to discern morality in persons. His conversations with her gave him the initial inspiration to study character.

Rousseau continues his narrative, after describing his childhood and youth, with a philosophical meditation about the way his memory functions. He found that his memory in general, and particular images from the past, were more powerful in his mind than the immediate impressions of present objects. He realized that his earliest memories continued to have an influence on him. Experiences that imprinted themselves on his mind late, rather than replacing former memories, became linked to them. First impressions and initial ideas exercised a lasting influence upon those that followed. Rousseau realized that if he wanted to reveal his soul to the reader, it was necessary to acquaint him or her with those first impressions and initial ideas. Only then would the reader be able to pass correct judgement on Rousseau's later ideas.

At twenty-one, Rousseau considered himself as having become a man, but a man with a childishness that remained with him throughout his life. When he returned to de Warens she favored him as a man, and for a while he was her lover. Till then he had never even considered such a relationship, and he looked upon the new association with de Warens as calculated instruction by a tutor. He described her as having a sensitive disposition but a cold temperament. Aware of the contradiction, he added, "It may be that Nature was wrong and that this combination ought not to have existed; I only know that it did exist."

As the lover of Madame de Warens Rousseau had to perform certain household duties, but he had time to continue his study of music and to read. His friendship with M. de Conzié, one of de Warens's visitors, stimulated his interest in literature and philosophy; their common interest was in Voltaire. Reading the works of Voltaire inspired Rousseau: "The pleasure which these readings afforded me inspired me with the desire of learning to write elegantly, and of attempting to imitate the beautiful coloring of this author, which enchanted me." He was particularly eager to study Voltaire's *Philosophical Letters*.

His growing interest in philosophy caused him to complain that he could not dedicate himself adequately to study because of de Warens's habit of entertaining visitors. He was not happy with the way things were, and he fell ill. To decrease the number of visitors and reduce de Warens's great financial burden, they decided to move temporarily to a smaller estate that belonged to M. de Conzié. Les Charmettes, though close to de Warens's own estate, was as isolated as Rousseau could wish.

Though this new pastoral life meant happiness around the clock, the country air did not restore Rousseau's health as the couple had expected. Moreover, he suffered an attack of "beating carotid arteries," pulsations and buzzing in his ears that forced him to stay in bed for a few weeks. The physician's treatment did not give him much relief and the symptoms of the attack remained with him, although less severely, for the rest of his life. The attack convinced him that he did not have much longer to live, and he transformed his attitudes and way of life: "This accident, which should have killed my body, only killed my passions; and I bless Heaven every day for the happy effect which it produced upon my soul. I can certainly say that I never began to live, until I looked upon myself as a dead man."

In this mood he looked toward religion for hope; initially, his chief theologian was Madame de Warens. De Warens's profession was to be a good Catholic, and she claimed subservience to all decisions of the church. Rousseau found that she was misled by her sophisms, but she did not consider her beliefs in the least inconsistent with Catholic doctrine. For example, she could not imagine hell, but she nevertheless believed in purgatory.

Rousseau found the religious direction he was looking for through his physician, M. Salomon, who was a convinced Cartesian. Rousseau discovered that Salomon's sensible talk about the order of the world and his agreeable, instructive conversations helped the patient more than all of the doctor's medical prescriptions: "I took great delight in M. Salomon's conversation; it seemed to me that, while in his company, I was acquiring a foretaste of that higher knowledge, which was reserved for my soul, when it had lost the fetters which confined it."

Rousseau started to look for books that would help him understand Salomon better. He found the books of the Oratory and Port-Royal Schools, which combined devotion and science, best suited for this purpose and read over and over again *Entretiens sur les Sciences* by Father Lamy. He studied with great enthusiasm and found that his devotion to philosophical studies caused him to forget his sufferings; therefore, he was less affected by his illness. But the expectation of an early death remained with him for the rest of his life.

At the age of twenty-five Rousseau began to study the encyclopedia diligently, finding that its short articles eased his mind. This type of reading suited Rousseau, because he quickly became bored and his attention wandered after a few pages. Nonetheless, he studied the logic of Port-Royal, Locke, Malebranche, Leibniz, and Descartes. He nearly always found that these and other authors contradicted each other.

His studies were intended to create a storehouse of ideas, regardless of whether the ideas were false or true. After only a few years of studying in this way—that is, "thinking exactly as others thought, without, so to speak, reflecting"—he found himself in possession of a "fund of learning" that enabled him to think without the assistance of others.

Rousseau considered himself a semi-Jansenist during this period because of his intensive study of Jansenist writings, although their harsh theology frightened him. His friendship with a Jesuit confessor counterbalanced the depressing influence on him of the Port-Royal doctrines of arbitrary grace.

Rousseau thought it wise of him in those days not to think about the future. He enjoyed the present, and diverted his thoughts from his physical condition by performing some light manual labor and by his studies; his health eventually improved greatly. To a great extent Rousseau attributed his ailment to hysteria, which he calls "the ailment of happy people."

Rousseau criticized physicians and philosophers for not understanding his illness, as they only believed in the truth of what they were able to explain. Since they could not explain Rousseau's malady, for them it was as if nonexistent. Theologians, however, did understand his illness. He attributed to his studies of philosophy and theology not only a healing effect on body and soul, but also the practical advantage of having learned how to think and make comparisons. He described how his newly acquired philosophical knowledge and skills helped him to draw up a list of virtuous principles. And when he found himself in a situation where passion almost overcame him, he was able to think the matter through and to act in accordance with his new principles.

Rousseau finally decided to leave Madame de Warens. He recognized that in spite of his misfortunes, the virtues that had been cultivated in his youth had developed because he had nourished them by studying. Nevertheless, the Romantic, Classical, and Rational seeds needed "the leaven of adversity in order to bear fruit."

Rousseau became a tutor, but without success. Having again failed in a profession, he returned for a short while to Madame de Warens, but found himself out of place: She had taken a new lover and made different household arrangements. He then decided to sell his books and try to make his fortune in Paris with a revolutionary system of music notation.

Apart from recalling the few shameful and painful memories, Rousseau enjoyed writing the first part of *The Confessions*. Unlike the time he later calls the happy years of "ignorance"—that is, the time in which he wrote the first section of *The Confessions*—the following section, describing his memories of Parisian high society, reveal a more informed but less pleasant side of life.

Two years passed before Rousseau started to write the second part of his *Confessions*. He began by explaining that so far *The Confessions* had been written solely from memory, and that he "must have made many mistakes."[8] Nevertheless, the rest of *The Confessions* also would be written from memory, although in describing his period at the "Hermitage" he buttresses his memory with the aid of letters. He admits that he easily forgets misfortunes. Since he has enough trouble with a mind prone to frightful visions of the future, he must forget the unpleasantnesses of the past. He might therefore have omitted or transposed facts or mistaken a few dates.

Dent finds that where the accuracy of Rousseau's narrative can be checked, to a great extent facts are correctly recorded. Hartle disagrees with Dent and finds that Rousseau subordinates truthfulness to his philosophical purpose in writing *The Confessions*. Hartle judges Rousseau's self to be an "imaginative construction" and therefore his *Confessions* must also be an "imaginative construction." Kelly also declares that *The Confessions* are fiction: "Rousseau presents a moral fable."[9]

Rousseau's real object in his autobiography is neither to write fiction nor to create a narrative of data that can be judged factually, but to compose a truthful narrative of himself by himself: "to contribute to an accurate knowledge of my inner being in all the different situations of my life." And he could not be mistaken in the history of his soul. Or perhaps one should say that in the history of his soul he could not be proven to be mistaken. It also cannot be proven that Rousseau created an "imaginative construction" of himself. Another peculiarity concerning Rousseau's memory is its transient quality: "It only serves me so long as I am dependent upon it. As soon as I commit its contents to paper it forsakes me, and when I have once written a thing down, I completely forget it."

Rousseau was disappointed by his first contacts with the intellectuals of Paris: "I was always astonished at the readiness with which, by the help of a few sonorous phrases, they refuted without having understood me." He was more fortunate in his contacts with the Parisian ladies. Madame de Broglie gave him a book entitled *The Confessions of the Comte de* ——— to instruct him in the protocol of salon life in Paris. The author of the book became a good friend of his, and he carried the confessions of the Comte with him for more than twenty years.

Rousseau exchanged Paris for Venice, where he was the French ambassador's secretary from 1743 to 1744. He found that in this period more philosophical seeds were sown in his heart. However, Rousseau was again disappointed by circumstances. This time his disappointment was with the religious as well as the secular institutions of society. His criticism of his ex-employer, the ambassador, and the government institutions reverberated with the injustice he suffered at their hands: "The . . . uselessness of my complaints left in my mind the seeds of indignation against our foolish civil institutions, whereby the real welfare of the public . . . [is] always sacrificed to an apparent order." Rousseau maintained that this "apparent order" sanctioned the public authority's oppression of the weak. The Jesuits, and particularly a certain Father Castel, did not escape his sensitive eye: "I saw that he followed faithfully one of the grand principles of his society—always to sacrifice the weaker to the stronger."

It was some comfort to Rousseau to make at least one good friend in Venice, the Spaniard Ignacio Emmanuel de Altuna. When Rousseau returned from Venice to Paris, de Altuna visited him and was his companion for half a year. Rousseau was proud of his friendship with de Altuna; he always gloried in his friendships with prominent people, as evidence, so to speak, with which to refute the arguments of his "enemies" that he was a man devoid of friends.

After Ignacio de Altuna left for Spain, Rousseau met Thérèse, who provided him with a substitute for "Maman," Madame de Warens. His friendship with Thérèse, their love, and their marriage after twenty-three years of intimacy had a stabilizing and consoling influence on

Rousseau's turbulent life. The important role Thérèse played in his life and work is obvious, since Rousseau was of the opinion that their union was decisive for his morality and character.[10]

In spite of Rousseau's own statement about the moral content of his relationship with Thérèse, Schwartz contends—and in doing so he also refers to Starobinski—that Thérèse was merely a sexual, "physical" object for Rousseau that helped him to overcome his vice (i.e., masturbation). Schwartz maintains that Rousseau's relation with Thérèse differs from Émile's relation with Sophie, in Rousseau's book *Émile,* in the following aspect: "Rousseau's love for Thérèse is not 'moral' in the sense of being particular. . . . But it is moral in that she consents to his love, in that their love is reciprocal."[11] Schwartz finds that Émile's relation to Sophie is such that it determines Émile's moral being, because Sophie is apparently not a "physical" object.

Another eminent friend was Diderot, who had asked Rousseau to write articles for the encyclopedia. When Diderot was arrested for having written some politically offensive passages, Rousseau's emotional life was so affected by the thought that his friend might be imprisoned for life that he almost went mad. Rousseau may have been so alarmed by this event because his sensitive and suspicious mind found a justification for his own paranoid fantasies in Diderot's imprisonment.

Rousseau identified with the sufferings of his philosophical mentor and visited him almost every other day in prison. On his way to visit Diderot in the Vincennes prison Rousseau became inspired to write a prize essay for the Academy of Dijon.

Diderot encouraged him to write the essay, *The Discourse on the Sciences and Arts,* and with it a new chapter opened in Rousseau's life. It is to these events that Rousseau attributes the beginning of his misfortunes. Although *The Discourse on the Sciences and Arts* won the prize of the Academy of Dijon, Rousseau himself judges it in his *Confessions* as "altogether destitute of logic and arrangement, . . . the weakest in argument, . . . the poorest in harmony and proportion."

Thérèse's third pregnancy was another occasion for Rousseau to engage in philosophical self-scrutiny. He considered his duties as an unmarried father in the wider context of his duties as a human being. Even among his friends there were quite a few who thought him an unnatural father, a man without feelings, who had sent his children to the Foundling Hospital to get rid of them. Rousseau confesses that his own conscience bothered him, although only occasionally. He resisted his pricks of conscience and the accusations of friends and enemies alike by looking upon himself as "a member of Plato's Republic." He had done what he believed best for his children and wished that he himself had had the same care his offspring received.

In 1752 Rousseau became seriously ill and his physician said that he might have only another six months to live. This knowledge encouraged Rousseau to be more determined than ever to live according to his philosophical beliefs: "I employed all my strength of mind in breaking away from the bonds of the opinion of the world, and in courageously carrying out everything which appeared to me to be right." He began, therefore, to dress soberly and made use only of a round wig. Either the physician had been mistaken or Rousseau's new determination seems to have healed him. Whatever the case may be, Rousseau lived on.

In 1753 the Academy of Dijon proposed as the subject of its new prize essay *The Origin of Inequality amongst Mankind*. Rousseau was struck by the courage implicit in this title, and he withdrew to the forest to reflect on the subject. In the forest he discovered the true image of man: "I demolished the pitiful lies of mankind; . . . comparing the man, as man has made him, with the natural man, I showed him in his pretended perfection, the true source of his misery."[12] Through these meditations Rousseau felt that his soul ascended to the Divinity.

Grimsley observed that Rousseau's belief that people only have to use their faculties to find God was exceptional among his contemporaries: "He decisively rejects the idea of a Church claiming a unique revelation, for, in his view, this falsely presupposes that members of a particular ecclesiastical organization have a way of finding the truth that is denied to other people."[13]

When he finished *The Origin of Inequality amongst Mankind*, he gave it to Diderot to read. Diderot praised it, but few other readers in Europe at that time understood it. Rousseau knew intuitively that he would not receive the Academy of Dijon prize again, but he did not regret having undertaken to write on the subject. The "excursion and occupation" with it had been beneficial for his health and temper; he found that he was stronger and better. The period during which he worked on *The Origin of Inequality amongst Mankind* taught him that he was better off without physicians and medicine. Accordingly, he began to ignore the fixed rules the physicians had prescribed for him. Whenever he felt strong enough he walked in the Bois de Boulogne. Detesting life in Paris, disgusted with its social and literary societies, he longed for a home in the countryside.

Rousseau decided to move back to Switzerland and he thought it appropriate to return to the religion of his native country. In 1754 he settled in Geneva, and his request to become a Protestant again was granted him. He observed that after having read the Bible for so many years he had learned to reject fallacious interpretations of its contents. Philosophy had taught him to select what was essential in religion from "the petty and rubbishy forms with which it has been obscured." However, Rousseau's return to Geneva was of short duration.

He went back to Paris to make some final arrangements for leaving, when Madame d'Epinay offered him the Hermitage, her mansion at Montmorency. He accepted her offer and with Thérèse and her mother moved to the rural mansion. Rousseau recalls the period at the Hermitage as having been the last happy days of his life. However, Rousseau felt that Diderot and others accused him of having ignoble sentiments when he left Paris for the Hermitage in 1756.

In the following five years Rousseau produced his major works: *Julie, The Social Contract*, and *Émile*. Throughout *The Confessions* Rousseau explains how his writings related to specific events of his life: *The Social Contract* was inspired by his Venice period, the Savoyard vicar in *Émile* resembles M. Gaime, *Julie* was inspired by his affair with Sophie d'Houdetot at the Hermitage, and the landscape described in *Julie* resembles that of the lake of Geneva.

Rousseau found that he must have been born for the rustic state of retirement he enjoyed in the Hermitage. He observed that these new circumstances transformed him into a shy, courteous, and timid person. This was just the opposite of what had happened during the time he designated as the "first revolution" in his life; that is, during the Parisian years, which had made him audacious, proud, and undaunted. Returning to the countryside a "second revolution" took place that caused him as it were to return to his former character. But unfortunately he never was the same again, and went to another extreme: "From that time my soul, in a state of agitation, no longer kept its center of gravity, and its oscillations, ever renewed, always destroyed it." Nevertheless, he considered the "second revolution" to have restored him to nature.

Rousseau's agitated mind started to suspect Grimm and Diderot, two of his Parisian friends, of spying on him with the help of Thérèse's mother. There was only one friend, Madame d'Houdetot, who Rousseau considered so trustworthy that he even became passionately involved with her. At forty-five Rousseau described himself as a lovesick shepherd. His fluctuating emotional life created a new reality that he was unable to grasp. Comparable to his flight into the realm of imagination during his apprenticeship with M. Ducommun, he again sought refuge in a fictional world: "The impossibility of grasping realities threw me into the land of chimeras, and, seeing nothing in existence which was worthy of my enthusiasm, I sought nourishment for it in an ideal world, which my fertile imagination soon peopled with beings after my own heart."[14] His gloomy state of mind was fruitful soil for his novel *Julie*.

Robert Elbaz believes that from early childhood on Rousseau developed the concept that he had a double and he indulged in imaginary role playing. The models for these roles were found in his surroundings or were of his own making. Contrary to my understanding, Elbaz finds that "Rousseau believes in the models he creates; it takes a long time and many cures to free him of his conviction."[15] But, as indicated in *The Confessions*, Rousseau was quite aware of his own mental flights of fancy and was eminently able to control the imaginary worlds he created. What seemed less completely under his control was the idea or perhaps the illusion that he was persecuted and spied upon. This obsession seemed to cause unnecessary upheavals in his life, such as leaving the Hermitage.

Rousseau had considered Diderot as a close friend and was seriously traumatized by a sentence from Diderot's *Fils Natural*, which he thought had been written in disapproval of his solitary way of life. His belief that Diderot had been gossiping about his affair with Madame d'Houdetot caused a final break in their friendship. He had spoken only to Diderot about his secret affair, so it must have been through Diderot that their mutual friends in Paris all heard the story. His misfortunes were becoming more apparent to him when he decided that Diderot, Grimm, and Madame d'Epinay—his hostess—were conspiring against him: "I saw all my friends leaving me, without knowing how or why." Accordingly, he left the Hermitage and moved to a lodging in the gardens of another protector, M. de Prince Conde.

Rousseau found that his leaving the Hermitage, where he discovered that he had been deceived in the choice of friends, had a fatal influence on his work as well as on the rest of his life. Reflecting on his work from the Hermitage period, he recognized not only the portraits of his ex-friends, but also that he had tried to cure himself of his passion for Madame d'Houdetot. In these writings he had expressed his feelings and thoughts about the persons who once had been close friends. Rousseau's troubles, as always, seemed to inspire him; after he completed *Julie*, he put the finishing touches on *The Social Contract* and continued with *Émile*.

His publisher Rey urged him to write his memoirs. He was encouraged by the idea and decided that his memoirs, in contradistinction to the autobiographical essays of the "false ingenuousness of Montaigne," would be a work of unexampled veracity that would "enable the outside world to behold a man as he really was in his inmost self." The proof Rousseau gave of his own truthfulness was that he accused himself of shameful behavior and wrongdoing, while Montaigne only meditated on his own fine character. Further evidence of Rousseau's sincerity was his description of the kiss he demanded from the little granddaughter of Madame de Luxembourg. In *Émile* he had condemned such forced affection. Being reminded of his own condemnation of such coercive acts, he cursed his "incredible stupidity."[16]

Julie became Rousseau's great literary success, and the public thought that he was the hero of what was considered an autobiography written in the style of a novel. Susan Jackson elucidates the point that in his foreword to *Julie* Rousseau neither denies nor affirms the possibility of his novel being an autobiography: "Neither possibility is absolutely foreclosed." Moreover she finds that Rousseau appeals to his public to read *Julie* "holistically, profoundly, dynamically, even inexhaustibly autobiographical."[17]

I find that Rousseau in this stage of his life says "yes" and "no" to self-disclosure. This can be explained, on the one hand, by the need Rousseau felt to cure himself through writing *Julie*, while on the other hand he was restrained through ethical motives to write the truth. Only in a fictional style could he conceal and disclose truth. Grimsley considers that this is a vital stage in the development of Rousseau's self-awareness. It was just Rousseau's "infatuation with Mme. d'Houdetot and the sense of having fallen short of his own moral standards . . . [that] now made it necessary for him to deepen the examination of his own life and penetrate its real character."[18]

In *The Confessions* Rousseau contradicts rumors that he is Saint-Preux or any another character in *Julie*. He tells of having written the book in a state of "feverish ecstasy," and that his subjects were not real but "beings of the imagination."[19] Rousseau thought that only those possessing a sixth sense, a moral sense, could understand *Julie*. Jean Starobinski indeed understands *Julie* to be an ideological novel, in which "the quest for a moral synthesis does not prevent constant slippage into passional ambivalence."[20]

Rousseau was not told why the publication of *Émile* was suspended. The mystery surrounding this affair frightened him and he observed that he began to fantasize as to why his "last and best work" had been deferred. He suspected that the Jesuits, Jansenists, and philosophers all opposed and delayed the publication of *Émile*. Although he realized the madness of these paranoic thoughts, certain facts and circumstances nevertheless give them an air of probability and seemingly demonstrated the truth.[21]

The book was finally published, but it did not receive the same public approbation as Rousseau's other works. Moreover, the French court and Parliament decided to arrest Rousseau because of the heretical ideas expressed in the section of *Émile* called "the Creed of a Savoyard Priest." Some of Rousseau's influential friends intervened, however, and delayed his arrest, helping him to escape.

The night before he began life as a fugitive he was reading, as usual, from the Bible, which he had read through some five or six times. That night Chapter 19 of the Book of Judges would be the last chapter he would read. It inspired him to write the poem the "Levite of Ephraim," whose tragic story seemed to symbolize Rousseau's own life. This poem became his favorite work, although he did not feel it was his best work. He favored it because he found consolation in writing it, and the creative activity was some compensation for his sufferings.

If one takes it for granted that Rousseau wrote the truth about himself, one must then consider that his memory seems to mislead him concerning not reading the Scriptures anymore. Or he might have meant that he never returned to his rigid habit of reading Scripture every night, since Grimsley reports that during Rousseau's stay in England "he sought comfort in the study of the Bible, of which he had always been an assiduous reader."[22]

After his flight, Rousseau asked himself what would have happened if he had decided not to follow the advice of his friends and had remained in France. He tried to discover by a process of logical induction if their warning had been part of the plot against him. It seemed to him that if he had remained at home quietly nothing would have happened. For the next eight years Rousseau found himself deciphering "intrigues," and he finally discovered the "prime mover" of every conspiracy against him. Nevertheless, he did not think his investigations were successful and found himself surrounded by a profound darkness, a darkness impossible "to penetrate, so as to arrive at any kind of truth."

At this stage of his life writing *The Confessions* became an "act of hope," a creation through which somebody might one day understand what Rousseau himself could not comprehend; that is, the "mystery" of the "betrayal" by his friends.

A measure of tranquility seems to have returned after Rousseau took refuge on the island of Saint-Pierre. There he bade farewell to the world as it were, and desired to spend the rest of his life in the quiet peacefulness of the island. From then on he dedicated his life to perpetual leisure: "This is the life of the blessed in the next world, and, from this time forth, I fixed upon it my supreme happiness in this."

Different from the tedious idleness of society, the idleness of solitude was like a ceaseless childlike activity. Through active idleness Rousseau became a passionate botanist. He abandoned himself to aimless reveries, which produced in him blissful states and elicited ecstatic exclamations, such as, "O Nature! O my mother! behold me under thy protection alone! Here there is no cunning or knavish mortal to thrust himself between me and thee." But it did not take long before he was banished from this newly found paradise too. Rousseau continued his flight, this time to an unknown destiny.

Rousseau then goes on to summarize his stay in England and return to France, which he planned to write about in a third part of *The Confessions* if he ever had the strength for it. He planned to have his memoirs published postmortem, but he gave occasional readings from them during his lifetime. In the same manner in which he concludes *The Confessions*, he concluded those readings in Parisian salons by declaring "I have told the truth."[23] Rousseau denounced as neither truthful nor just all those who after having become acquainted with his honest scrutiny of his own life would still consider him a dishonorable man.

Rousseau's self-analysis and narrative explicitly show the following philosophical developments and their practice in life: the influence of philosophical self-education during Rousseau's childhood and early manhood; his observations about and analysis of his memory; his notion of self, which is not identical with the mechanical deterministic and scientific self concepts that were fashionable among his fellow philosophers, but based on consciously observing thoughts and feelings; his ability to deduce moral, sagacious, and practical lessons from his life experiences; an increasing modifying influence of ethical principles on his life; his self-identification with philosophers and his rejection of certain philosophers and philosophies at the end of his life; skills in self-scrutiny and self-apology; and recognition of his own "mad" fantasies and the attempt to analyze them logically. Though Rousseau is supposed to be the father of Romanticism, it is not difficult to sense in *The Confessions* an early Existentialist conception of life as well. Or, as Dent articulated Rousseau's "Existentialism," "Aside from those passages of obsessive self-concern where Rousseau writes with a troubled mind, *The Confessions* is [not] . . . the depiction of a case-story. Rather we sense here the extraordinary force of the presence of another living being; we witness the celebration of the miracle of existence."[24]

PHILOSOPHY AS AUTOBIOGRAPHY

In this section I examine some of Rousseau's major writings and their consistency with the description of philosophy in his autobiography. I compare *The Confessions* to other works of Rousseau, such as *The Preface to the Narcissus, Émile, Rousseau, Judge of Jean-Jacques: Dialogues*, and *Reveries of the Solitary Walker*.

The Preface to the Narcissus

In *The Preface to the Narcissus,* written at the very beginning of Rousseau's career, about three years after *The Discourse on the Arts and*

Sciences, some of the paranoid ideas Rousseau suffered from are already apparent. He describes himself as persecuted by a multitude of antagonists, who rather than combatting his philosophical ideas focus their attacks on his person.

In *The Confessions*, Rousseau's self-accusations and self-justifications aim to appease and reconcile his adversaries. At the time Rousseau wrote *The Preface to the Narcissus* the conflict with his adversaries was just beginning, and Rousseau attempts only to correct their erroneous arguments and misapprehensions.

Rousseau's argument in *The Preface to the Narcissus* is that there should be no discrepancy between an author's opinions, his or her way of living, and the ideas that are expressed in his or her works. Rousseau had known authors who did not identify with the ideas they advocated in their writings, but argued only for the sake of argument. In spite of such discrepancies between text and author, Rousseau believed that such texts should be judged by the value of their content. His ideal authors were the Classicists, "the true philosophers," who did not write philosophical books for the sake of vainglory, but wanted to inspire people to live in accordance with the laws of humanity.

In *The Preface to the Narcissus* Rousseau repeats the essential arguments of *The Discourse on the Arts and Sciences*. He explains that the opposition of his adversaries is wrong because they do not understand that reflecting and thinking are two different things. Thinking and acting are natural and helpful to human beings, but reflecting is not. Rousseau associates reflection with book knowledge, which makes man unhappy, impairs one's health, mars reason, and corrupts morals. Study is fitting only for the genius: "If all men were Socrates, science would not be harmful to them, but they would not have need of it."

Rousseau tries to show that the contradictions he is accused of are no more than the creation of those who do not understand him. For example, he did not argue in favor of making an end to the arts and sciences as his opponents claimed. He had even suggested that the arts and sciences be supported. He finds them useful, but not for purifying morality. However, the arts and sciences can be indirectly useful in the area of morality through distracting people's attention from evil purposes, thereby preventing them from doing wrong. His critics are advised to study his principles more thoroughly and to observe his conduct more carefully; they will then find no grounds for accusing him of inconsistencies.[25]

By expounding his principles better in *Émile*, and by explaining his life and the development of his ideas in *The Confessions*, Rousseau tried to enlighten his opponents with respect to his actual teachings and personality.

Émile

Émile is not only a protest against established methods of education, but also an attempt to propose a better alternative. Rousseau's method is child centered, devoted to what children can learn while disregarding what grown-ups ought to know. The alternative method is based on Rousseau's observations, and is a collection of his scattered thoughts, which he recorded with little concern for order or continuity.

Émile's first experience must be freedom: He must be free to develop natural habits, which presumably will equip the child with lasting self-control. Rousseau distinguishes his own thoughts on child education from those of contemporary philosophers such as Abbé de Saint-Pierre, Hobbes, and Locke. He prefers the educational systems of Plato and Seneca. Because those ancient philosophers were closer to nature, they understood that "childhood is the sleep of reason." Rousseau discovered that true happiness for children as well as for adults consists in their possession of liberty. People in primitive societies found natural happiness in a perfect equilibrium between the reign of power and will, but eighteenth-century people had to free themselves and their children from all the fantasies and desires that extended far beyond the natural achievements of humankind. It is because of these unnatural fancies that persons suffer many ills, while all of society is sickened by modern hubris. Rousseau's counsel to humankind is to "live according to nature, be patient, get rid of the doctors; you will not escape death, but you will only die once, while the doctors make you die daily through your diseased imagination."

Émile's education is achieved through stimulating the child's desire to learn. Instead of teaching him habits and obedience, the child is encouraged to think for himself, which is the one habit Rousseau finds necessary for living. Émile's education is supposed to turn him into a philosopher. An education like Émile's creates a pupil who philosophizes and asks Socratic questions (i.e., he "never asks a question without a reason for it, for he knows he will be required to give his reason before he gets an answer"). Natural education makes the world an object of curiosity, and the child's surroundings become an instructive text demanding his thought and consideration.

Émile's emotional development starts in self-love and love for those around him. Affection, however, is rooted in the need of the other, and Rousseau finds this a weakness. Affection has to evolve from this all-too-human "amour-propre" into a virtuous "amour de soi." Émile is brought up more or less as a recluse, his exemplary life similar to that of Robinson Crusoe. At an early age the child is taught that the "really happy man is a hermit."

Rousseau believed that the emergence of sexuality and the passions initiated manhood and were a second birth, a road to freedom. Only then has the time arrived to begin Émile's formal education, for which Rousseau recommends Plutarch and other classical authors. These should not be studied to develop Émile's memory, but to develop in him the art of thinking and judgement. Émile will naturally have more respect for the works of the ancient philosophers than for those of the seventeenth and eighteenth centuries, because he senses that the ancient philosophers are close to nature. Rousseau calls Émile's exercise in thinking "a course in practical philosophy, a philosophy better understood and more thoroughly mastered than all the empty speculations with which the brains of lads are muddled in our schools."[26]

So far, Émile's education resembles Rousseau's description in *The Confessions* of his own development. During childhood Rousseau had been left much to himself and had enjoyed the freedom of self-education. Only at the age of twelve, as noted earlier, did he receive lessons from a tutor for a short while. In early manhood he opted for self-imposed intellectual training, through which he learned scholarly discipline. Frederick Green noticed that Rousseau, at thirteen, "in the absence of any systematic instruction," had gathered through his readings "a remarkable fund of what schoolmasters used to call general intelligence."[27]

The ideas presented in the section of *Émile* called "The Creed of the Savoyard Priest" resemble Rousseau's religious quest as described in *The Confessions*. And in *Émile* Rousseau discloses that the educational example in the "Creed" is based on his own experience. By studying philosophy Rousseau had not been freed from his doubts as he had hoped, but they had actually multiplied. Accordingly, he maintains that philosophy and theology were inadequate for an understanding of life and God. Instead of following the manifold contradictory philosophical ideas of others, he decided to follow the ideas revealed by his own intellect: "Let me follow the Inner Light; it will not lead me so far astray as others have done."[28] He considers that the best use of reason is in the adoration of the "Being of beings," and in the yielding of reason before the Supreme Being.

The role of philosophy in Rousseau's religious quest is the classical role of philosophy as theology's "handmaid." Grimsley notes that "the whole of the second part of *Profession de foi* is permeated by a strongly rationalist element, since Rousseau sees reason as a safeguard against religious intolerance and fanaticism."[29]

Ultimately, reason and metaphysics are found to be deceptive, while his experiences had taught him that the instincts of the soul are the right guide for life. Rousseau's disregard for metaphysics and any other philosophy that does not have practical implications is evident from *The Confessions, Émile,* and *The Discourse upon Inequality*. Apparently this makes Maurice Cranston understand Rousseau's educational thought "to be above all a scheme for moral education . . . and yet at the same time he proposes methods of moral education which depend on the concealment of truth and which are plainly designed to deceive the child."[30] By instinct Émile is guided to a cosmopolitan utopian vision in which the nations of the world dispense with their national boundaries. People of all nations become globe-trotters to "verify, compare and examine for themselves the various religions to be found."[31] The experience of other cultures and religions is a necessary and integral part of teaching human beings respect and love for all religions. I find here again a strong analogy to Rousseau's description in *The Confessions* of his own wanderings and the way his journeys changed his understanding of and attitude toward religion.

Émile's education is completed with the subduing of his sexual passions. Although he is engaged to Sophie, he must leave her to experience travel and life in foreign countries. This life of wandering teaches Émile what it means to be solitary. After having been disciplined by means of this solitary life style, Émile returns to Sophie. In the future they will share their solitude. Rousseau might have adopted the idea of subduing the passions from ancient and religious thought, but it also might have been a lesson based on his own life experiences as described in his *Confessions*. After his own passions had been fully aroused he decided that he had to leave Madame de Warens for the sake of his further development. In *The Confessions* Rousseau expresses his attraction to Port-Royal philosophy; the solitary lifestyle of the Port-Royal communities, also called "Solitaires," seems to have had a lasting influence on his own life and educational precepts.

Rousseau, Judge of Jean-Jacques: Dialogues

After Rousseau's return to Paris he was forbidden to give readings from *The Confessions*. Rousseau felt he was treated like a barbarian, totally rejected and misunderstood. He abandoned all "proper" philosophical work, with the exception of *Considerations on the Government of Poland*. Instead, he concentrated on botanical studies, an opera, and two autobiographical works. The two autobiographical works, *Rousseau, Judge of Jean-Jacques: Dialogues* and *Reveries of the Solitary Walker*, are a continuation of his attempts to come to terms with his adversaries. Kelly correctly remarks that Rousseau shared the classical view of philosophers as exemplary figures rather than simply as intellectuals. Hence, autobiography suited Rousseau's aims better than any other literary vehicle that would convey only his thoughts.[32]

Rousseau, Judge of Jean-Jacques: Dialogues is a long satire Rousseau wrote to contradict the arguments, opinions, prejudices, lies, and misunderstandings derived from his work and person. Rousseau's strategy became that of the jester. The dialogues very appropriately bear as an epigraph the words of Ovid: "Here I am the barbarian because no one understands me." It is not clear whether *Rousseau, Judge of Jean-Jacques: Dialogues* should be understood as anything but satire; however, many contemporary critics of the dialogues disregard the satiric element. For example, Kelly suggests, "Rousseau now undertakes to educate his audience about how they should act as his judges. Thus the *Dialogues* can be regarded as a manual for the readers of the *Confessions*."[33] However, Kelly recognizes Rousseau's assessment that it is impossible to educate the public on how to judge him.

Nevertheless, the sarcastic element in the dialogues is obvious from an exemplary mock disclosure about Jean-Jacques's love of botany. His hobby is more than just a pastime; Jean-Jacques collects plants because he knows how to poison people; yes, even to poison people by just looking at them.

Rousseau likewise makes fun of his critics' claims that there are contradictions and inconsistencies between his work and his personal behavior. Rousseau explains how *The Confessions*, instead of reconciling him with his adversaries, gave the latter a hold on his soul. What he had acknowledged as flaws his adversaries called his vices, his faults they called crimes, and the weaknesses of his youth they found characteristic of his adult life. Rousseau satirically raises questions concerning his adversaries' perception of reality. He finds that if they could see Socrates, Arestides, or even God himself, they would perceive them as infernal monsters.

Philosophical themes from Rousseau's other works are recognizable in spite of the tone of ridicule and hyperbole. Examples are his criticism of the "sophistication of religion" or his contempt for the "convenient philosophy of the happy and the rich."

In the epilogue to the dialogues, called "The History of the Preceding Writing," Rousseau changes his sarcastic tone and writes in genuine seriousness. He describes how, confronted continuously with social difficulties, he was helped and comforted by his own thoughts: "Final ill success, which ought to have added the finishing touch to my despair, did not affect me like the prior ones. . . . A passage of *Émile* that I recalled made me return within myself and find what I had vainly sought outside."

Rousseau, Judge of Jean-Jacques: Dialogues was Rousseau's final attack on his adversaries before he surrendered and accepted what he considered his destiny: "Let men henceforth do everything they wish; after I have done what I must, they will torment my life in vain; they will not prevent me from dying in peace."[34]

Reveries of the Solitary Walker

In *Reveries of the Solitary Walker* Rousseau celebrates his personal victory over all his opponents. He had not been able to convince his opponents that their opinions of him were wrong, or to change the influence his enemies had on the public, but all this could not touch his private well-being. On the contrary, these sufferings had brought him closer to himself and to nature.

Rousseau is no longer addressing his adversaries or the public; he now writes for himself: "Such reflections as I have in future I shall preserve in writing; every time I read them they will recall my original pleasure. . . . I shall forget my misfortunes, my persecutors and my disgrace." He no longer wants to explain his writings or himself to others, and this is the main reason he does not consider *Reveries of the Solitary Walker* as an appendix to *The Confessions*. But, just as he did with *The Confessions*, he compares this last autobiographic enterprise too with the autobiographic, philosophical essays of Montaigne.

Whereas in *The Confessions* and other works Rousseau had failed to unravel the conspiracy against him, in *Reveries of the Solitary Walker* he finds an explanation through shifting the realm of his inquiry from the human to the divine. The plot against him is now explained as a "divine secret." Although he continues to reject Jansenist and Augustinian "fatalism," he accepts that he was destined by God to suffer, although he is innocent. But there is hope in his sufferings; sooner or later "his turn will come."

As an old man of sixty-four Rousseau looked back at his life. He examined and summarized large sections of *The Confessions*, comparing himself to Diogenes searching for a man who is a true philosopher. Rousseau found most of eighteenth-century philosophy "other-centered." Other-centered philosophy serves the interests of the philosopher without the philosopher believing in or practicing the doctrines he or she teaches. Rousseau posits a "self-centered" philosophy, aimed at self-knowledge and the achievement of inner enlightenment. His philosophical search revealed to him the principles of a liberal, theistic, natural religion, such as he described in the "Creed of a Savoyard Priest."[35]

Amélie Rorty Oksenberg sees in Rousseau's philosophy a political, psychological–educative, and affectional–social therapeutic experiment. She finds it is an attempt in which Rousseau failed: "And all three therapeutic strategies have the same problem: they presuppose the conditions they are meant to achieve; they depend on the intervention of a benign, paternalistic, unflawed Legislator–Tutor; and they introduce elements and structures that undermine the direction of therapy."[36] It seems to me that Rorty Oksenberg fails to comprehend that the young Rousseau had wanted to become a religious minister, and had finally found religious and philosophical self-fulfillment in writing and living according to his own theistic "Creed." After Rousseau failed to answer his religious calling, this could be understood as a personal rectification, but is it therapy? Rousseau wrote in *The Confessions* that writing *The Origin of Inequality amongst Mankind* had a curative effect on him, and that he had written *Julie* with a therapeutic purpose in mind. By his own testimony, these therapeutic projects were personal (not political) and successful.

In *Reveries of the Solitary Walker*, just as in the epilogue to *Rousseau, Judge of Jean-Jacques: Dialogues*, Rousseau described how his own writings indeed comforted him during his hours of darkness: "Then it is that, being incapable of the thought processes which would be necessary to reassure myself, I feel the need to recall my former conclusions; I remember the painstaking attention and the sincerity of heart which led me to them and all my confidence returns."

In *Reveries of the Solitary Walker* Rousseau asserts that reliable evidence for having spoken the truth in *The Confessions* is established through the fact that he had been guided by the voice of conscience, rather than the light of reason. He had followed the guidance of his conscience instinctively, before he had been able to adopt this as a rule he discovered through reason. Through his reveries he was able to discern that the voice of conscience had protected him from falsehood. His autobiographic narrative had a moral end in view, as in fables: "Their aim is or should be to present useful truths in a form which is pleasing to the senses, there is hardly any attempt in such cases to conceal the factual untruth . . . and the person who tells a fable simply as a fable is in no sense a liar." The rule of conscience followed in *The Confessions* had prevented him from contradicting genuine memories, but sometimes when his memory had formed an incomplete picture he had "dreamed up" matters to supplement it. However, these "imagined" things were such as could have existed in reality.

Rousseau reflects on the blissful days he experienced on the island of Saint-Pierre. He asks, "What is the source of our happiness in such a state?" It seems to him that this happiness is found in days of pure being, when the feeling of existence is unmixed with any other emotion. Those days of pure existence were deeply engraved on Rousseau's memory. By recalling his blissful state on the island of Saint-Pierre he is transported daily "on the wings of imagination and tasting for several hours the same pleasures as if . . . still living there." In *The Confessions* Rousseau described how he would escape in imagination into a fictional world created by the books he read; in *Reveries of the Solitary Walker* to escape thus he returned to his own writings or to memories. Rousseau believed that his afflictions taught him the self-love that men in their natural state possess. His adversaries had done him more good than if they had spared him their blows.

Rousseau's final, unfinished meditation is an homage to Madame de Warens. He found the determining direction of his whole life in his tender feelings for "Maman" de Warens. His feelings for her had shaped his soul in its ideal form.[37] In *The Confessions* Rousseau had written that his romanticism could not be corrected by logic. His romantic view of life—possibly due to his inherited sensitive nature and cultivated by the novels from his mother's library—remained; indeed, to his last days it was a vital source in his life and writing.

Rousseau's philosophical writings and novels—examples taken from his work over the years 1753 to 1778—center around principal themes that resemble events and subjects described in *The Confessions*: self-justification; the importance of philosophy as practice rather than as theory only; a search for true philosophy and religion; an intellectual development leading from rational and scholarly knowledge to an instinctual personal wisdom; liberal, self-directed education; and authentic and moral relationships.

PSYCHOANALYSIS FROM NATURE'S PERSPECTIVE

From traditional psychoanalytic perspectives Rousseau's family relationships are problematic, if not pathogenic. Yet from Ronald D. Laing's psychoanalytic perspective Rousseau's family life can be considered acceptable and sound. Also, Mila Morgenstern shows Rousseau's interpretations of the family as appropriate for our times. For example, Rousseau considered that the family structure has to provide authenticity for each member. Likewise, Rousseau relates authenticity in the private realm to that within the public realm, by which he empowers the role of women in daily life in a significant manner. Rousseau confronts the sacred institution of family life by defining it "as the product of a 'revolution' [leading to the socialization of Savage Man] but also insists that it is a 'natural structure.'"[38]

Laing echoes Rousseau's recognition of the political origin and consequences of family life: "The dynamics and structures found in those groups called families in our society may not be evident in those groups called families in other places and times. The relevance of the dynamics and structure of the family to the formation of personality is unlikely to be constant in different societies, or even in our own." Laing differentiates between the family of origin and the "family" that is the internalized family, or the family as fantasy. This last one is as it were the real, the efficacious family. The system internalized is not a construct of particular roles a priori existent, as in the Freudian understanding of relationships: "If self depends on the integrity of the 'family', the 'family' being a shared structure, self's integrity is then dependent upon self's sense of this as a structure shared with others. . . . To be in the same family is to feel the same 'family' inside."[39]

In Rousseau's case the fact that he continued until his last day to relate to Madame de Warens as "Maman" seems to indicate where he located his real family to be; that is, not in Geneva. Not the fact that Rousseau had not known his biological mother, but that another woman had adopted him is significant, and caused him—consciously—to aspire to distinction. Later, Thérèse shared in the Rousseau fantasy family, and she is explicitly named a substitute for de Warens. This might explain why Rousseau (if the children he is supposed to have had with Thérèse were indeed his own children) sent his children to an orphanage. Rousseau's own adoption experience is repeated as it were through his offspring. His children should share in a similar ideal fantasy family as he considered himself to have been raised in. From a more traditional viewpoint, the way Rousseau handled being a father could be understood as the result of his own traumatic adoption experience, and a need to relive this experience through giving his own children for adoption.

Thomas Kavanagh considers that Rousseau's relation to Madame de Warens is not a mother–son relation; instead, it distinctly resembles a pre-Oedipal symbiosis: "Rousseau's allusion to the shadow of 'incest' hanging over his feelings toward Madame de Warens should not so much be read as a reference to mother–son incest as to that between a sister and brother standing before their mutually recognized yet always denigrated father."[40]

Psychoanalytic and psychiatric interpretations of Rousseau's character are abundant. The Rousseau scholars Ronald Grimsley and Jean Starobinski relate extensively to these interpretations in their work. Grimsley dedicates about seventy pages in *Jean-Jacques Rousseau: A Study in Self-Awareness* to Rousseau's psychological development. Grimsley also adds his own knowledge of psychoanalysis to this study: "His mother's premature death from purpuric fever when he was only a few days old may well have laid the foundations of a radical anxiety at the very beginning of infancy. Some psycho-analysts, following Freud's suggestion, insist that the act of birth—and specially of a difficult birth—may be enough to provide the baby with its first real experience of anxiety, and it has been maintained that this initial emotional impact may evoke anxiety of a 'persecutory' kind." In his analysis of Rousseau Grimsley draws mainly on the psychoanalytic and psychiatric diagnostic works of Victor Demole, Suzanne Elosu, René Laforgue, Adolf Heidenhaim, Susan Isaacs, Gasperd Valette, and Louis Proal.

Grimsley finds it plausible that Rousseau's natal and postnatal condition created in him a lasting anxiety, and in later life a desperate struggle to overcome these feelings. Grimsley also observes that the early death of Rousseau's mother was followed by a "close emotional dependency on his father." Other significant persons, such as Rousseau's Aunt Suzanne and her servant, are held responsible for "spoiling" him and adding to Rousseau's sense of insecurity, anxiety, and "a tendency to overcome anxiety through an attitude of retreat and submission."

To make things more complex, Rousseau's confession that in his father's eyes he replaced his mother is thoroughly scrutinized. This confession leads to the psychoanalytic suggestion that Rousseau "may have come to believe—unconsciously and irrationally—that it was wrong for him to enjoy life, and especially everything connected with sex." Moreover, another psychoanalyst suggests that Rousseau experienced a need "'to make reparations and to suffer' and this conviction, in its turn, influenced his attitude towards sex; he felt it was wrong to enjoy erotic experience and that to have normal relations with a woman was equivalent to murdering her."[41]

The unanimity of these suggestions with Rousseau's description of himself in *The Confessions* and other autobiographical works is quite remote. Though Rousseau does not deny all kinds of suffering, such as anxiety, hysteria, and some paranoia as well, he wanted to enjoy life and seems to have been able to enjoy life, including sex. Rousseau's finding ecstatic bliss and inner harmony in solitude is considered an autistic escape mechanism by a majority of analysts. Rousseau's intense, childlike joy in reverie and collecting plants is classified as an unjustifiable pathological state of being.

It seems relevant here to refer to the excellent study of the psychiatrist Anthony Storr on solitude. Storr relates to the the lives of Kant, Wittgenstein, and Newton as having shared a Rousseauian inclination for solitude. But Storr concludes, "The psychopathology of such men is no more than an exaggeration of traits which can be found in all of us. We all need to find some order in the world, to make sense of our existence. Those who are particularly concerned with such a search bear witness to the fact that interpersonal relationships are not the only way of finding emotional fulfillment."[42]

In line or out of line with the alleged sexual-frustration hypothesis concerning Rousseau, it is also believed that he was masochistic: "He was inclined to what may be called a 'moral' masochism, through which he obtained a secret, if sometimes distressing, pleasure in the idea of a self-abasement and humiliation which made him the passive object of other people's feeling." Toward the end of Grimsley's book there are two pages of psychiatric diagnostics applying to Rousseau, and Grimsley settles for the claim of paranoia. He places this claim in a Freudian framework through referring to the case study of Dr. Schreber.

According to Freud, former friends are turned into "enemies" and "persecutors"—in Rousseau's case this happened with Diderot, Grimm, d'Alembert, and Hume—because they are the objects "of a forbidden wish—namely homosexual desire."[43]

Unlike Grimsley's classical psychoanalytic orientation, the account Starobinski presents in *Jean-Jacques Rousseau: Transparency and Obstruction* is considered phenomenological. According to the book's introduction, Starobinski's approach has much in common with the work of Husserl and Sartre: "Existence is ontologically both relative and relational; there is no Self without the Other. Thus the empathetic reading, although a crucial moment, constitutes only one moment in the critical process." Typical for this approach is that the "phenomenological critic is looking for latent meaning contained in the work and not a hidden cause." Like in Sartre's Existential–psychoanalytic writings (such as the biographies of Flaubert and Genet), Starobinski's aim is to reveal Rousseau's "fundamental existential choices." Starobinski writes against the "regressive" psychoanalytic interpretation that Rousseau's *Confessions* is the sublimated expression of exhibitionism (Rousseau describes in *The Confessions* that in his youth he had been caught in what seems to have been just a one-time public "striptease" performance). Similar to classical psychoanalytic studies, Starobinski finds Rousseau's deprivation of maternal love as characteristic for his whole development. But the Oedipal triangle in Rousseau's life is questioned. He shows, for example, that contrary to René Laforgue and other psychoanalysts, Rousseau did not find in love triangles "the opportunity to relive the experience of being a guilty son hoping to restore a lost intimacy." The role Rousseau seeks in love affairs, and in life generally, is not that of dependency, but that of the teacher, the master, the protective mentor.

When Starobinski surveys listings of a diagnosis attributed to Rousseau (for example, dementia, psychopathic personality disorder, neurosis, paranoia, *folie raisonnante*, and uremia-induced organic brain disease) it seems to him that a contemporary psychiatrist would say that the correct diagnosis would be paranoid delusions. And though Starobinski seems to succumb to this diagnosis, he does question if Rousseau's opus exhibits his disease or is merely the reaction against the disease.

In the final chapter of *Jean-Jacques Rousseau: Transparency and Obstruction*, Starobinski uses psychoanalytic terminology for reasons of convenience. Rousseau is reported to have had a sadomasochistic personality structure. Much attention is given to Rousseau's urinary-tract problems, and Starobinski is sympathetic to the psychoanalytic reading of it as "receptive urethral eroticism."[44] The sudden shift of framing Rousseau into traditional psychoanalytic discourse seems to me a minor weakness in Starobinski's otherwise fascinating analysis.

The conclusions of philosophical psychoanalysis (i.e., my inquiry into the dynamics of consistency and continuity of Rousseau's thoughts and life as he recorded them in his autobiography and other writings) are different from the lessons learned from Augustine's life and work. Likewise, my conclusions differ greatly from the average psychoanalytic understandings, because it is not my aim to reach a conclusive nor a clinical diagnosis concerning the philosophers in question. To arrive at an in-depth understanding of Rousseau it is necessary to display first of all his self-awareness and self-knowledge.

From childhood on Rousseau's life was characterized by seclusion; as a child he already experienced the loneness of the solitary individual, which he found was an excellent condition for developing meticulous self-awareness. Except for his first Parisian period, Rousseau sought a quiet life in which he could be absorbed and undisturbed with himself and his work.

Rousseau described his self-awareness as dating back to the age of five. As a self-conscious child he was aware of the extent to which reading novels influenced his emotional life. In *The Confessions* he described the influence books had on his emotional, intellectual, and spiritual life, and his reading transformed his youth and manhood. Rousseau's sensitive nature was also fertile soil for developing self-awareness and a clear perception of the world around him. As years passed his self-awareness would quite naturally broaden and deepen.

However, in *Jean-Jacques Rousseau: A Study in Self-Awareness*, Grimsley contends that Rousseau's self-awareness was developed mainly later in life: "The personal writings themselves . . . are merely the culmination of a long process of psychological development. . . . As he grew older, he became increasingly aware of himself as a man who was confronted by the need to resolve certain enigmatic and contradictory traits in his own character."[45] Where Grimsley's terms, "later" and "older," are vague, I find that at least in the course of Rousseau's writing career his personal self-awareness goes back to his earliest works; for example, in *The Preface to Narcissus: Or the Lover of Himself*. Grimsley's study of the development of Rousseau's self-awareness includes only a sporadic discussion of *The Confessions*, while in this context great importance is attributed to *Julie*. Grimsley considers that Rousseau's self-awareness increased during the time in which he wrote *Julie*.

From *The Confessions* it is clear that Rousseau not only had memories of himself as a child, but that he was aware of how childhood imaginings and ideas from the books he read influenced the rest of his life. For example, his identification with Plutarch's heroes created in him a "free and republican spirit." Rousseau's childhood reflections on everyday experiences are remarkable for their critical judgment, examples being his relation with the Lamberciers and M. Ducommun.

His critical understanding of his situation is followed by a change in his behavior. Rousseau's "flights into imaginary worlds" apparently also taught him to apprehend the real world from a detached and critical distance. Therefore, at an early age he could make rapid and definitive decisions, such as his decision to leave Geneva.

Rousseau was aware that as a youth he interpreted other people's behavior and drew moral lessons from their actions; for example, from his father's behavior. Until Rousseau started to write down his thoughts, he experimented freely with different ways of life: He became a practicing Catholic, he learned and applied new moral principles from M. Gaime, and so forth. Curiosity and readiness to experiment with events and ideas he encountered were characteristic of Rousseau. This experimental and practical attitude toward life is described as an educational philosophical method in *Émile*. Awareness of how his own feelings and memory were formed ascribed great importance to childhood experiences and impressions.

Through his educational method he seems to try to reduce the influence of childhood impressions on the memory by limiting their number to those impressions the child would have been exposed to in its natural surroundings. Lessons learned from his own childhood and youth are found as educational models in *Julie* and *Émile*. Though Rousseau identifies himself as the tutor in *Émile*, and Émile is educated according to Rousseau's own educational methods, it is not clear if he was aware that Émile's "Socratic" education is an idealized form of his own upbringing. It is likely, though, that such an analogy existed in his self-perception, since Rousseau had fond memories of his childhood and idealized his own upbringing as exemplary.

When Rousseau first became interested in the study of philosophy it seemed beyond his reach. However, when an illness gave him an opportunity to read philosophy books, he found this study beneficial to his health. Philosophical thought and meditation had a calming and curative effect on his body, emotions, and mind. Rousseau differentiated between philosophies that he found disturbing and vain (for example, those of the Jansenists and the Philosophes) and true philosophy, which has a beneficial influence. Vain philosophies are those involving only thought, while true philosophy is thinking directed toward action and life. Thus, Rousseau's main criterion for true philosophy was that thought should be for practical ends. His dedication to his own ideas and to their practice in life was so great that he found his personal honor and integrity depended on living in accordance with his own philosophy.

In *The Confessions*, Rousseau observed a relation between his own well-being and practicing philosophy, not only in social living but also in the intellectual activity of writing; writing *The Origin of Inequality amongst Mankind* and *Julie* was beneficial to him. Guy Lafrance finds Rousseau's theme in *Julie* more than an "ideology." He also contends that the same moral ideas found in *Émile* and other writings of Rousseau are developed in *Julie*.[46]

Rousseau's determination to live according to his own morals and principles, such as he recorded in the "Savoyard Creed" and other named works, helped him to recover from illness and depression. His diagnosis of his own sufferings as hysteria, as an emotional sickness that needed a philosophical cure rather than the medical treatment the physicians had prescribed for him, was a remarkable self-observation on his part. And yet even today, philosophers and other scholars pay little attention to Rousseau's self-diagnosis and self-prescribed philosophical remedies. Studies of Rousseau's illnesses seldom illuminate his awareness of the emotional origin of much of his suffering.

For example, Starobinski considers that "Rousseau was for all practical purposes unaware of being mentally ill." However, in spite of Starobinski's belief that Rousseau was ignorant of his own mental condition, he does observe that Rousseau suggested a practical, philosophical cure for himself and others: "But how is man to heal himself of history? Not by rejecting it. The answer is found in *Émile* and in the *Social Contract*, works in which man (individually or communally) dedicates himself to overcoming history by means of art."[47]

If Rousseau's critics would only read *The Confessions* not as fiction but as a reliable text, and in addition would differentiate between Rousseau's satirical and sincere tones, they would perceive quite a different portrait of him. *The Confessions* as an accurate self-portrait depicts Rousseau's profound awareness of his own emotional distress, whatever the origin and nature of his deprivation might have been. Furthermore, it is evident that, fully aware of what he was doing, he created a philosophical understanding of himself and a philosophical way of life that was an antidote for his sufferings.

I will proceed in this philosophical psychoanalysis of Rousseau by revealing patterns of philosophical activity and how these contributed to or diminished consistency and continuity in the life described. The consistency of Rousseau's works and the personal practice of his ideas in life were issues that Rousseau continually addressed in his writings. From the beginning of his career there were critics who accused him of contradictions between his ideas and his way of life. Rousseau's attempts to prove the consistency of his theories, as well as the fact that his theories were consistent with his way of life, went through three different stages.

In the first stage he took his antagonists seriously and tried to be more precise in explaining his theories and himself and how they interrelated. We find examples of this in *The Preface to Narcissus: Or the*

Lover of Himself, The Confessions, and *Émile*. Perceiving that this approach failed, he tried a satirical approach, such as in *Rousseau, Judge of Jean-Jacques: Dialogues*. The last stage of apologetic strategy was that of public resignation. For example, the *Reveries of the Solitary Walker* is a self-justification written for himself only. Elisabeth Zeil-Fahlbush presents a cogent argument for consistency in Rousseau's writings and analyzes the application of his ideas to his life. She concludes that Rousseau's thinking is not a detached, separate philosophical system, but that in his writings he works out ideas he experienced in his daily life.[48] Writing for him was a practice that developed consistently with life, and it introduced a greater, more complex consistency between thought and life.

In his apologetic texts Rousseau argued that a correct understanding of him would show his writings to be consistent with his personality and way of life. He admitted that physical weakness and imperfection of character sometimes prevented him from being as completely consistent as he wanted to be, and he believed that his goodwill made up for any inconsistencies. Rousseau was as consistent in his thoughts and actions as it was in his power to be. He noticed that illness and persecution helped him to return to the essence of his own thoughts. He also became aware that only with the "help" of his adversaries was he able to practice the austere and ecstatic elements of the "Savoyard Creed."

For Rousseau, consistency was not just a matter of logic, but a specific state of consciousness comparable to a transcendental or mystical experience, beyond controversy and conflict. Green does not think that Rousseau's description indicates mystical ecstasy. He finds the latter's experience on the road to Vincennes a "semi-mystic conversion," while he describes Rousseau's ecstasy in the *Reveries of the Solitary Walker* as merely "a state of self-hypnosis and a curious variety of conscious states."[49] However, *The Confessions* show clearly the religious contents of Rousseau's ecstatic wanderings in the forest. He felt, as it were, "lifted up" into a religious experience through which he encountered the "Supreme Being." This transcendent experience could not be attained through logic or philosophy, although these he considered as helpful signposts on the way to the source of supreme consistency, which he located in the "Being of beings" and the "natural self." Basil Munteano maintains that Rousseau's search for unity was not obtained through a dialectic synthesis of antitheses. Rousseau's syntheses are in Munteano's view only imaginary, and he names Rousseau's transcendental experience, "l'unification illusoire de l'extase."[50]

Rousseau believed that if he could explain this true natural self to his adversaries they would understand that the so-called contradictions in his character and writings were merely some small human deficiencies. Although Rousseau acknowledged that he had done things in life that he was later ashamed of, his *Confessions* are not the confessions of the ordinary monotheist; they are the confessions of a pantheist. He does not plead guilty before God and humanity in the hope of receiving absolution. On the contrary, by revealing his own natural goodness, his true, natural, consistent self, he tried to convince his adversaries to be reconciled to him.

In the *Reveries of the Solitary Walker* Rousseau describes how he found that the oneness of self and nature transcends all conflicts and paradoxes. Through "reverie" he induced in himself a state of absence of emotions, a state of mind in which he found perfect tranquility. Rousseau's juvenile flights into imaginary worlds through reading books, studying, writing, composing, and his solitary lifestyle were all similar to his practice of "reverie," a practice designed to free him of disturbances, conflicts, paradoxes, and emotions.

Robert H. Bell observes that Rousseau "confidently asserts the coherence of character." In Rousseau's coherent character Bell recognized a conventional, even orthodox concept of identity. Rousseau's soul would resemble the Augustinian and Cartesian "given, substantial and immutable" soul.[51] I agree with Bell concerning the coherence of Rousseau's character, but I do not think it was "given" to him. Rousseau's natural self had to be achieved through continual self-education and practice of philosophy.

Rousseau believed that reasoning could generate many inconsistencies that could not be resolved through reason. He therefore rejected the possibility of creating a harmonious philosophical system only on the basis of logical premises.[52] Instead, he developed a philosophical–theistic skepticism in which the mysterious knowledge of the "Supreme Being" homogenized the inconsistent and the consistent. From the perspective of this higher, "divine" logic, Rousseau found no inconsistencies in the arguments put forward in *The Confessions* or in his other writings.

Rousseau made use of two techniques for making adjustments when he discovered inconsistencies between his thought and his actions. First, when he had sufficient emotional, mental, and physical strength to modify his behavior, he would try, and usually succeed, to make the desired change in his way of life. For example, he tried and indeed succeeded in curing himself of his passion for Sophie d'Houdetot. Nevertheless, there are also inconsistencies that he found beyond his personal strength and intellect to reconcile. "Public embarrassment" seems to have legitimized behavior he would otherwise have rejected as immoral; Rousseau's excuse for falsely accusing a girl of having stolen a ribbon was the desire to avoid public embarrassment. Or his justification for fictional aspects he introduced in the story of his life, which he compared to the imaginative truth of a fable, was justified by his moral purpose in telling the story.

Second, in *The Confessions* Rousseau strove to prove that in spite of these few inconsistencies, his unique personality was in harmony with his own thoughts and Nature. He recognized the contradictions in Madame de Warens's character, but to him they seemed natural. Also, contradictions he discovered in himself were not perceived as inconsistent with his true being; that is, with his self in its natural state.

Rousseau questioned himself about the following contradictions: Why did he not live according to the laws of his beloved Genevan Utopia, and why did he not live in Geneva? The only reasonable answer he could give was the same as the one he used to explain his persecution: He was so destined! It is true that there were many occurrences in Rousseau's life that impressed him with the futility of existence and made him receptive to fatalism. Grimsley observes that Rousseau's fatalistic concept of life was not limited to himself: "Rousseau also considers that man's alienation from himself and his failure to find spiritual fulfillment were the result of a fatal accident that had diverted him from his true destiny."[53] Rousseau might have interpreted in his own life as destiny incidents such as his mother's death when he was an infant, his sensitive nature, his religious calling, and his poor health. These were just a few of the impediments that frustrated his natural desires and his development.

Rousseau responded to the frustration of his natural tendencies by the exigencies of life through passive and instinctive actions. Since the only possession of the poor wanderer Jean-Jacques Rousseau was himself, he could only retreat into the solitude of self. When rational adjudgment of his behavior seemed impossible, Rousseau's second recipe for attaining consistency in his life was by way of passive flight. In the *Reveries of the Solitary Walker*, however, he explained that his passivity was not without activity; on the contrary, it was a spontaneous way of achieving creativity.

He found the strength to overcome obstacles, contradictions, and inconsistencies through escaping into an internally perceived freedom; from this inner stronghold he tried to change himself and his circumstances. *The Confessions* is the history of a "fleeing" self, which escapes the detached examinations of others and in part of Rousseau himself. His acknowledged partial self-awareness, however, did not impair his ability to draw a true, if imperfect, self-portrait.

Nevertheless, his self-portrait is a better representation of who he really was than anyone else could have depicted, as others could not know his inner world as he did. Where he was prevented from knowing the full truth about himself, he hoped somebody with a heart like his would reveal the truth he himself was unable to grasp.

Starobinski showed that Rousseau considered his own heart transparent as crystal, clear and fluid as water, and bright as the sun. His transparency was a result of his inability to hide his emotions, either from himself or from others.[54]

Huck Gutman rightly observed that Rousseau's self was a "self as subject." During Rousseau's time at the Hermitage he became aware of this "self as subject": At age forty-five he underwent a "second revolution" when he realized that by reason alone he could no longer grasp the conflicting reality of his inner world. An objective vision of his situation and personality was consciously replaced by a vision grounded in subjective experience: Reason, together with the imagination, instincts, and the moral guidance of Rousseau's conscience, became the new means to resume living. Gutman considers *The Confessions* a "technology of self" in which Rousseau developed "vital techniques in the constitution of the self as a subject." Gutman also finds that the "self as subject" is the "basis for the revolutionary desire to transform society so that it would be conducive to the liberty and equality of all."[55] Rousseau's lifelong flight from internal and external conflicts and inconsistencies became an intellectual–mystical reverie, which in turn produced a revolutionary and homogeneous social philosophy.

In *The Confessions* Rousseau's understanding of memory imposes a powerful sense of continuity on the understanding of his development. He found that his early experiences and memories had a lasting impact on later experiences and memories, and he believed that others would be able to understand him only if they knew those early memories and could see his life as a continuum. Certain early experiences Rousseau found of greater importance for the understanding of his life than others; those experiences he called "seeds." As a botanist, he used a metaphor in which generative development is clear.

He recognized that through the extensive reading he had done in his youth three kinds of seeds were sown in his self: romantic, classical, and rational. Another type of "seed," which he did not mention, was the religious seed. Born in Calvinistic Geneva and the grandson of a Protestant minister, there must naturally have been a religious influence on the young Jean-Jacques. Amidst many external changes and difficulties, the "seeds" he enumerated became "plants," and blossomed, through his writings.

The idea and importance of living according to a particular philosophy must have had relevance for him from the age of seven, when he identified himself with Classical Greek and Roman heroes. Not only reading had an ongoing formative effect on him; his early experiences, feelings, and thoughts shaped his life, as a flowing stream shapes a pastoral scene.

However, a better metaphor for envisioning continuity in Rousseau's life seems to be comparing his development to the construction of a pyramid. The broad, square base of youthful learning and experiences undergoes a gradual selective orientation and meets at a common vertex (i.e., Rousseau's "Savoyard Creed").

In *The Confessions* Rousseau described a continuous philosophical development in his life, but in the course of this development he had undergone two inward personal revolutions. His "Parisian" revolution turned him into a reluctant extrovert, who previously had been accustomed to provincial surroundings and a quiet way of life. Taking part in Parisian salon and society life affected him more deeply than his first initial entry into society in Madame's de Warens's household, when he already felt the need to withdraw to a more peaceful place in the country. Rousseau's early experiences had created a love for solitude in him, although he succeeded, for short periods, in changing from an introversive to an extroversive lifestyle. Essentially he so disliked the extroversive way of life that it even made him ill. Both Rousseau's departure from Madame de Warens's villa at Chambéri and his escape from Paris to the Hermitage were preceded by illness. His recovery seems to have depended on the prospect of a quiet existence in natural surroundings where he could dedicate himself to study and writing.

His lasting inclination for solitude apparently originated in his sensitive nature, which he explained in the *Reveries of the Solitary Walker* as follows: "Always too strongly affected by what I see or hear, and particularly by signs of pleasure or suffering, affection or dislike. . . . It is when I am alone that I am my own master, at all other times I am the plaything of all who surround me."[56]

Rousseau's first revolution had to be followed by a retreat, which he experienced as another revolution. His complaint that he had lost his center of gravity in this "second revolution" shows that his new solitude in the countryside was ineffective in freeing him from his bonds with Paris. The retreat at the Hermitage could not cure him of the oppressive emotions, fantasies, and memories he had developed during the "first revolution."

The solitude he longed for at that time he could only regain when he returned to Paris, after much suffering and restless wandering. Only when he came back to Paris and had again abandoned himself to his "destiny" did he seem to regain his equilibrium.

In the *Reveries of the Solitary Walker* he maintained that the sufferings inflicted on him safeguarded his talents and helped cultivate them. Finally, Rousseau regarded his lasting relationship with Madame de Warens as the most powerful and most constant influence in life. It is not only romanticism when Rousseau credits her with "shaping" his soul. Schwartz noted that "Madame de Warens, who is older than Rousseau, combines the functions of Sophie and the tutor [in *Émile*] in Rousseau's education."[57] In *The Confessions* Rousseau described how Madame de Warens, as his own "tutor," continually motivated him and imbued him with the determination to develop himself further; or in Rousseau's last written words, "I decided that a rich store of talents was the surest protection against poverty, and I was resolved to employ my leisure hours in making myself able, if possible, one day to repay the best of women for all the help she had given me."[58]

It is obvious that attaining continuity and consistency played an important part in Rousseau's consciousness and in his daily life. However, the inner harmony he claims to have achieved through continuity and consistency, by dint of his inner practice of philosophy and written works, is often ignored, doubted, or rejected as such by philosophers and psychoanalysts alike.

NOTES

1. Christopher Kelly, *Rousseau's Exemplary Life: The "Confessions" as Political Philosophy* (London: Cornell University Press, 1987), 45.
2. Jean-Jacques Rousseau, "Preface to Narcissus: Or the Lover of Himself," in *The Collected Writings of Rousseau*, vol. 2, ed. R. D. Masters and C. Kelly (London: University Press of New England, 1992), 198.
3. N.J.H. Dent, *A Rousseau Dictionary* (Oxford: Blackwell, 1992), 56.
4. Jean-Jacques Rousseau, *The Confessions of Jean-Jacques Rousseau* (New York: Modern Library, 1945), 252, 591.
5. Ann Hartle, *The Modern Self in Rousseau's Confessions: A Reply to St. Augustine* (Notre Dame: University of Notre Dame Press, 1983), 11.
6. Rousseau, *The Confessions of Jean-Jacques Rousseau*, 3, 6.
7. Ronald Grimsley, *Rousseau and the Religious Quest* (Oxford: Clarendon Press, 1968), x.
8. Rousseau, *The Confessions of Jean-Jacques Rousseau*, 7, 11, 12, 14, 16, 17, 40 56, 57, 87, 93, 125, 176, 180, 181, 205, 221, 236, 240, 245, 246, 251, 256, 269, 274, 283.
9. Dent, *A Rousseau Dictionary*, 56; Hartle, *The Modern Self in Rousseau's Confessions: A Reply to St. Augustine*, 10; Kelly, *Rousseau's Exemplary Life: The "Confessions" as Political Philosophy*, 239.
10. Rousseau, *The Confessions of Jean-Jacques Rousseau*, 284, 361, 291, 336, 335, 341, 426.
11. Joel Schwartz, *The Sexual Politics of Jean-Jacques Rousseau* (Chicago: University of Chicago Press, 1984), 105–106.
12. Rousseau, *The Confessions of Jean-Jacques Rousseau*, 358, 359, 362, 367, 372, 374, 400–401.
13. Grimsley, *Rousseau and the Religious Quest*, 69.
14. Rousseau, *The Confessions of Jean-Jacques Rousseau*, 401, 405, 461, 431, 441.

15. Robert Elbaz, *The Changing Nature of the Self: A Critical Study of the Autobiographic Discourse* (London: Croom Helm, 1988), 94.
16. Rousseau, *The Confessions of Jean-Jacques Rousseau*, 501, 534, 553.
17. Susan K. Jackson, "Claiming the Patent on Autobiographical Fiction," in *Reading La Nouvelle Héloïse Today, Pensée libre* 4, ed. O. Mostefai (Ottawa: North American Association for the Study of Jean-Jacques Rousseau, 1993), 203.
18. Ronald Grimsley, *Jean-Jacques Rousseau: A Study in Self-Awareness* (Cardif: University of Wales Press, 1968), 160.
19. Rousseau, *The Confessions of Jean-Jacques Rousseau*, 567.
20. Jean Starobinski, *Jean-Jacques Rousseau: Transparency and Obstruction*, trans. A. Goldhammer (Chicago: University of Chicago Press, 1971), 115.
21. Rousseau, *The Confessions of Jean-Jacques Rousseau*, 587.
22. Grimsley, *Rousseau and the Religious Quest*, 30.
23. Rousseau, *The Confessions of Jean-Jacques Rousseau*, 658, 666, 669, 682.
24. Dent, *A Rousseau Dictionary*, 59.
25. Rousseau, "Preface to Narcissus: Or the Lover of Himself," 191, 195, 197.
26. Jean-Jacques Rousseau, *Émile*, trans. B. Foxley (London: Everyman's Library, 1974), 1, 30, 71, 49, 46, 140, 153, 142, 182, 173, 204.
27. Frederick C. Green, *Jean-Jacques Rousseau: A Critical Study of His Life and Writings* (Cambridge: Cambridge University Press, 1955), 8.
28. Rousseau, *Émile*, 226, 231.
29. Grimsley, *Rousseau and the Religious Quest*, 47.
30. Maurice W. Cranston, *The Noble Savage* (London: Penguin Press, 1991), 179–180.
31. Rousseau, *Émile*, 270.
32. Kelly, *Rousseau's Exemplary Life: The Confessions as Political Philosophy*, 252.
33. Ibid., 240.
34. Jean-Jacques Rousseau, "Rousseau, Judge of Jean-Jacques: Dialogues," in *The Collected Writings of Rousseau*, vol. 1, ed. R. D. Masters and C. Kelly (London: University Press of New England, 1990), 189, 240, 241, 252, 255, 256.
35. Jean-Jacques Rousseau, *Reveries of the Solitary Walker*, trans. P. France (London: Penguin, 1979), 32, 45, 55.
36. Amélie Rorty Oksenberg, "Rousseau's Therapeutic Experiments," *Philosophy* 66 (1991): 421.
37. Rousseau, *Reveries of the Solitary Walker*, 61, 69, 76, 89, 91, 153, 154.
38. Mila Morgenstern, "Rousseau for the Twentieth Century: New Interpretations of the Family," in Mostefai, *Reading La Nouvelle Héloïse Today, Pensée libre* 4, 223, 224.
39. Ronald D. Laing, *The Politics of the Family and Other Essays* (New York: Vintage Books, 1972), 3, 13.
40. Thomas M. Kavanagh, *Writing the Truth: Authority and Desire in Rousseau* (London: University of California Press, 1987), 11.
41. Grimsley, *Jean-Jacques Rousseau: A Study in Self-Awareness*, 24, 25, 26, 27, 28.
42. Anthony Storr, *Solitude* (London: Fontana, 1989), 167.
43. Grimsley, *Jean-Jacques Rousseau: A Study in Self-Awareness*, 53, 191.
44. Jean Starobinski, *Jean-Jacques Rousseau: Transparency and Obstruction*, xxvii, xxx, 170, 177, 201, 375.
45. Grimsley, *Jean-Jacques Rousseau: A Study in Self-Awareness*, 1.

46. Guy Lafrance, "L'Éthique de *La Nouvelle Héloïse* et du Vicaire Savoyard," in Mostefai, *Reading La Nouvelle Héloïse Today, Pensée libre* 4, 141, 147.

47. Starobinski, *Jean-Jacques Rousseau: Transparency and Obstruction*, 371, 367.

48. Elisabeth Zeil-Fahlbush, *Wissen und Handeln: zur Begruendung der praktische Philosophie bei Rousseau* (Bonn: Grundmann, 1979), 11.

49. Green, *Jean-Jacques Rousseau: A Critical Study of His Life and Writings*, 97, 367.

50. Basil Munteano, *Solitude et Contradictions de Jean-Jacques Rousseau* (Paris: Nizet, 1975), 210.

51. Robert H. Bell, "Rousseau: The Prophet of Sincerity," *Biography* 3, 4 (1980): 301.

52. Ezequiel de Olaso, "The Two Skepticisms of the Savoyard Vicar," in *Skepticism in the Enlightenment*, ed. R. H. Popkin, E. de Olaso, and G. Tonelli (Dordrecht: Kluwer, 1997).

53. Grimsley, *Rousseau and the Religious Quest*, 136.

54. Starobinski, *Jean-Jacques Rousseau: Transparency and Obstruction*, 254.

55. Huck Gutman, "Rousseau's Confessions: A Technology of the Self," in *Technologies of the Self*, ed. L. H. Martin, H. Gutman, and P. Hutton (Amherst: University of Massachusetts Press, 1988), 99–121.

56. Rousseau, *Reveries of the Solitary Walker*, 148.

57. Schwartz, *The Sexual Politics of Jean-Jacques Rousseau*, 102.

58. Rousseau, *Reveries of the Solitary Walker*, 155.

CHAPTER 6

The Philosopher in Revolt

One gets rid of a neurosis, one doesn't get cured of one's self.
Jean-Paul Sartre, *The Words*

A PHILOSOPHICAL NARRATIVE FOR ALL

In *The Words*, Jean-Paul Sartre analyzed his life according to his Existential psychoanalytic method. This method I described briefly in Chapter 3. In this chapter not only Sartre's practice of Existential psychoanalysis will become manifest, but intermittent further explanations pertaining to it will add to its theoretical dimension.

In *The Words*, Sartre reveals himself as a person with a lifelong involvement in writing. He began writing at the age of eight and continued to do so until he was sixty-eight, when blindness prevented him from working as he had been accustomed to. From 1926 to 1963 Sartre wrote letters to his companion Simone de Beauvoir. He called his letters to her "the transcription of immediate life" and a witness to his life.[1] Sartre intended these letters to be published postmortem, and except for those that might have violated the privacy of friends who were still alive, they were indeed published after his death.[2]

Another autobiographical source is Sartre's *War Diaries*.[3] His early novel, *The Nausea*, and the trilogy *The Paths of Freedom* (i.e., *The Age of Reason, The Reprieve*, and *Iron in the Soul*), also contain autobiographical elements. Readers of Sartre's letters may recognize some close friends of his in the fictional images that appear in these novels as

Ivich, Bost, Brunet, and Zuore.[4] In *The Words* Sartre confesses that the person behind the figure of Roquentin in *The Nausea* was himself: "I used him to show, without complacency, the texture of my life."[5] However, Roquentin as self-image is just one of Sartre's evanescent images. The self he describes in *The Words* is what I call "the essential Sartre." For example, he envisions himself as reborn time and again. He rises from ashes, not out of his past, but out of nothingness: He subordinates the past to the present, the present to the future; Sartre transforms "a quiet evolutionism into a revolutionary and discontinuous catastrophism."[6] However, in "Sartre on Sartre," Robert Champigny finds that the manner in which Sartre "pictures his childhood should reveal the way he tries to totalize himself at the moment."[7]

Sartre's letters, diaries, and early novels are all in a variety of ways autobiographical, but they are not, like *The Words*, autobiography proper. Yet in "Self-Portrait at Seventy" Sartre said that *The Words* is no truer about himself than *The Nausea* and *The Paths of Freedom*. He considers *The Words* a kind of novel, "a novel that I believe in, but a novel nevertheless."[8]

In the interview "On *The Idiot of the Family*," Sartre describes his aim in all of his Existential psychoanalytic novels: "to show the formation and the personalization of the individual, that is to say, how he moves toward the concrete from the abstract conditioning of the family structures." His method is philosophical and not scientific as is Lacan's psychoanalysis, in that Sartre uses notions instead of concepts. Concepts define persons from the outside, while notions define them from the inside. Consequently, to understand people one needs empathy. The self in Sartrean psychoanalysis appears in human thought as the unification of reflected consciousness.[9]

Hugh Silverman believes that there is an application of Sartre's progressive–regressive self-reflexive method and his third episteme from the *Search for a Method* to himself in *The Words*, and consequently asserts that "the self must appear within the very words that one uses" and that the result is a "product of human activity, human praxis."[10]

It is not because Sartre described his childhood that *The Words* is his autobiography per se, but because he described how self is unified in reflected thought, and how his mature self opposed the abstract conditioning of the family structures it received in childhood.

In Sartre's interviews about himself and his work after he became blind (i.e., "Self-Portrait at Seventy," "Conversations with Jean-Paul Sartre," and "Today's Hope"), he acknowledged Beauvoir's "Conversations with Jean-Paul Sartre" as the continuation of his autobiography *The Words*.[11]

His other autobiographical and biographical writings are characterized by the fact that they were inspired by, and are witnesses to, a change in him. *The War Diaries, The Nausea,* and *The Paths of Freedom* were written during the Second World War, a period Sartre called his passage from youth to maturity. Through these autobiographical texts he expresses the way his life changed, the major turning point occurring when he abandoned his prewar individualism, and "the idea of the pure individual and adopted the social individual and socialism."[12]

In *The Words* Sartre not only bears witness to the developments and changes in his life, but seeks to invoke and institute change in himself and others by repudiating the bourgeois way of life and by denouncing literature that is not committed to liberation and social progress. He intended his autobiography to be as revolutionary as Marx's *Capital;* it is not just a description of a "lost" life, but an attempt to change that life. It is an Existential psychoanalytic praxis.

That Sartre's project was never completely implemented does not mean that it is without value. The choice of being is the foundation of the existential project, and it is this choice that is of paramount importance.

Douglas Kirsner is of the opinion that after *The Words* Sartre was cured of literary myths.[13] I find, though, that Sartre wrote *The Words* over a period of ten years and during that time he produced literary works such as *Kean, The Condemned of Altona,* and *The Freud Scenario.* Then, after *The Words,* he also published fiction. However, most of his life after 1953, when he began to write *The Words,* was concerned with political and social criticism, interviews, and political action.

Sartre knew that he could not stop writing fiction, and that he certainly would not stop working on *Flaubert,* which he was convinced was an opus as revolutionary as *The Words.* Though Sartre may have failed partially in realizing his revolutionary project, he clarified—"purified"—his intentions by writing about his writing neurosis, his cure of his madness, and his good intentions. In "The Purpose of Writing" he states that the "need to write is fundamentally a quest for purification."[14]

In this sense *The Words* has much in common with a classical religious confession: The sinner confesses his or her failings and believes thus to have been delivered of them. Yet it is likely that the change that has occurred is only partial, although at least from a religious standpoint the change of intention is the most important.

Sartre writes negatively about his childhood in the hope of intensifying and furthering the changes that occurred in him from 1939 to 1945. *The Words* is not just an account of Sartre's life until he was twelve years old; in the context of his childhood he describes episodes and discusses issues deriving from his adult life. For example, he compares his first experience of social adhesion—during the hours he spent in the cinema as a child with his mother—to his experience of social adhesion during the Second World War: "The only other time I have witnessed that nakedness, that sense of everyone's direct relationship to everyone else, that waking dream, that dim consciousness of the danger of being a man, was in 1940, in Stalag XII D."[15]

Sartre divided *The Words* into two sections: "Reading" and "Writing." Although the book follows an apparent chronological order of Jean-Paul's early development in reading and writing, I find three major themes in the otherwise achronological and associative account of his life: Sartre's "incomplete Oedipal complex," God and the unnatural, and death and immortality.

The "Incomplete Oedipal Complex"

The section "Reading" begins by introducing and describing Sartre's paternal and maternal background. The tragic death of his father, fifteen months after Jean-Paul was born, left a permanent mark on his life. The theme of Sartre's family relations or his "most incomplete Oedipal complex" has often been construed as indicating that Sartre intended his autobiography to substantiate a classical psychoanalytic interpretation of life.[16] Sartre, however, rejected the Freudian unconscious and other ego hierarchies. Consequently, he rejected the Oedipal complex as well as other unconscious complexes, and he would certainly not have described his childhood in Freudian terms. Despite the obvious anti-Freudian tendency in Sartre's autobiography, scholarly explanations that seek to conceal his philosophical self-interpretation beneath classical psychoanalytic understandings are not lacking.

For example, Jeffrey Mehlman claims that the apparent absence of sexuality in the Schweitzer–Sartre household caused the absence of the normal Oedipal triangle.[17] Although Mehlman does not provide his readers with a psychoanalytic explanation of Sartre's difficulties in recalling his childhood, nevertheless one might easily make use of Mehlman's account as a source for a psychoanalytic explanation, in that he finds that for Sartre, "to recall . . . childhood is first of all to remember a general embarrassment about sex."[18] I find, however, that in the liberal, humanistic atmosphere of the Schweitzer–Sartre household the puritanism suggested by Melhman is difficult to imagine. The child Jean-Paul was allowed to read Flaubert's *Madame Bovary*, Corneille's tragedies, and other literature in which lovers, sensuality, and sexuality are certainly present.[19] Janine Hochland offers another Freudian perspective on *The Words*. To her, Sartre's confession in *The Words* that "as a brother he would have been incestuous" and the way he expresses his feelings for his mother make it "quite possible that Sartre's problem is precisely that of an *unresolved* Oedipus complex, symbolized in various literary situations."[20]

However, Kate and Edward Fullbrook suggest that Sartre tried deliberately to neutralize what would likely be interpreted as an Oedipal relationship with his mother by describing her as a sister figure.[21] They also suggest that Sartre's stepfather, who married his mother when Sartre was twelve, had been the authoritative influence in the new family structure, and one of the major causes for Sartre's incipient and then permanent rebellion against hierarchical power structures and paternalism of any kind.[22] But, as I will show further on, Sartre himself found the very absence of authority in his early family life the source of his revolutionary character.

According to Philip Thody, Sartre presumably suffered from the absence of the Freudian reality principle. Thody considers that from Sartre's account of his "unsatisfactory" childhood one may conclude that children "should be given security and firm discipline by their parents, and this discipline should be reinforced by the lessons which they learn from the other children in their own age group."[23] Thody's conclusion seems to me to contradict Sartre's firm belief in anti-authoritarianism; his discontent is not due to the lack of authoritarian and peer discipline but is because he had been alienated from humankind through his particular destiny.

In *The Words* Sartre describes Freudian themes such as incest, rebellion, and narcissism with deliberate irony. For example, he does not forget to add incest fantasies to his confession about his childhood, to which he attributes the literary variations on the theme in *The Flies, The Paths of Freedom*, and *Altona*. But incest appealed to him only if it remained platonic![24] Likewise, when he readily subscribes to a psychoanalytic verdict that declares him to be without a superego, he can only speak ironically. Apparently, however, Sartre's irony was originally sharper, as we learn from the following: "In 1963 I needed only three months to revise the first version [of *The Words*] and remove the somewhat too ironical tone I had given it."[25]

After the death of Sartre's father, his mother and grandparents behaved as if he never had had a father: "I was given to understand that I was a child of miracle."[26] Sartre attributes his "levity" and freedom from "the canker of power" to not having had even the shadow of a father. For example, in "Self-Portrait at Seventy" he denies ever having used power, although he had been in positions of authority.[27] Sartre did not consider his grandfather as a replacement of paternal authority. He metaphorically describes the male authority of his early childhood as follows: "the God of Love with the beard of the Father and the Sacred Heart of the Son."[28] He believed that if his mother and grandmother would have wanted to punish him by putting him on bread and water, his grandfather would have brought him jam. Sartre found that his freedom from submission to any rules till the age of ten, when for the first time he was sent to school, implanted the liberalism so characteristic of his early individualism and later socialism.

When Sartre diagnoses himself as suffering from a neurosis, he does not imply the classical Freudian neurosis rooted in an unfortunate infantile sexual development, but rather a kind of anti-psychiatric neurosis that can develop through negative reciprocal relations with one's social surroundings. Sartre suffered from a kind of neurosis wherein madness itself was the solution to the problem. His anti-psychiatric orientation is also apparent in that he compared his personal schism between an actual life and a literary fantasy life with the schizophrenia of a psychiatric patient.

The patient is described as hospitalized and crying out from his bed: "I'm a prince! Arrest the Grand Duke!" But when the nurse tells him to blow his nose, he does so. And when "the prince" is asked what his profession is, he confesses that he is a shoemaker. Immediately after this moment of insight, however, the shoemaker turns into "a prince" again. For two years, from the age of nine to eleven, when his lonely fantasy world had to make place for the study of grammar, arithmetic, and dictation, Sartre seems to have been cured of his writing neurosis. But then he went completely mad. First, the First World War caused him to relapse into childhood fantasies, but there was a difference: He had become aware that the nature of fantasy was different from the nature of reality. Second, his enrollment in the Lycée Henry IV gave Sartre young, live playmates. He finally "had been delivered from the sin of existing." In the light of actually living, his dreams of literary glory and immortality seemed bleak.

However, Sartre recognized that his new active life was only a superficial change. Inwardly his writer's mandate still existed. Between 1914 and 1916 he had lost sight of himself, but tasting actual living brought him closer to his destiny: His mandate became his character, it flowed from his head into his bones; he and his madness became one. At the end of *The Words* Sartre considers that "one gets rid of a neurosis, one doesn't get cured of one's self."[29]

God and the Unnatural

Most scholars neglect the themes of God and the unnatural as treated in *The Words*. But the ironical manner in which Sartre deals with religion does not justify overlooking its influence on his early development.

Rivca and Haim Gordon show that the major themes of Sartre's early philosophy found in *Being and Nothingness* can also be found in *The Words*. However, they do not exclude the possibility that *The Words* represents "more than one phase and period of Sartre's thought."[30] This seems feasible, since Sartre's aim of "becoming God," as he expressed it in *Being and Nothingness*, was completely altered in *The Words*. Sartre's ideal instead became to be an ordinary human being.

God's existence is an issue that might have evoked the first philosophical questions in the young Sartre. God, symbolizing the supreme authority, was a matter of concern to Jean-Paul because in his grandparents and mother he observed diverse attitudes toward Him. His mother and grandmother, as nonpracticing Catholics, went to mass to hear good music. His grandfather, of Protestant descent, always joked about Catholicism as well as about his own religion.

The manner in which Sartre first heard about God did not induce in him either belief in or fear of the Divinity. On the contrary, his "religious education" taught him that religion was insignificant and even bestowed on him a familiarity toward God. Jean-Paul addressed the Almighty in prayers until God disappeared—by accident. As a child, and later in life too, Sartre identified with God. He found that his family's lack of religious conviction prevented him from being religious, from even becoming a monk. Instead of fulfilling the religious potential that he recognized within himself, he came to believe in atheism. The strong convictions and the fate of an outcast, so characteristic of early twentieth-century atheists, appealed more to the young Sartre than the religious skepticism and indifference he encountered in his grandparents' home. In his late fifties Sartre realized that he had missed his vocation: "I needed God, He was given to me, I received Him without realizing I was seeking Him."[31]

Until the age of seven the long-haired and angelic-looking Jean-Paul probably felt he had been destined for a supreme purpose, something like a divine calling. When by mistake he missed the call of God, Sartre appropriated the divine mission his family seemed to approve of: the profession of writer. As an alternative revelation Sartre experienced a "fundamental illusion": writing made him powerful; "all things would humbly beg for a name; to name the thing was both to create and take it." At first his grandfather was skeptical about his choice of becoming a writer. But when a friend of the family proclaimed that Sartre would be a writer, that he was meant to be one, Jean-Paul's destiny was sealed. His grandfather still tried cautiously to divert Sartre from a literary career by showing him the bourgeois security the teaching profession could give him, while also leaving him opportunities to write.

Sartre found that it was this very caution that drove him to literature. He felt that he was the product of a collective family demand. Later in life, when gloomy over his writer's profession, it gave him some comfort to believe that it was his destiny.

Although elsewhere Sartre blames the absence of God and the meaninglessness of life for his writing neurosis, he found fault here with his educators: "I had not chosen my vocation; it had been imposed on me by others. Actually, nothing had happened: some words tossed off by an old woman and Charles' machiavellism. But that was enough for me to be convinced."[32] This existential "primal" scene resembles a formative episode out of Sartre's Existential psychoanalysis of Jean Genet: "A voice declares publicly: 'You're a thief.' . . . What happened? Actually, almost nothing: an action undertaken without reflection, conceived and carried out in the secret, silent inwardness in which he often takes refuge, has just become objective. Genet learns what he is objectively."[33]

Virtue was natural to Jean-Paul the child. The juvenile actor tried to please his grandparents and mother and thereby prevent scandal. Sartre's desire to please went so far that it attained the inhuman, the unnatural, the divine. His is the image of the child prophet who proclaims divine truth; of him the Psalmist says, "Truth flows from the mouth of babes and sucklings." Sartre must have been conscious that his desire to please could be diagnosed in a classical psychoanalytic manner as originating from a narcissistic personality disorder. Accordingly, he asked himself if he was narcissistic and answered as follows: "Not even that. Too eager to charm, I forget myself. After all, it doesn't amuse me very much to make mud-pies, to scribble, to perform my natural functions: in order for these to have value . . . at least one grown-up must go into raptures over my products."[34]

Sartre recognized how unnatural his virtue was when he understood that it was rooted in the excessive love of his grandparents and mother, a love he compared with the unnatural love certain people have for children and animals, a love hostile to human beings because of its excessiveness. Until the age of ten Sartre was surrounded only by adults; he felt their gaze preserving his "nature as a model grandson." He felt that the gaze of the adults turned him into a fake child, into an actor, into nothingness: "I was nothing: an ineffaceable transparency."[35]

Next to identifying himself with God, he identified with animals, although Sartre disliked animals. Sartre's identification with the unnatural might explain his dislike of all that was pure nature. His dislike of animals and nature seemed to transcend the boundaries of what an English BBC broadcaster recognized as a typical French conflict: a Cartesian split between mind and matter, nature and culture, which may cause most Frenchmen to be less attached to pets than their English neighbors.

In his conversations with Beauvoir, Sartre conveyed a lifelong aversion to the natural; it found expression, for example, in his dislike for unprepared and uncooked foods. Tomatoes appeared too natural. In general Sartre found that food "must be the result of work performed by men. Bread is like that. . . . [It is] a relationship with other men."[36] Sartre felt at home in the unnatural, in otherworldly surroundings. Books were his pets and his countryside. The mirror reality found in the library of his grandfather was his playground.[37] His peer group and playmates were Corneille, Victor Hugo, Goethe, Flaubert, and

Chateaubriand. His familiarity with great writers was the lasting influence of these playmates on his life.

Questioning his grandfather about books and writers, he was made to understand that "humanities led us straight to the Divine, all the more in that added to them were the beauties of nature." The sixth floor had become Sartre's permanent home, his natural watchtower, were he could inhale the rarefied air of good literature. Sartre's mother tried to counter the grandfather's humanistic influence on Jean-Paul by first giving him fairy tales to read, and then other children's books. Sartre actually enjoyed these action stories more than the incomprehensible stories of his immortal literary friends. This marked the beginning of his double life; as long as he lived he preferred a detective story to a philosophy book, although reading philosophy and literature remained important to him. Sartre believed it was because of the happy endings of those fairy tales and cartoons that he possessed a "deep seated phantasmagoria: optimism."

Sartre understood his unnaturalness as the absence of meaning in living. He only knew "the conceit of a lap-dog." His family's adoration, and his lack of any reason for living, created pride in him: "Since nobody laid claim to me seriously, I laid claim to being indispensable to the Universe." He explains how his dream of traveling on a train without a ticket revealed his pride. When the conductor asked for his ticket, he justified his trip by claiming to have an important secret destiny: He travels for "reasons that concerned France and perhaps all of mankind." Sartre's awareness of the effects of his family's idolization of him eventually helped him escape the consequences of his pride, which he condemned as the plea of wretches.

Sartre found that his unnatural surroundings, his games with his ghostlike literary friends in the sixth-floor library, alienated him from other human beings. He did not identify himself with his grandfather, a neighborhood kid, or a policeman, but with a poodle, a fly, and God. As an actor he kept creating himself: "I am the given and the gift. . . . I have no rights, since love heaps blessings upon me; I have no duties, since I give out of love. Only one mandate: to please; everything for show."

Sartre traced his place in society to his childhood experience; he stood aside from society, a position comparable to that of the church. He existed alongside the secular power as a prince of a priestly order. He described his grandfather as a holy man, surrounded by books written by saints and prophets. Sartre followed in their footsteps; he decided to write for God, for the purpose of saving the world. Although at the end of *The Words* Sartre claims to have systematically thought in opposition to himself and to have destroyed his belief in literary martyrdom, salvation, and immortality, important writers continued to have an influence over him that he could not understand. He confesses that on his final judgment day he is answerable only to the great creators of literature, to "those that are only answerable to God." Sartre was aware that his faith in the heroes of the bourgeoisie (i.e., the timeless authors) was inconsistent with his critique of bourgeois literature.

Sartre considered that his dual religious affiliation, Protestant and Catholic, prevented him from believing in any religion, but it created faith in him for other matters, such as philosophy and literature. When at the age of twelve Sartre had come to the conclusion that God did not exist, he nevertheless let the Holy Ghost remain, "the one who guaranteed . . . [his writer's] mandate." At the age of fifty he realized that writing had been his opium of religion. He finally became the atheist he had always wanted to be: "I collared the Holy Ghost in the cellar and threw him out; atheism is a cruel and long-range affair: I think I've carried it through."

Sartre might have identified himself with Pascal's thinking reed had he been born in the seventeenth or eighteenth century. But having been born in the twentieth century he compared himself with a weed that grew on the compost of Catholicism. He attributed his neurosis, which he compared with blindness, to the slow decay of twentieth-century Christianity. However, he at last outgrew the idolization of his literary saints and the superficial bourgeois way of life: He came to realize that he was as good as all men and no better than any.

Death and Immortality

At the age of nine Sartre witnessed the beginning of the First World War and shared the French anti-German sentiments. He found himself scarred by the defeat of the French in the war. The evil he experienced through the war flawed his small literary paradise. Sartre defined his life from 1905 to 1914 as Good without Evil, a life undefined by opposites, and he concludes, "If one is defined only by opposition, I was an undefined person."

In his imagination Sartre participated in the battle against the national enemy. Whereas soldiers killed with guns, he slaughtered his opponents with his pen: "I regarded works of art for a long time as metaphysical events, the birth of which affected the universe." Eventually, the soldier in Sartre became the tragic image of Parsifal, an expiatory offering.

At the age of ten Sartre felt chosen; because of his predestination he was unable to experience the events of war reported in the newspapers as events that concerned him, as things that could happen to him. Although he could imagine losing one of his limbs, that would not touch his innermost self: "My misfortunes would be only tests, means for writing a book . . . rungs on the ladder that was leading me to my glorious end."

Sartre had made the acquaintance of death before the First World War. Although his father's death was an issue bypassed in his upbringing, he looked upon himself as the son of a dead man; it was "to a dead man that he belonged." At the age of five he felt as if death lay in wait for him. He saw it in the evening on the balcony, it peered through the windows; even walking down the street he met death. For a while he met death every night in bed and later it appeared in disguises such as the voice of his mother singing, or in books like *The Venus of Ille*. However, death became entirely real for Sartre only at the age of seven: "I met real Death, the Grim Reaper, everywhere, but it was never there. What was it? A person and a threat. The person was mad. As for the threat . . . shadowy mouths could open anywhere . . . and snap me up." Sartre believed that at the age of seven he suffered from a genuine neurosis. He explained that those feelings of terror originated in his sense of being superfluous. Sartre located the origin of his madness in a philosophical issue, a desperate quest for the meaning of life. He felt condemned for his uselessness, and expected his judgment at any moment.[38] In *The Words* the "shadowy mouth" that could snap him up any moment belongs to the grim male reaper, Death. Although in their article "Holes and Slime: Sexism in Sartre's Psychoanalysis" Margery Collins and Christine Pierce indicate that mouths and holes are associated with femininity in Sartre's psychoanalysis, *The Words* contains a male counterpart that can devour him.[39] Sartre believed that authentic faith in God could have helped him overcome his lack of meaning in life and his fear of death. He could have received immortality from God without having to escape into a fictional world. However, as stated before, Sartre's God appeared as absent.

There is more on death and the dead in *The Words*. Grandmother Sartre died when he was five. Then there is Bercot, a classmate whom Sartre calls his brother, who died at the age of eighteen. Another classmate, Benard, also died. Maybe because Benard, like Sartre, was the only son of a widow, his death affected Sartre much more than the death of Bercot. Sartre asked himself, "Did I have an inkling of Evil, of the absence of God, of an uninhabitable world? I think so: if not, why would Benard's image remain so painfully clear in my rejected, lost, forgotten childhood?"

Sartre's final analysis of the origin of his continuous writing habit was that it was a flight, a revolt against life, an escape into a kind of suicide. Sartre understood his choice of becoming a writer at the age of seven as a dismissal of life. He decided that he would live as if dead, because only the dead were rewarded with immortality. He found that his childhood resembled that of the great immortal dead, such as

Jean-Jacques Rousseau and Johann Sebastian Bach. When he compared himself to his friends at the age of twenty, he found that they possessed a zest and love for living he did not. He had only a passion for the past; he, the dead one, "tried to live backwards."

However, death is always covered in the glory of future fame. When Sartre wrote *The Words*, even then, death was as if nonexistent to him. He considered himself immortal, although it seemed a reality he had to accept and not something he still desired. At his death his writings would be him: "I, twenty-five volummes, eighteen-thousand pages of text, three hundred engravings, including a portrait of the author."[40] When Sartre became aware that he had established a lasting name for himself in philosophy and literature, a kind of eternity, he must have realized that he had achieved the purpose of his neurosis and could now live without it. Having delivered himself of his neurosis, Sartre realized that as a writer he was not the Immortal Almighty.

Jane Tompkins rightly observes that *The Words* is "a turning point" in Sartre's philosophy of self.[41] In Sartre's new humble vision of himself as a writer he was an average, powerless person. Nevertheless, writing books was valuable because it offered human beings a critical mirror by which they could attain self-awareness.

In this analysis of *The Words* I have shown how Sartre applied his philosophical–literary method of Existential psychoanalysis to himself. His autobiography was not intended as another literary masterpiece, but as a literary–philosophical praxis that had to cause a change in his own life as well as in the lives of others. Sartre's effort was successful, since he at least succeeded in radically changing his own life through it.

PHILOSOPHY AS LITERARY AND POLITICAL ENGAGEMENT

In this section I analyze Sartre's works to ascertain whether they are consistent with the philosophy found in his autobiography. I choose from Sartre's opus *What Is Literature, The Freud Scenario, Conversations with Jean-Paul Sartre*, and *Hope Now*. These works are indispensable for evaluating the development of crucial philosophical issues and themes indicated in my reading of *The Words*, such as Existential psychoanalysis, writing, reading, God, immortality, and death.

What Is Literature

The four essays in *What Is Literature* were first published in 1947 in *Les Temps Modernes*. In these essays Sartre discussed the following issues: what is writing, why write, for whom does one write, and the situation of the writer. These issues remained of vital interest to Sartre throughout the rest of his life. In the introduction to *What Is Literature*, Wallace Fowlie observes that Sartre turns "his treatise into something that resembles a psychoanalytical history of contemporary literature," and a political guide for writing books.[42]

In *What Is Literature* the questions asked by Sartre about writing are directly related to Sartre's works of Existential psychoanalysis. In these analyses he tries to understand the existential project of the writer. In these studies Sartre not only analyzed the lives of writers like Baudelaire, Genet, and Flaubert, but he also analyzed the life of Sigmund Freud.

Sartre regarded *What Is Literature* as a reply to those who questioned his project of an engaged literature; it is an apology for engaged literature by means of a discussion of the nature of literature. Hazel Barnes points out that during the war, in Sartre's Christmas play *Baronia*, written for the inmates of the Stalag XIID prison camp, Sartre's literature was already engaged: It was used as a form of political action.[43] Barnes finds that Sartre's career was divided between literature and philosophy, but he bridged the gap between them: there is philosophy in literature. It is typical for many existentialist philosophers to unite the theoretical with the literary; for example, Kierkegaard, Marcel, Camus, and Beauvoir all wrote philosophical fiction.[44] Benjamin Suhl finds Sartre's "practice of literature and of literary criticism as concomitant to his philosophy."[45] Kirsner finds, contrary to Barnes and Suhl, that for Sartre literature is a regression, a form of play. Literature is different from political and philosophical writings, which relate to the real world of radically alienated persons. He suggests that Sartre's enthrallment by literature may be understood in a psychoanalytic way: "Sartre could pour out the pure milk of paradise instead of being reliant on the tasteless and nauseating milk that he finds in the outer world."[46]

Sartre shows in *What Is Literature* that propaganda is different from engaged literature in style and content. He views the prose writer as a person who wants to reveal the world by his or her words. For an engaged writer, words are action, since he or she intends to change the world by revealing it. The power of this disclosure is that it says what has not yet been formulated or "what dares not tell its name." Sartre finds that the writer's choice of the subjects to be disclosed is of greater importance than the literary style used for disclosure. However, the necessity remains of giving the reader aesthetic pleasure. Only when a feeling of aesthetic joy is awakened is a literary work achieved.

The "dead lions" of literature, like Rousseau, Montaigne, or Chateaubriand, are united in that they had a message, an argument that contained their personal feelings. If they would have been alive today, their message would have induced love or hatred. In Sartre's definition of good literature, the message is "a soul made objective."[47] However, the writer's message is time bound. Montaigne's skepticism and Rousseau's humanism do not disclose the repression of contemporary readers. Moreover, most professional critics have no intention of bringing the writer's message alive; on the contrary, by showing only the internal contradictions of the lives and the writings, the message is made worthless.

Iris Murdoch finds that Sartre had a greater interest in issues than in persons, which she finds characteristic of rationalism. But she finds that the stress of issues is not a quality of great novelists, however fitting it may be for a good dramatist.[48] In the interview "The Purpose of Writing," Sartre himself seemed to be in agreement with Murdoch when he stated that drama was the most suitable form for his work. In this interview Sartre described philosophy as concerned with people: A person is "at once an agent and an actor, who produces and plays his drama while he lives the contradictions of his situation, until either his individuality is shattered or his conflicts are resolved."[49]

However, that the writer with a message wants to achieve a particular purpose does not explain why the literary project was chosen as an activity to achieve that objective. Behind the different aspirations of writers Sartre expected "a deeper and more immediate choice" common to all. The choice that unites good authors is the choice of freedom: "The author writes in order to address himself to the freedom of readers, and he requires it [freedom] in order to make his work exist."

Reading and writing are dialectically correlated. Reading is the synthesis of perception and creation, but Sartre admits that he could say the same about the enjoyment of most other forms of art. Reading as directed creativity requires the freedom of the audience, and the author must enforce this freedom, through which one can differentiate between good and bad novels. A bad novel is an act of bad faith. For example, a novel in praise of anti-Semitism cannot be good because it denies the freedom of a people. A good novel may denounce racism violently and not lose its value because it enforces the freedom of the human race: "The bad novel aims to please by flattering whereas the good one is an exigence and an act of faith." The creation of such literature is a philosophical and ethical activity because the authors are guardians of ideal values. The engaged writer speaks for liberties denied, forbidden, or outlawed.

Thus, the question arises of to whom the author addresses himself or herself. Does he or she write for slaves, free people, or a universal reader? Sartre answers this question by showing that every good book encompasses a historical situation to which it proposes a "concrete liberation on the basis of a particular alienation." It is a particular historical situation that the writer wants to change or to preserve. Accordingly, one can recognize the image of an ideal reader, who resembles the novel's heroes or heroines. For example, Sartre could portray the image of Nathanael by reading *Les Nourritures terrestres*: "I can see that the alienation from which he is urged to free himself is the family, the real-estate he owns or will own by inheritance, the utilitarian project, a conventional moralism, a narrow theism."

Although Sartre's engaged literature has an ethical aim, it does not preach morality, but it renders a mirror image to the reader that has to make the projected situation unbearable. Literature with the ethical aim of liberating society is not a means but an unconditioned end. Literature is alienated from itself when it is not autonomous and is under the influence of the power structures and ideology of its era. Sartre admits that all writers are "situated" and to an extent under the influence of ideology and class. He predicts that only in a classless society will the end of the dialectical development of literature occur.

Consequently, the next vital concern is about the situation of the modern writer: Sartre characterizes the situation of the writer before the Second World War by the absence of Evil in political realism and philosophical idealism. The notion of Evil had become the property "of some Manichaeans—Anti-Semites, fascists, anarchists of the right." The war and the occupation caused the rediscovery of the absolute at the heart of relativity itself. Evil was no longer just an appearance. Accordingly, the postwar writer understood that "Evil, fruit of a free and sovereign will, is, like Good, absolute."

The evil felt during the war brought these writers to touch limits, extreme situations, that made them different. Sartre considers postwar writers metaphysical writers because they created a literature of extreme situations. For Sartre, "metaphysics is not a sterile discussion about abstract notions which have nothing to do with experience. It is a living effort to embrace from within the human condition in its totality." The postwar writer abandoned the literature of *exis* (being) for a literature of praxis: "Praxis as action in history and on history; that is, as a synthesis of historical relativity and moral and metaphysical absolute, with this hostile and friendly, terrible and derisive world which it reveals to us." The public of the postwar author is the bourgeoisie, which also had been the public of the prewar writer. But since the message of the postwar writer is antibourgeoisie in content, the contemporary writer really has no public to address. Whereas the bourgeoisie had found a reason for living in the old books, the postwar writer offers this public their own picture of "victims, doubtless, and innocent, but, still and all, tyrants and guilty."

The first duty of the postwar writer is to "re-establish language in its dignity." Sartre found it necessary to distrust the incommunicable, and he found that what could not be discussed was the origin of violence. Restoring confidence in language and thought—Sartre observed that "we think with words"—is a first step in demystifying false consciousness like Nazism and other ideologies.

Sartre's literature of praxis describes, narrates, or explains situations, but the key expression for this new literature is perception. Perception "itself is action, if, for us, to show the world is to disclose it in the perspectives of a possible change, then, in this age of fatalism, we must reveal to the reader his power, in each concrete case, of doing and undoing, in short of acting."

These issues are obviously the axis of *The Words* and of all of Sartre's work; for example, Sartre's division of *The Words* into two sections (e.g., "Reading" and "Writing"). In *What Is Literature* Sartre explained the meaning of "reading" and "writing" and how these activities are interrelated. Reading and writing are paths to freedom. In *The Words* Sartre described his own personal history and proposed a "concrete liberation on the basis of . . . [his] particular alienation."[50] The new guardian of ethical values denounced the old bourgeois values of his grandparents and parents and committed himself to a revolutionary future. In line with Sartre's literary theory, *The Words* has a revolutionary message; it is a literary and metaphysical praxis.

The Freud Scenario

In *The Freud Scenario*, which he wrote in 1958, Sartre applied his psychoanalytic method to the founder of psychoanalysis, Sigmund Freud. In 1962, when he saw the first production of it, he withdrew his name, on the grounds that the movie was a mutilated version of the film script.

The psychoanalyst Jean-Baptiste Pontalis and others considered *The Freud Scenario* a turning point in Sartre's own method and his understanding of Freud; it seemed to them that Sartre had become more Freudian over the years.[51] However, it is clear from Sartre's writings and from Barnes's conversation with Beauvoir in 1984 that Sartre had "great respect for Freud but did not regard the scenario as indicating or inducing any change in his attitude."[52] The central theme of *The Freud Scenario* is not the classical theme of father–son relations, but positive versus negative reciprocal relations. Sartre's notion of reciprocity can be defined as follows: "In reciprocity, each may make himself a vehicle of the other's project, so that the other will make himself a vehicle of one's own. . . . Or each makes himself the means of the other for one joint end, which will be unique and transcendent." However, reciprocity can be positive as well as negative; it is the basis of all relations, reification and alienation included, although these are its negative forms. In lacking or refusing reciprocal relations, "each refuses to serve the end of the other, and recognizing his being as an objective means in the project of the other as adversary, he puts to profit his own instrumentality for the other, to make of him an instrument of his own ends: this is struggle or conflict."[53]

Reciprocity is a characteristic found not only in Sartre's later work, as in *The Critique of Dialectical Reason*, but also in his earlier work, *Being and Nothingness*. Adrian Mirvish points out explicit evidence in *Being and Nothingness* "to support the idea that Sartre does in fact have a fully fledged notion of reciprocity, even if this is sometimes paradoxically to be found among claims that suggest the contrary."[54]

Sartre's treatment of Freud's life story is as radical as *The Words*, and *The Freud Scenario* is in accordance with Sartre's own psychological concepts. Barnes finds the most striking evidence of Sartre's using his own theory "his subtle, all pervasive stress on the self-directing intentionality of the patients' behavior," but she nevertheless finds that Sartre did not challenge the basic concepts of Freud's theory.

I do not agree with Barnes's analysis in two aspects, although these differences may merely be subtleties that can be explained through my interpreting *The Freud Scenario* in an antipsychiatric context. Barnes, for example, finds that Sartre portrayed neurotic behavior as explainable either as the result of the unconscious or as a manifestation of the bad faith of an intentional consciousness. In bad faith one does not make something of oneself as the authentic individual does, but sees oneself as others do.

Barnes does not find fiction created for the sake of illuminating Freud's character in the scenario: "There is absolutely nothing comparable to that unforgettable, shattering scene when a cruel adult points a finger at the cowering Jean Genet and passes sentence—'You are a thief.'"[55] To me, however, Sartre explained Freud's life and theory around a shattering scene, the incident in which an anti-Semite attacked Jakob Freud in the presence of his son Sigmund. Later, at home, the six-year-old Sigmund picked up a book on Roman history and showed his father a picture subtitled "Hamilcar makes his son Hannibal swear to avenge the Carthaginians."[56] He persuaded his father to assume the role of Hamilcar and to make him swear vengeance. Sigmund–Hannibal then took an oath to avenge his father, the hero Hamilcar, and all humiliated Jews.

Ernest Jones and Freud give different versions of the story.[57] Sigmund Freud was not present at the time of the attack on his father, but when he was ten or twelve years old his father told him about it. However, both Jones and Freud associate the story with Hannibal's oath and his place thereafter in Freud's fantasies.[58] Sartre used his own imagination to illuminate the story and the consequences of the event for Freud's life and work. According to Barnes, the Freud of the scenario closely reflects Jones's biography of Freud, and Sartre used the material freely. I, on the other hand, find that Sartre contradicts Jones, as well as Freud's autobiographic account, in some very cardinal instances.

Nevertheless, Sartre remained within Freud's definition of psychoanalysis because Freud agreed that any form of inquiry having as its starting point the two facts of transference and resistance may call itself psychoanalysis.[59] Stuart Charmé recognizes that "when the phenomenon of transference is seen in its widest sense, it begins to resemble what Sartre calls the constant symbolization of a person's fundamental project in new context."[60] In spite of remaining within this Freudian psychoanalytic boundary, it seems to me that Sartre's understanding of transference and resistance is essentially different from that of Freud.

In the scenario, Sartre explains Freud's rejection of what is called "the seduction theory." In his history of the psychoanalytic movement, Freud wrote that he was influenced to believe in the traumatic origin of hysteria by such leading physicians as Breuer, Charcot, and Chrobak. Accordingly, he related his patients' symptoms to passive sexual experiences in early childhood: that is, to seduction. He eventually abandoned his early belief in the seduction theory and instead adopted the theory of infantile sexuality, which he considered the "outcome of psychoanalytic work, a theoretic inference legitimately drawn from innumerable observations."

As described by Freud at the beginning of his career—when he followed the teachings of the medical authorities and believed in the seduction theory—he was an accepted member of the medical establishment. But when he presented his own scientific discoveries to the Neurological Society he was received with silence, which he interpreted as resistance. To understand the truth, his colleagues had to overcome the very same obstacles as his patients, although he did not consider the former neurotic. He then entered into what he called his "splendid isolation," and explicitly claimed not to have been "subject to influence from any quarter."[61] Freud considered his dream analysis to have been of major importance for his self-analysis, since his own dreams led him back to all the events of his childhood.

Jones finds Freud's self-analysis essential for the development of his theory of infantile sexuality and the Oedipal complex. He writes that in February, after Freud's father died, Freud was accused of seduction. Three months later Freud had an incest dream that convinced him that the seduction theory was erroneous.[62] Jones describes how Freud gradually gained insight and felt the greatest confidence in his own interpretation of dreams.

Masson presents evidence that Freud's seduction theory was disavowed because "the idea of sexual violence in the family was so emotionally charged that the only response it received was irrational distaste."[63] Masson finds that Freud might still have had faith in the seduction hypothesis, but that he abandoned it due to a failure of courage. Though Sartre's dramatic treatment was written some three decades before Masson's research was published, it resembles Masson's thesis in showing that the abandonment of the seduction theory was not based on scientific inquiry, as Freud and Jones claimed. Sartre does not explain Freud's change of mind as a lack of courage; on the contrary, he explains it in the context of the historical, almost mythological hero image of Hannibal, an alternative Oedipal figure. This I demonstrate by referring to some scenes from Sartre's scenario.

Freud begins his self-analysis through a conversation with his friend, the nose and throat specialist, Dr. Wilhelm Fliess. Freud had earlier expressed his concern that the seduction theory was an unbearable truth. Something was wrong with it, because several of his patients tried to commit suicide after hypnosis during which they expressed unconscious memories. Freud then decided that he should apply his theory to himself and asked Fliess to be his analyst.

Fliess resists, ill at ease and indignant.

FLIESS Are you mad? I'm not a psychiatrist.

FREUD So what? If I want to analyse my case, I must speak in someone's presence.

He forces him to sit down . . . : You don't have to do anything except listen to me. . . . I need a witness."[64]

Freud does not recognize the need for a dialogue in self-analysis; there is no mutual relation between the two friends. I consider that in this and other instances of negative reciprocity Sartre portraits Existential psychoanalytic resistance. After Freud expresses total insecurity in himself and his theory, in an authoritarian manner Fliess tells him to correct the "error of detail" he might have made in the seduction theory.

In the following scene Freud has a session of self-analysis with Cecily, his only remaining patient. Freud's facial expression is now different: "Still somber, he has lost the aggressive moroseness that we have come to associate with him. . . . He is sad, but seems open." Freud proposes that he and Cecily search together for the reason behind the free associations of their ideas. In this session the relations are reciprocal, but Freud makes it clear—somewhere in the middle of the session—that their dialogue is only a means of arriving at self-analysis. If he attains his goal he will again place himself in the role of the witness, the objective observer of the truth. After a couple of such reciprocal "antipsychiatric" sessions, Cecily says she had wanted to kill her mother; she accuses the child Cecily of having been a little monster. Freud responds, "No. She was a child. That's all. I've won. . . . Thanks to you, I think I understand both of us. And that I can cure us." Notice that in the first session of mutual self-analysis Freud and Cecily would cure each other; now Freud says, "I can cure us." This is not the first time in the scenario, in spite of the great respect for Freud that one senses in Sartre, that Freud appears to be manipulative and dishonest with others and with himself.

As one can guess, Cecily's memory of having wanted to kill her mother reveals to Freud that "Oedipus is everybody." Freud now opens up about his relations with his father, about his jealousy because his father slept with his mother, his search for other fathers, and his abandonment of the pseudofathers if he recognized in them any sign of weakness; he realizes that now, through his understanding of all this, he must revise his theory: "In neuroses, I've viewed the parents as guilty and the children as innocent. That was because I hated my father. It's necessary to reverse the terms."

Freud's last words in his self-analysis with Cecily are, "I was jealous! Jealous! And out of jealousy I accused him of having been incapable of raising or even feeding a family. But it wasn't true: it was anti-Semitism that ruined him."[65] I find this last sentence to be the bottom line of Sartre's analysis of Freud. He shows Freud as an authentic Jew, conscious of anti-Semitism and of the need to fight it.[66] And this context—human interaction in the context of the social system in which a person is implanted—explained why Freud suppressed the seduction theory; perhaps consciously, but if not, then in bad faith.

In the course of the scenario Sartre has Dr. Sigmund Freud recall his Hannibal oath several times. In one of the scenes at the beginning of the scenario he tells his fiance Martha about his commitment to avenge his father and "us." The meaning of the word "to avenge" has changed, it now means "to become the best doctor in Vienna." When he is not successful in hypnotizing his patients, he expresses his feelings of frustration by destroying a wall decoration portraying Hamilcar and Hannibal.

But Sigmund–Hannibal remains alive, as evidenced by the following episode. After Freud presents his seduction theory to the Medical Society he encounters unscientific responses, such as "psychiatry for pigs!" and "old maids' fancies," and also anti-Semitic responses like "Back to the ghetto!" Though this episode is a Sartrean fantasy about Freud, it nevertheless discloses much about Sartre's Freud, since in response to the racist vocabulary he knocks off a colleague's top hat and returns the insults with no less becoming rhetoric. He explains this action to his wife as "I've just settled an old score."

Finally, the traumatic experience is referred to near the end of the scenario in a scene showing Freud visiting his father, who seems to be on his deathbed. Old Jakob shows himself to be pleased at Sigmund's professional achievements and calls him "my little Hannibal," which causes father and son together to relive the traumatic racist attack.[67]

It is obvious that Freud's struggle against anti-Semitism is closely related to the image he has of his father. His father is a hero whom he has to protect and avenge. Though his father may in actuality be weak, his imaginary father is the blameless, Moses-like image of Hamilcar, a father who cannot be, should not be, accused of seduction. If, nevertheless, his father would have seduced his sister, for his own sake Freud would close his eyes to it. Sartre shows that Freud changes his early theory not so much because he lacks the courage to face criticism from colleagues, but in view of the consequences of the seduction theory in his own private life. As a scientific hypothesis Freud's theory must be universally applicable. To purify the omnipresent father image from accusations of incest, Freud confesses to hating his father, though there are no expressions of overt hatred in his behavior. His hatred is invisible, or if you like, unconscious—or Freud is deceiving himself.

Freud's hatred is similar to the feelings and intentions King Oedipus might have had, since the king cannot be accused of having killed his father out of hatred because he had no idea that the man he killed was his father. Moreover, Oedipus did all he could—with the exception of suicide—to avoid the predicted death of his father. It is thus not surprising that Sartre's Freud adopts Oedipus, the tragic but faithful son of Laius, as an additional self-image.

Sartre shows Freud's explanation of self to have gone astray in that he attempted to make his theory applicable to every individual. Freud was aware that not all fathers are seducers, and that one need not be neurotic to have been the victim of seduction. In spite of this observation, Freud could not dialectically conceive of his early or later theories as containing elements of truth for only certain specific individuals. A human understanding of persons demands a dialectical and pluralistic understanding of human experiences within the context of the social system in which a person is implanted. At the same time, it is important to remember that Sartre's Freud, though not committed to reciprocal relations, has his breakthrough to self-understanding in a reciprocal relation with a patient. Sartre shows that negative reciprocity, such as racism and other types of discrimination and manipulation and other kinds of violent behavior, indeed traumatize people and cause inner conflicts, confusion, and outward struggle.

Comparably, in *The Words* Sartre accentuated the influence social contexts had on his own life. Both Freud and Sartre revolted against the social structures they experienced as oppressive and harmful. Nevertheless, Freud's "vengeance neurosis" caused by negative reciprocal relations is not cured, and Freud countertransfers negative reciprocal relations and maintains them in his psychoanalytic work. Whereas in *The Words* Sartre contends that he was cured of his "writing neuroses" by applying his philosophical–literary method of fiction writing to himself, in *The Freud Scenario* he reduces Freud's scientific method to a pseudoscientific exertion that misses the mark.

Conversations with Jean-Paul Sartre

Through the interviews that Sartre held at the end of his life (i.e., *Conversations with Jean-Paul Sartre* or *Conversations* and *Hope Now*), one can observe his own awareness of changes and contradictions in his work.[68] Sartre called *Conversations* the continuation of *The Words*, although it differs from his autobiography proper; it has more in common with an intellectual autobiography. Most appropriately, Barnes called *Conversations* an "autobiographic interview."[69] Although among the topics of *Conversations* Barnes summarizes Sartre's thoughts on literature, death, and God, she elaborates primarily on the other issues discussed in the interviews, such as Sartre's preference or dislike of certain foods, his sexual tastes, and his changing notions of freedom.

Reading and Writing in Conversations

In these conversations Sartre defined the relation between philosophy and literature, as he did in *What Is Literature*. Philosophy is in literature. Sartre aimed at writing books "that would reveal to the reader things he had never thought of before." At the beginning of his career he wanted to express the truths he cherished through novels like *Nausea* rather than by writing philosophical books about his ideas. Writing is the creation of something meritorious, and in addition, the creation represents the writer: "The man is present in his book, and the man's value comes to him from the book." Philosophy has no absolute value in itself, because it is subject to circumstances that change. Consequently, Sartre finds philosophy a means in the service of literature. Through philosophy Sartre found "the dimensions necessary for creating a tale." Sartre finds it "rather odd" that philosophy became so important to him that he even became the author of books on philosophy.

In a critical evaluation of his own work, Sartre expresses himself favorably about the collected essays *Situations*, a series of critical reflections on life in general. But he is not so pleased with his literary and philosophical works proper. He defines *Situations* as "articles related to my philosophy but written in a very simple style and speaking of things that everybody knows about." Although Existential psychoanalysis, like Sartre's analysis of Jean Genet, belongs to the literary style of the novel, it is also philosophical work because in it

Sartre's uses philosophical concepts. His writings against bourgeois literature and his political activities against bourgeois society did not detract from the value of literature. On the contrary, through political activity he aimed at creating a world in which literature could express itself freely.

Sartre's first home had been his grandfather's sixth-floor library. After leaving his grandparents' home he borrowed books, and until the age of forty did not own the books he read. At that time, after his stepfather's death, his mother wanted him to live in her apartment. It was only after he moved in with her that he succumbed to his love of books and began to establish his own library, with, for example, the complete works of Colette, Proust, and others.

Writers who Sartre found were influential in his adult life were Kafka, Proust, Morand, and Dos Passos, and the philosophers Husserl, Heidegger, and Marx. In addition, he read history: "Anecdotal and biographical history. . . . In any case it went with the philosophical concept that one ought to be interested in history, that it formed part of philosophy." Sartre found that the biographies of writers like Emile Zola, who as they approached their fifties became political activists, were decisive as guides in his life: "A writer's life was shown as having a youth, a middle part which was the production of his works, and a later part in which he engaged in politics in his capacity as a writer and in which he intervened in the country's affairs."

History became important to Sartre during the war, when he discovered the meaning of being part of history and experienced the meaning of being an individual within a collective. His life, like the life of most of his fellow citizens, was compounded of incidents or "collective occurrences." Sartre's newly discovered historical awareness coincided with belief in progress. He agreed with Comte's optimistic dicta, "Progress is in the bringing out of a hidden order," but at times he also believed in the possibility of failure and the cessation of progress.

In 1952, when he started to write *The Words*, he felt completely isolated politically. The war had created a historical and political consciousness in him, but he was not yet actively involved with politics: "I didn't look upon it as essential. I wrote that politics was a human dimension. But in fact it was scarcely one of mine." In the first version of *The Words* Sartre intended to describe his entire life from a political viewpoint, something comparable to his analysis of Flaubert, which he considered a political work. But he stopped writing his own life story after the account of his childhood and reworked it about ten years later.

Another explanation for Sartre's interest in autobiography and biography is that such personal texts were disdained by the bourgeois and petit-bourgeois, the people who comprised his family background. Writing such "personal things" was revolutionary.

Sartre found that choices he made during the Second World War, such as joining the French Army and the Resistance, had changed his life entirely. But of all choices he ever made, writing remained the most important; writing always remained his fundamental choice. In *The Words* Sartre explains his fundamental choice as having eventuated through his mother's and grandparents' personal influence, his family's social position, a lack of meaning in life, and alienation. These multiple interpretations could be typical of what Sartre called in *Conversations* "worked-over phrases": "[In *The Words*] I wanted there to be hints, implications in every phrase, one or two implications. . . . It was full of tricks, of clever dodges, of the art of writing, almost of plays on words." Yet these "plays on words" may reveal the complexity of Sartre's childhood experience better than a statistical account of data. At the end of *Conversations* Sartre states that writing is still the most meaningful activity in his life, even the very meaning of his life.

Looking back at his lifelong literary–philosophical project, Sartre was most partial to his essays *Situations*. This might well be because these essays are most consistent with the practical purposes found in *What Is Literature* and *The Words*.

Freedom and Existential Psychoanalysis in Conversations

In his early works, such as *The Transcendence of the Ego, Emotions: Outline of a Theory*, and *The Psychology of Imagination*, Sartre presented a philosophical description of the ego, a description that is based on the experience of one's subjectivity. From then on he considered the ego and feelings transcendent, as psychic objects lying outside of consciousness. Sartre indicates that in his philosophy the notion of freedom is based on his personal experience of it. His conception of the ego's freedom has a vital bearing on his Existential psychoanalysis.

As a child he felt free, and he therefore made it an aim to cultivate freedom in himself: "The idea of freedom evolved in me. It lost those vague and contradictory aspects that it has in all people when they take it for granted to begin with, and it grew more complex. It became explicit. . . . I shall die as I have lived, with a deep feeling of liberty." In one of his early texts, *The Transcendence of the Ego*, he considers the contradiction implicit in the ability to describe the ego as a quasi object (the reappearance of comparable inclinations under analogous circumstances) and as the creative power to create oneself by oneself. Sartre maintains that to be free is fundamental to all human beings, but different people desire freedom in varying degrees.

When he was eleven years old he felt for the first time that someone's free will—in this case the bigger schoolboys at La Rochelle—could oppose and oppress him. This experience contrasted sharply with the free upbringing he received in the Sartre–Schweitzer household. The persecution he suffered at school turned his feelings of freedom inward. It was in his second year at the Lycée Henri IV that he learned the philosophical meaning of the word freedom.

At that time, Sartre identified the gratuitous act to a certain degree with freedom, but his concept of freedom was that of Stoicism: Freedom and consciousness were the same, yet he found that not all his acts were free. On this point he admits that he had changed. Consequently, he stopped believing that human beings are free in every situation, although he found that if one simplifies his later theory of freedom, for the sake of convenience one still can maintain that all people are free. What Sartre exactly means by "people are free" is this: "One is responsible for oneself even if one's acts are provoked by something external. . . . Every action includes a proportion of habit, of received ideas, of symbols; and then again there is something that comes from our remotest depths and that is related to our primary freedom."

His early notion of freedom caused him to be against Fascism: "In my opinion a man must decide for himself—in conjunction with others perhaps, but for himself. Yet in fascism he is dominated by men placed above him." Likewise, he found the doctrines of socialism problematic for their lack of individualism and personal freedom, and consequently he began a lifelong search to combine socialism and the idea of liberty.

During 1942–1943 it became clear to Sartre that his early idea of absolute inner freedom was invalid in situations where one could not act freely. Instead, he came to believe that "one freedom is enchained by another freedom or by other freedoms." During those war years he found it unacceptable for one person to be free if others were not. From 1945 to 1950 his conception of freedom was that in particular situations freedom is abolished, while on the other hand freedom is a reciprocal bond that unites people.

In 1974, looking back on how freedom evolved in him, Sartre found that in general his experience of freedom did not change: "I was oppressed at the time of the war. I was a prisoner. . . . Yet I lived through being a prisoner in my own way with a certain freedom." Sartre associated his personal history of freedom with finding himself responsible for almost everything that ever happened to him. The fact that he did not consider his actions to have been determined by others or by external influences but by himself bestows on him his sense of freedom. He and other human beings are of a dialectic nature: "being and nothingness, being and becoming, the idea of freedom and that of the exterior world that set itself against my freedom as it were. Freedom and situation."

Sartre's later definition of freedom is "freedom represents something that does not exist but that gradually creates itself." This definition applies to all human beings, but it is modified by circumstances, social background, development, and knowledge. Sartre's book on Genet presents a good example of the freedom intrinsic to the ego in Existential psychoanalysis. In Genet's life Sartre observes a transformation "that was the work of freedom. . . . This change might very well not have taken place. . . . [It came] from the use of his freedom. It transformed the meaning of the world and gave it another value. . . . It was freedom choosing itself that brought the transformation about."[70]

With all due respect to Hazel Barnes's vast legacy in Sartrean scholarship, I have been unable to justify her claim that Sartre had changing notions of freedom, although I must admit that Sartre slightly modified his basic notion of freedom by eliminating Stoicism from it. Though one could consider this modification "a change," it seems to me a minor adjustment and not a different philosophy or different notion of freedom.

Barnes contends that Sartre's self-image of a free agent was "inextricably bound up with the self-assurance bestowed by his childhood happiness, no wonder that the defense of it became a prime motif of even his involuntary behavior." Was Sartre then in bad faith when he confessed his personal freedom to Beauvoir in *Conversations*? When Sartre explained his occasional enjoyment of liberal amounts of liquor at the age of sixty-nine with "C'est agreable," Barnes upholds Beauvoir's understanding that Sartre's drinking habit was an escape, not a free choice.

Barnes finds that "the excessive use of alcohol may have been not escapist in the usual sense, but rather for the sake of feeling his imagination creative. For Sartre, to be without creative imagination was not be himself."[71] Sartre's subjective experience of freedom, and his subjective perception of other issues as well, differs from the exterior view "the others" have of it.

Finally, there are two statements in *Conversations* that substantiate the anti-Freudian self-analysis found in *The Words*. First is Sartre's awareness of his "most incomplete Oedipal complex": He remembers having loved to play with little girls when he was a boy, having had some "vague feelings" for some of his mother's friends, and "a fairly sexual feeling for . . . [his] mother" when he was thirteen. At the Henri IV Lycée Sartre became aware of a vague homosexual inclination. According to Beauvoir, "It was a very slight inclination." He kept his marriagelike contract with Beauvoir faithfully until his last days. Second is Sartre's "total absence of narcissism": Sartre agreed with Beauvoir's explanation that his consciousness was directed toward others and the world, while he did not concentrate on and was not concerned with his self-image.

Conversations shows that Sartre's existential freedom was not something he experienced only as a child, but that it was the dominant and lasting revolutionary theme of his life. As Sartre admits the influence of biographical writings on his life, one may assume that his autobiography and biographical novels are attempts to influence his readers, to be a critical mirror to them. The revolutionary intention of *The Words* was to elicit change, to liberate himself and others; it is a literary–philosophical and Existential psychoanalytic practice.

God in Conversations

In *Conversations* Sartre began his negative discussion of God, his atheism, by repeating some of the material found in *The Words*. He remembered that at the age of eleven he had conceived new ideas about God, and he was solving these questions about God by himself. Then suddenly, in the midst of the daily routine of waiting for some neighborhood girls to take the tram with them, he had "a momentary intuition": "I don't know where the thought came from or how it struck me, yet all at once I said to myself, 'But God doesn't exist!'"

Sartre realized that it was an intuition that had determined his life and he never questioned this intuition until the age of sixty. Is this an indication that at sixty Sartre reconsidered the existence of God? I find that Sartre overcame some reluctance when Beauvoir started questioning him on this topic, which she chose to discuss only at the end of *Conversations*. His first few answers are ambiguous and it is as if he indeed preferred to finish the last chapter of *Conversations* as he intended, without the subject of God, with the following words: "Displeased at dying that particular day rather than ten years later, but content. And up until the present, death has never weighed upon my life and probably it never will."

In the continuation of this chapter, the section on *Hope Now* (i.e., the conversations with Benny Lévy) may explain Sartre's initial resistance to discussing this apparently sensitive subject with Beauvoir. However, Sartre is agreeable and tells her that as a child he never heard about atheism, but his grandfather did convey to him that one had "to discover one's own way of thinking." Consequently, the child Sartre had his own little storeroom of ideas, contrary to the respectable "religious" ideas of the members of his family. When he grew up he learned about atheism and changed his early idealist revelation of it into a materialist idealism that could be explained. During his study of philosophy in high school and university, Sartre discovered that there was a lack of atheists' philosophy books, in that all "the great philosophers have been believers more or less." It was then that he envisioned the creation of an atheist philosophy, "a philosophy of man in a material world."

During his time in prison camp Sartre had close contact with a group of imprisoned priests. It is striking to observe that at the end of his life Sartre did not recall the severe criticism he had received from devout Christians throughout his career, but instead recalled a short reconciliatory story about an Abbé Leroy. Leroy, one of the prison camp inmates, told him that he thought Sartre would not be turned away from Heaven but that he would learn to know God either in his lifetime or after his death. Moreover, Leroy "would not accept a place in Heaven if . . . [Sartre] were turned away." Nevertheless, this did not prevent Sartre from continuing to profess atheism and saying that in *Being and Nothingness* he vindicated his disbelief in God. But here too there is an ambiguity in the way he answers Beauvoir's questions on God. *Being and Nothingness* provides proof of God's nonexistence, but the reasons for the denial of God's existence are now said to have been other than those Sartre argued for in *Being and Nothingness*: "The real reasons were much more direct and childish—since I was only twelve—than theses on the impossibility of this reason or that for God's existence."[72]

And though Sartre cannot believe in God, he notes that he has ideas that refer him back to God: the idea of destiny, the origin of which can only be explained through the existence of a creator, and the idea of Good and Evil as absolutes. Although professing a humanist ethics, in his notions of absolute Good and Evil Sartre traces his childhood catechism lessons. He predicts that this and other such God consciousness will only gradually lose its power over people.

Of all his plays Sartre liked *The Devil and the Good Lord* best. When the play had just been published, Beauvoir wrote the following: "In fact, Sartre was once more confronting the vanity of morality with the efficacy of praxis. This confrontation goes much further than it had in his previous plays; *The Devil and the Good Lord* is the mirror of Sartre's entire ideological evolution."[73]

Where Beauvoir finds its major theme to be the vanity of morality, in *Conversations* Sartre stresses that for him the conflict of major importance in *The Devil and the Good Lord* is between the Church (or God) and people. The theme in *The Devil and the Good Lord* is the problem of bad faith versus authenticity in a particular social context: Belief in God is a metaphysical and social deception, the alienation of an authentic human being among other human beings.

Although the play is set in the sixteenth century, "a time when it was normal to believe in God," its hero, the priest Heinrich, is confronted with the existential choice of whether to leave the church. It is characteristic of Sartre's "evolution" to describe the lack of social (religious) freedom as the cause of Heinrich's inability to change his fate as a free individual. Though Heinrich disagrees with many views maintained by the church, his loyalty to the church is such that he can leave it only when the church excommunicates him.

Sartre explains faith in God as originating in, and pertaining to, past centuries, whereas he finds that the twentieth century is marked by a lack of intuition of the divine. Nevertheless, he does not find the contemporary world atheistic, and believes that the few deliberate atheists are still too immersed in remnants of divine conceptions. But Sartre hopes that people will cure themselves, just as he did; from this perspective his own process of dealienation as found in *The Words* seems to have been written as a model cure.

In *Conversations* the practice of atheism emerges as one of Sartre's lifelong projects. The only difference in the treatment of this subject in *The Words* and *Conversations* is that in the latter Sartre is able to keep a partially detached and inquiring stance on this topic, as he also does in *Hope Now*.

Immortality and Death in **Conversations**

Some time about 1945 Sartre considered himself as having become a man of genius, an immortal, because of *Nausea* and *No Exit*. After having attained this new self-awareness, he felt free to dedicate himself to committed writing. Before 1945 he was still trying to attain salvation through the works he created: "I created something absolute which was, in short, myself. . . . An artistic creation outlives mundane things and therefore I, the author that it embodies, I outlast mundane things."

Committed writing addresses the actualities of a society, and aims to persuade the public of a specific viewpoint and to propose action accordingly. When the subject that the committed writer confronts is resolved in one way or another, the text is no longer operative. Nevertheless, Sartre considered the notion of posterity relevant also to his new manner of writing: "But behind my dream [of committed writing] . . . there was the notion of posterity—a posterity that can only come into existence together with a complete transformation of the work, which stops being active but which becomes a work of art like almost all objects which belong to the past."

Sartre found that a work of art inherently possesses an absolute, trans-human value, no longer because God looks at it, but because the author and his or her audience invest it with trans-human value. Sartre regarded this secular type of immortality as an illusion, but he retained it as a working illusion.

Having reached old age, Sartre had no need for illusions in facing death. He more or less agreed with Beauvoir, who found that he faced death with great equanimity. He compared death with a series of deprivations: He had to give up drinking, old age forced him to be occupied with all kinds of trivia, and he was less comfortable than he had been ten years before. This predeath process at sixty-nine eventually accumulated until it became complete deprivation. Sartre accepted death as natural, but as a person whose life had been devoted to culture, who treasured the unnatural, death opposed his life as a whole.[74]

At the end of *The Words*, Sartre expresses the same tranquility about facing death as in *Conversations*. However, in *Conversations* there is no recollection of Sartre's great childhood anxiety about death as he described it in the first section of *The Words*.

Hope Now

The *Conversations* between Sartre and Beauvoir were tape-recorded in 1974, but were not published until a year after Sartre's death in 1981. Benny Lévy's interviews with Sartre, *Hope Now*, convey Sartre's thoughts during the years immediately prior to his death. *Hope Now* was published in March 1980, about a month before Sartre died, and was meant to be the outline of the Sartre–Lévy book "Power and Liberty."[75]

Since *Hope Now* stirred quite a controversy, it is necessary to understand the background against which it emerged. The contents of *Hope Now*—its obvious objective—are often construed as irrelevant for understanding the ongoing process of Sartre's work because of issues such as Sartre's age, his health, and his relationship with Lévy. Sartre's close friends accused Lévy of abducting the "old man," and of having published ideas in Sartre's name that could not have been his. Nevertheless, Sartre approved of the publication of *Hope Now*, and did not change his mind about it later, even under the heavy emotional pressure of Beauvoir, who demanded that he repudiate it. Beauvoir's image of a dominating, manipulating Lévy is difficult to recognize in the dialogue of *Hope Now*. That *Hope Now* is not the product of Lévy's authority over Sartre can also be concluded from the evidence provided by Arlette Elkaïm-Sartre (Sartre's adopted daughter and now legal executor of his writings): "As I did with other interviews of that same period, I therefore read and reread their [Sartre's and Lévy's] dialogue to him, repeating word after word as well as the whole text several times. . . . Sartre added and corrected as he wished."[76]

Ten years after *Hope Now* was first published, Lévy wrote "The Final Word," a commentary on his interviews with Sartre. The 1996 English edition of *Hope Now* contains not only the Sartre–Lévy text but also two short essays by Lévy: "Presentation" and "The Final Word." This English edition also contains an introduction by Ronald Aronson in which he attempts to clarify why *Conversations*, and not *Hope Now*, should be viewed as the "objective" representation of Sartre's last thoughts. For example, Aronson maintains that it is a fact that the Sartre of *Hope Now* is only a shadow of the genius Sartre had been: "He has become an old man, and has lost most of his powers."[77] Sartre, however, did not give much thought to his physical afflictions and old age: "I see myself, I am aware of myself, as forty-five or fifty; I work like someone of that age. I don't feel old. Yet someone who is seventy years old is an old man."[78]

Although Aronson purportedly presented arguments for and against the credibility of the controversial text, and to that end also interviewed Lévy, I nevertheless find that Lévy's subjective perspective concerning the circumstances under which this text was created is markedly absent. A balanced perspective would give priority to the statements of the authors and editors of *Hope Now*.[79]

A Retrospective on the Context of Hope Now

My intention in the following interview with Lévy on the circumstances surrounding *Hope Now* is to make the text rather more acceptable than questionable.[80] The issues I discussed with Lévy were: Sartre's intellectual fitness during the last years of his life, the Sartre–Lévy relationship, and Lévy himself.

When Lévy began to assist Sartre with secretarial work, the two men had already known each other for about three years. Although Lévy became an employee of Sartre's, it was only natural that their mutual cooperation would continue. Lévy does not find it important to recall the exact date on which he began to work for Sartre, but he attributes great importance to the ten years of friendship and cooperation between Sartre and himself. Formerly their relationship had involved political cooperation on two projects: Lévy asked Sartre to become the editor-in-chief of the revolutionary periodical *La Cause du Peuple*, and Sartre, Lévy, and Gavi joined forces to produce dialogues for the book *We Are Right to Revolt*.

In the last seven years of Sartre's life his blindness and other health-related problems prevented him from working (i.e., writing) as he had before. But did this affect his intellectual powers? Lévy maintains that it affected Sartre's way of thinking. Sartre had never worked with outlines or plans. He would sit in front of an empty page and thoughts evolved as he wrote. All his life writing and thinking had coincided; separating the two activities created a hiatus in his thinking that could not be filled by reflecting aloud.

Sartre had many years of experience with extemporaneous participation in dialogues; interviews with him were numerous until 1979. Nevertheless, Lévy finds a difference between *Hope Now* and Sartre's former work. He construes this difference as a weakness: Sartre could no longer argue with subtle nuances in great detail or depth.[81] His arguments had become more general and less complex, although he knew how to defend his convictions. This weakness generated an unexpected strength in that it liberated Sartre's spontaneous thinking and added the beauty of unadorned thought to his reflections.

When Lévy began to work with Sartre, the older man habitually fell asleep. Cohen-Solal reports from her conversation with Lévy that when he began working as a secretary he considered resigning because the task seemed impossible. He had the impression that his job was "to fend off sleep, lack of interest, or, more simply, torpor . . . involved was a sort of resuscitation."[82] Lévy had to adapt himself to working with him under these new circumstances. Initially Sartre intended to collaborate with Lévy on another volume of his Existential psychoanalysis of Flaubert, the promised and very promising volume on Flaubert's *Madame Bovary*. But Sartre's attempts to rouse Lévy's interest in the subject were not successful, and they soon found it impossible to continue with *The Family Idiot*.

They began to work on the book "Power and Liberty" instead, and in 1979 decided to produce the text of *Hope Now* in response to expanding new-right political activism. But when they started this collaboration, Lévy became seriously doubtful of the possibility of producing the work at all, despite the fact that for the past three years they had worked together to record more than forty tapes for "Power and Liberty." After a few sessions with Sartre, however, Lévy's doubts disappeared completely and within half a year *Hope Now* was ready to go to press.

Looking back at this period, Lévy now thinks that it was because of their former political cooperation that he could no longer hear "Sartre's voice" during their final years of collaboration. He acknowledges that he, like most of Sartre's other friends, had not understood the philosopher. To some extent he too continued to interpret Sartre in light of his former thoughts and writings. Today Lévy's essential memory of Sartre is the older man sitting in his easy chair and denouncing the limitations of his former works. In spite of his physical condition, Sartre still believed he could produce something new, something better than he had created until then, and Lévy accordingly helped the blind writer to create something new.

During this period Sartre's voice was not that of the political activist—as Lévy had originally expected, since their theme was the future of left-wing politics—but of the Existential psychoanalyst. Lévy expressed this psychoanalytic aspect in the "Presentation" as "I was present at the birth of 'the Soul,' as it is defined in *Phaedo*: detachment from one's interests and the reconstitution of self."[83] Lévy's voice in this discourse can be compared with that of Socrates; his aim was to reveal corruptness, not only in right-wing politicians, but also in the extreme militant left.

The Sartre–Lévy relationship was an intimate one in the platonic sense of the word. Since in Sartre's days homosexual relations became more fashionable among numbers of prominent intellectuals, it seems to me necessary to stress that their intimacy was entirely platonic. After all, in *Conversations* Sartre stated that as a youth he had become aware of a vague homosexual inclination.[84] Sartre dedicated his first biography, the Existential psychoanalytic novel *Baudelaire*, to Jean Genet and later wrote a biography of Genet, the homosexual poet and writer. However, Sartre's most extensive and unfinished biographic work is about Flaubert.

Flaubert, Genet, and Baudelaire would seem to share not only their profession as writers, but also their particular inclinations toward homosexuality.[85] In other texts by Sartre one can find additional homosexual characters as well as a suggestive ambience. Hence, I cautiously posit the possibility that Sartre did not lose his vague "teenage" homosexual inclination later in life. At least one may conclude that he tended to introduce varying aspects of homosexuality in his writings.

Cohen-Solal claims that Sartre's close friends agreed that the Sartre–Lévy relationship was an escape, "as if in Victor [Lévy], Sartre had found the ideal friend with whom to indulge a number of illegitimate pleasures to which his other friends had no access."[86] Against this background I dared to question Lévy as to whether Sartre discussed those vague teenage homosexual inclinations with him, just as he tried to articulate them in *Conversations* with Beauvoir.[87] Lévy declared himself totally unacquainted with this subject, but he did recall Sartre telling him that he personally regarded homosexual relations as repulsive. It would be an easy solution now to explain the "mystery" of the Sartre–Lévy relationship in the context of repressed or sublimated homosexuality, but this is not what I suggest. I find it surprising, and quite revealing with respect to general attitudes toward homosexuality, that even my rejection of kinds of homosexuality as a possible rhizome in the relationship is considered offensive and inappropriate by some people. In their view, one should not mention homosexuality at all, and above all not in relation to Sartre and Lévy. One also finds that many index listings on Sartre and his writings carefully avoid the subject. With absolutely no intention of hurting anybody's feelings by investigating this issue, I nevertheless think it important to acknowledge that Sartre wrote without scruples about homosexuality.

Sartre and Lévy discussed not only political and philosophical topics; their daily dialogues involved all details of their lives. For example, the pregnancy of Lévy's wife was analyzed day after day. From a phenomenological viewpoint Sartre could not define the ontological status of the embryo, while Lévy introduced him to the clear answers offered by Judaism.

An often misunderstood aspect of the Sartre–Lévy relationship was the equality and frankness with which they treated each other. If they did not agree, each tried to convince the other, as is customary in the best philosophical traditions, of which the Babylonian Talmud and Plato's dialogues are only two ancient examples. Consequently, sometimes Lévy and sometimes Sartre changed his point of view. Lévy recalls an occasion when they had thoroughly discussed a controversial issue and had not reached agreement. After several months, however, Sartre changed his mind on the matter, saying that he had been wrong and Lévy right.

Examples of occasions wherein Lévy changed his mind, or accepted Sartre's view, concerned the publication of *Hope Now*: Lévy felt uncomfortable with the title of the text but accepted the name Sartre chose. (Lévy differentiates between "good hope," a concept that is used in the Jewish New Year prayers, and "bad hope.") Then Sartre insisted that *Hope Now* be published under Lévy's own name rather than his alias. He recognized that Lévy's adopted name symbolized the wish to hide his personal—Jewish—identity behind a facade, behind the pose of a political activist. Against Lévy's resistance to revealing himself, Sartre insisted on bringing that hidden self into the open. Lévy objected, maintaining that under the name Pierre Victor he was known as an author and political activist. But he eventually changed his opinion in favor of Sartre's point of view. Lévy believes that the wide range of their discussions, including their disagreements, was extremely beneficial to his own personal development.

Is such a mutual influence characteristic of a relationship in which individuals try to manipulate one another? Is it not more like a sincere relationship between friends? In the Sartre–Lévy relationship I perceive a mutuality that stimulated each of them to develop in new, albeit different, directions. The reason Sartre so appreciated Lévy might have been precisely because of the possibility of the truly reciprocal relationship Lévy's personality seems to have offered him.[88]

When Lévy started to work for Sartre he had become interested in learning about Jewish tradition, but was far from committed to Orthodox Judaism. He attended evening courses on Judaism, and what he learned at night he discussed at work with Sartre the following morning. Sartre thus became familiar with the wisdom of the Jewish sages.

Lévy, a Maoist at the time, had lived the life of a secular Jew. Although he indicated that he could well have had romances with non-Jewish women, he nevertheless fell in love with a Jewess, and later married her. This might possibly be explained by an earlier fundamental choice on his part to be Jewish, although Lévy seems to be unaware of having made such a choice. At present, he professes Orthodox Judaism and Existentialism. From his point of view the choice of the woman he married, as well as all his other choices, fall within a framework of inevitability, that is, Divine Providence (*Hashgachah*).[89] His wife and family were one influence that led to a search for Jewish identity, but another important influence was Sartre. Lévy cannot say that Sartre tried to analyze him in accordance with the Existential psychoanalytic method. Nevertheless, he felt as if Sartre was his analyst, and the outcome of those intimate, analytic discourses were significant for his personal life. (In earlier writings, as noted before, Sartre claimed the ideal, truly constructive relation between analyst and analysand was one of reciprocity.)

Was Sartre's personal interest in the Jewish religion then only a kind of psychoanalytic strategy to encourage Lévy to accept his Jewish identity? I suggest that Sartre's interest in Jewish destiny was not "role-playing" for Lévy's sake, but very likely for his own sake as well. The man who had declared in *The Words* that he had missed his religious vocation finally allowed himself to consider religious beliefs from a serious philosophical perspective. In addition to discussing Judaism with Lévy, Sartre began to study Jewish texts with Elkaïm-Sartre. For a whole month she recited to him chapters dealing with benedictions and prayers from *Masechet Berakhot* of the Babylonian Talmud. And Beauvoir read Jewish history to him.

I suggested to Lévy that when Sartre recognized that "there is a profound Jewish reality as well as a Christian reality" he came to accept the metaphysical link of the Jew—as well as members of other monotheistic religions, I assume—with the infinite.[90] Lévy rejected the conception that Sartre had become an ex-atheist, and pointed out that the philosopher had always repudiated Christian metaphysics. Lévy agreed with me that Sartre's childhood left him with an aversion to the Christian faith.

Moreover, Lévy added, exposure in his childhood to anti-Semitism instilled in Sartre erroneous concepts about Judaism. A few months before his death Sartre confessed to Lévy that in a certain sense he had been anti-Semitic, just as all non-Jews, whom he felt were anti-Semitic in the depth of their hearts—not in the sense of Nazis and racists, but in an anti-Judaic, antireligious sense. At first Lévy could not believe Sartre's confession, but explanations from Rabbinic sources on anti-Semitism convinced him that Sartre's statement was true. Lévy refers to the Talmudic dicta (Shabbat, 89 a), which explains the name "Sinai" as "*sina*" (hate), meaning that all those who did not receive the Mosaic Law of Mount Sinai—mainly the non-Jews—hate those who did receive it—the Jewish people.

In spite of Lévy's acceptance of this "ontological anti-Semitism," it seems to me impossible to rule out a degree of irony in Sartre's confession. Such ontological anti-Semitism would consequently also apply to secular Jews who reject Orthodox Judaism and instead accept Sartrean-like humanistic and democratic values. There are indeed some Orthodox Rabbinic authorities who apply this particular Talmudic dicta to radical secular Jews. To confuse any critique or rejection of Orthodox Judaism with a kind of anti-Semitism seems to me a poor and somewhat paranoid defensive response to criticism.

Although Lévy considers this confession on Sartre's part a breakthrough in his own relationship with Judaism and sees "great progress" in Sartre's understanding of the issue, he nevertheless finds that Sartre showed no spiritual interest in knowing the God of Israel. In messianic Judaism he simply recognized his own utopian, humanistic ethics, whereas in Christianity he could not find the ethics he sought. Under the circumstances of the last years of his life, Sartre seems to have initiated a personal encounter with Judaism. But, Lévy stresses, it was an encounter with Judaism as a philosophy, not with Judaism as a religion.

I suggest that during the years in which Lévy worked for Sartre the latter applied his newly discovered ethical and metaphysical dimension to his Existential psychoanalytic method, and practiced it not only on Lévy, but on himself as well. Throughout Sartre's life his mental attitude had been one of observation and analysis, of himself as well as of others; he maintained this attitude in his old age. Sartre's last psychoanalytic project, however, was not realized in his lifetime.

A year after Sartre's death Lévy completed the process in which the older man had encouraged him; he committed himself to Orthodox Judaism. While Sartre was still alive, Lévy felt that he could not make that commitment because he "was imprisoned by his great love for Sartre." Lévy has a very vivid memory of visiting Sartre two days before his death; in a hospital bed he found a man who did not know that death was near. Although gangrene had spread over his entire body, Sartre believed he would live another five years. To most people it might have seemed obvious that Sartre's life was drawing to a close, but he himself looked at it from another perspective, from the perspective of immortality, or as Sartre describes it in *The Words*, "In order to deprive death of its barbarity, I had made it my goal and had made my life the only known means of dying."[91] Lévy is still awestricken by the fact that Sartre did not seem to have tasted death; to Lévy he indeed was already posthumous.

This seemed exaggerated to me, and I questioned Lévy as to whether Sartre had not possessed a great talent for acting. But Lévy cannot envision Sartre with the shadow of death on him, although he thinks that a few hours before his death Sartre might have realized his actual situation; but Lévy was not a witness to this. During their last meeting Sartre said that he and Lévy would continue to work on "Power and Liberty" and publish it in September (was this his way of asking Lévy to finish the book, or was he trying to assert himself?). Elkaïm-Sartre and Lévy, however, decided not to continue either to process or publish the tapes on "Power and Liberty." Yet according to Cohen-Solal all the tapes were transcribed by a friend of Lévy's, and Elkaïm-Sartre read *eight hundred pages* back to Sartre. Sartre's "this won't do" with respect to particular phrases was understood by Elkaïm-Sartre as meaning that those sections—about twenty pages—had to be rediscussed with Lévy and read again to Sartre for his corrections and approval.[92]

Nonetheless, it seems to me that we still may hope that the echo of Sartre's voice will prevail in determining the destiny of "Power and Liberty," just as his living voice determined the publication of *Hope Now.*

The Objective of Hope Now

I will now show that the contents of *Hope Now* correspond with Sartre's earlier work, but slightly differently from the way Aronson claims. Aronson finds that Sartre "is most definitely not beginning afresh, but is at heart remaining consistent with his last thirty-five years."[93] I think that with *Hope Now* Sartre indeed started a new project, and not only because it was a response to a particular situation in 1979 and not a response to a situation that had existed in 1945.

Hope is the general theme of the dialogue between Sartre and Lévy. Appropriately, the first of the twelve sections addresses this theme, and the last section ends with Sartre's words, "I still feel that hope is my conception of the future." Sartre stressed that although he might not have touched on the subject of hope explicitly in his writings, it is there inherently; hope is part of the human beings he wrote about. He does not mean that people always succeed in their projects; on the contrary, human beings "never attained exactly what they had searched for." Nevertheless, "hope is in the way man acts, in the very fact of positing an end as having to be realized." Hope is the relation of a person to his or her goal and that relation exists even if one does not attain the goal.

At Lévy's request, Sartre exemplified this thesis with his own goals. Sartre found himself, as in *Conversations*, only partially successful. In general, however, he considered himself successful mainly because he always remained true to a particular line. In *Hope Now* that consistency finds expression in his desire for society, fraternity, and democracy as a way of life.

Sartre ascended from politics to ethics. He began to advocate the study of human beings, the primary relations among individuals, instead of a study of Marxists' tenets of productivity. He found that the primary relation of fraternity is based on a common origin, the kinship of all human beings, and a common goal, humanity. This eventual fraternity is prefigured by the "fact that there is an ethics." Sartre observed that most parents teach their children the ethics of everyday life, and accordingly he believed that human consciousness must have an ethical dimension that future revolutionaries would have to analyze.

Sartre's experience of the May 1968 revolution, and his years as a Marxist fellow traveler, taught him a theoretical principle that would necessarily affect the praxis of future revolutionaries. He found that revolutionaries failed to understand that in an ideal society relations among human beings should be ethical. It is only "through a kind of messianism that one can conceive of this ethics as the ultimate goal of revolution." One of Lévy's purposes throughout *Hope Now* is to stress new ideas, changes, and contradictions in Sartre's works. But, as Lévy understood only years later, Sartre was not concerned about these differences because he allowed "freedom grasped by truth" to undermine his former positions while maintaining a continuous line of thought.

The following are some examples of "changes" and "contradictions" that Lévy tried to indicate but Sartre denied or considered insignificant:

1. The relation of despair, anguish, and hope: Sartre's knowledge of despair and anguish was through the writings of others. But he felt he had to write about despair and anguish as Zeitgeist phenomena, although he was not acquainted with these from his personal experience. Failure, however, he did know from his own experiences in life. His strategy was to accept failure as part of life, while hope remained a necessary component of his actions. In *Being and Nothingness* Sartre did not confront despair and failure with the concept of hope. Nevertheless, he contended that hope was there, not as an illusion, but "as a manner of grasping the goal I set myself, as something that can be realized."
2. Sartre's role as fellow traveler: Lévy maintained that the role of fellow traveler was a failure, comparable to the failure of political party membership. Sartre disagreed, but found this discussion irrelevant since the kind of party politics that caused critical intellectuals to take on the role of fellow travelers seemed to belong to the past. Social evolution did affect political life and it changed the role of the political party. Sartre's conception of evolution was that through action—although action can be a series of failures—something positive will emerge: "Moving from failure to failure, would achieve progress."
3. Sartre's changed perception of the Jewish people: Sartre found that he did not change his views in this matter after writing *Anti-Semite and Jew*, although he now felt that he had presented a superficial description of Jews as the victims of anti-Semitism in the Christian world. Through his Jewish friends Sartre came to understand that Jewish existence is not con-

fined to the way he had described it. Looking back, he found that his description missed the reality of the Jew as "essentially metaphysical." In *Hope Now* Sartre acknowledged that he had begun to understand people differently through observing that the Jewish people had chosen to live, and still live, metaphysically. Sartre admitted that in his former philosophy he had deprived people of a metaphysical dimension: "There was a consciousness of self that I stripped of all individual characteristics that might have come from within." Sartre's recognition of this mistake allowed him to modify his Existential psychoanalytic approach to an Existential–metaphysical psychoanalytic method.

4. Sartre's understanding of revolution: At the end of *Hope Now* Sartre says that the ultimate goal of revolution is to create a society in which human beings are ethical, and that one can only envision that "through a kind of messianism."[94] He found messianism to be a typical invention of the Jewish mind. The new Sartrean messianism was a novel orientation in socialism, but was not much different from the libertarian socialism Sartre advocated in his 1975 interview with Contat, "Self-Portrait at Seventy." In "Self-Portrait at Seventy" Sartre already argued for "complete equality among members of a group, and ultimately among members of a society."[95]

In the 1976 interview with Leo Fretz, Sartre confirmed that the regressive analysis found in the *Critique of Dialectical Reason* would be the foundation for his future ethics. The Sartre–Lévy book "Power and Freedom" would be based on the first principles of morals as he had described them in the *Critique of Dialectical Reason*. His view expressed in *Hope Now* that the ideal society should be based on an ethical way of life was also posited in the interview with Fretz: "A society without power starts to become an ethical society, because a new form of freedom is established, which is the freedom of reciprocal relations of persons in the form of a we."[96] Continuity, in spite of some minor changes and new developments, indeed exists in *Hope Now*. In *Hope Now* Sartre found the understanding of human beings and their relationships crucial for any revolutionary and utopian project. Accordingly, *The Words*, as an exemplary understanding of one human being, is a highly relevant textbook for the revolutionaries of today and tomorrow.

I have shown so far in this section that Sartre's early literary–philosophical ideal was finally fulfilled when he wrote *The Words*. The critique of classical psychoanalysis, as Sartre practiced it in his autobiography, is also applied to Sigmund Freud, the founder of psychoanalysis, in *The Freud Scenario*. Freud's relationships with and understanding of human beings are criticized; Sartre considered replacing Freud's scientific approach with a subjective understanding of human beings. Positive versus negative reciprocal relationships in daily life and in professional situations replaced the psychoanalytic traditional necessities of transference and resistance.

In *Conversations* Sartre returned to the ethos of *What Is Literature* and *The Words*. The political activity he became involved in after writing *The Words* was not detached from or in contradiction to his lifelong project of writing; political activity had to make engaged literature an acceptable revolutionary practice.

In *Hope Now* one can discern Sartre's frustrated desire to continue his work on the final volume of his analysis of Flaubert. Instead, the values of Existential psychoanalysis were applied to society at large, and practiced in an actual relationship (i.e., his relationship with Lévy).

PSYCHOANALYSIS ON THE WRITER'S COUCH

It is remarkable that in spite of frequent attempts to attach to Sartre an assortment of psychoanalytic labels, there are no substantial studies about him by clinical psychologists, psychoanalysts, or psychiatrists. Ronald Laing and David G. Cooper described and explained Sartre's work, but there is no personal analysis of Sartre in *Reason and Violence*.[97] So far there are just three books by academics that extensively interpret Sartre and his work from a psychoanalytic perspective. This is apart from incidental psychoanalytic interpretative notes in papers or books on Sartre. For example, in Betty Cannon's *Sartre and Psychoanalysis* there is a comment on a narcissistic trauma that Sartre is said to have attributed to Baudelaire. Cannon considers Sartre's childhood narrative as somewhat akin to Baudelaire's: "At the time of the death of his natural father when he was six, the young Baudelaire is depicted as feeling himself justified in his existence through the adoring eyes of his mother, as was Sartre himself."[98] Cannon sees an additional potential narcissistic parallel in that both young boys enjoyed being part of an incestuous couple and were affected by their mothers' marriages with rivals.

Another psychoanalytic note to consider is Annie Cohen-Solal's report on her conversation with Jean-Baptiste Pontalis. Sartre once asked Pontalis, the renowned French psychoanalyst and collaborator with Sartre on the editorial board of *Les Temps modernes*, to analyze him. Sartre had begun to record his dreams and analyze them for work on his autobiography, which he initially thought to call *Jean sans terre*. Though it is not clear if Sartre's request was just a whimsical appeal for help, Pontalis took it seriously enough to reject it straightaway on the basis that he knew Sartre to well. Twenty-five years later Pontalis accepted Cohen-Solal's request to analyze Sartre's dreams for her Sartre biography. However, the outcome of Pontalis's examination is minimal, consisting of only a few statements. This time the excuse was "professional discretion."

Sartre's dreams presumably did focus on "the question of immortality, incompletion, recognition." And Pontalis interpreted the autobiography's initial title as "Jean sans père," while he joked about Sartre's deceased father and himself sharing the same first name.[99] The editorial working relationship between Pontalis and Sartre ended in conflict, and the conflict between the two men might have been reflected on in Sartre's article "Psychoanalytic Dialogue." Pontalis resigned from the editorial board after the publication of the article in *Les Temps modernes*.

It might be right in a traditional psychoanalytic fashion to translate "Jean sans terre" as "Jean sans père," but one could also ask for the meaning of the actual change of title from *Jean sans terre* to *The Words*. What in the first place might have caused Sartre to identify with this prince, John Lackland (1167–1216), the youngest son of King Henry II? Was it because of the reputation of John as vindictive, distrustful, and deceitful, though he was cultured and literate? Did Sartre identify with *Jean sans terre* because John's positive qualities were recognized only centuries later? Perhaps it was because of John's many quarrels with the papacy? Or was it because John, although the youngest son, became king and ruled over England for seventeen years? Or could the temporary title just have been a nickname given to the autobiography, just as Henry II nicknamed his son, ironically, "Lackland."

Cohen-Solal observes that the themes Pontalis recognized in Sartre's dreams are also important themes of *The Words*. These themes also happen to coincide with the three major themes that I recognize in *The Words*; the "incomplete Oedipal complex" (cf. incompletion), God and the unnatural (cf. recognition), and death and immortality (cf. immortality). It would have been interesting if a further comparison could have been made, but Dr. Pontalis could not say more than he did.

Andrew Leak and Douglas Kirsner are among the very few scholars who extensively analyzed Sartre and his work from a traditional psychoanalytic perspective. Another model psychoanalytic study I like to refer to is Josette Pacaly's book, *Sartre au miroir: une lecture psychoanalytique de ses écrits biographiques*.[100]

Leak argues that Sartre's texts are there to be psychoanalyzed because they are made of language, the medium in which psychoanalysis operates. Leak focuses on sexuality in Sartre's philosophical and literary works. In the context of my work I refer only to Leak's analysis of *The Words*. Leak indicates that Sartre had an ambivalent attitude toward his grandfather. Although the grandfather performed the role of father in the Schweitzer–Sartre household, he was not a genuine patriarchal substitute. A similar ambiguity Leak recognizes in Sartre's relation to his mother: "She and Poulou [Sartre's childhood name] appear to be locked into a sempiternal pre-Oedipal Eden whose harmony will never be destroyed by a brash Moses." In addition to the image of his mother as a virgin sister, she is the "potent phallic mother."

Nonetheless, Leak assumes that Charles Schweitzer, and Annie-Marie's second husband Joseph Mancy, imposed a male consciousness on the little Sartre: It was a men's world, and their little man belonged to their class. But Leak considers the influence of the male mediation as momentary: "The absence of the father leaves the child in the possession of the mother. The fate that threatens him—here [in *The Words*] summed up by 'féminisé' and 'affadi'—is engulfment, emasculation and mutilation." The mother–child dyad is translated into the Lacanian terms "le désir de la mère—the desire *for* and *of* the mother." Poulou's self-inscription into Lacan's symbolic order was through his use of language, by writing. His childhood writings were steps toward his liberation from the feminine dyad that he was trapped in. Final mediation was found when Sartre discovered "the role of the writer as socially valorised figure. This could be termed the entry into the 'Cultural Order.' Sartre talks of homosexuality as the way-out that Genet invents at the moment of suffocation; one could see the invention of writing as a similar way-out discovered by Poulou. The discovery of writing is thus tantamount, in the case of Poulou, to the reinvention of the missing father."[101] Yet Leak finds that in spite of this apparent progress Sartre remains locked into the pre-Oedipal stage of the imaginary.

In *The Schizoid World of Jean-Paul Sartre and R. D. Laing*, Kirsner analyzes Sartre from the perspective of the British object-relations school. He draws a close relation between narcissistic disorders and the schizoid problems he attributes to Sartre. Likewise, Kirsner assumes that "an exploration of Sartre's work using Erikson's categories would show how Sartre's world is based mainly around the first psycho-social stage of 'basic trust v. basic mistrust,' and to a lesser extent involves the second, 'autonomy v. shame and doubt.'"[102]Next, Sartre's committed literature is analyzed as combining the virtues of the theorist and the agitator. Kirsner utilizes H. Laswell's research, *Psychopathology and Politics*, to argue that agitators are narcissistic types.[103] Sartre is labelled as "the model child and impostor who has compulsive urges to express himself and his world orally; who systematizes at a highly abstract level, while at the same time actively attacking all in any type of authority; who depicts all relationships as mutually devouring."[104] Kirsner shows a measure of grace in his judgment of Sartre when he considers that the schizoid despair attributed to the philosopher is an overall characteristic of the world we live in.

Quite unlike the types of psychoanalysis done so far, I propose as a psychoanalytic study an inquiry into the dynamics of consistency and continuity of Sartre's thoughts and life as he recorded them in his autobiography and other writings. This is an attempt to find a unifying or dividing thread in his life and work. Charmé's work accentuates that "Sartre acknowledges that his life and his work probably contain a unifying thread, though he has never looked for it nor tried to establish it." Sartre compared this intellectual unifying thread to something like a system. "Sartre does not believe this system is linked together in some logical way that he is explicitly aware of, but it has a unity nonetheless."[105] My approach is also different from Existential psychoanalysis in that the objective to be disclosed is not the origin of a life, such as the Sartrean fundamental project, but patterns of philosophical activity: threads of intellectual development, change, continuity, discontinuity, consistency, inconsistency, and conflict.

Sartre considered philosophy an integral part of good literature. It was because of literature that he was interested in philosophy, the handmaid of all good writing. In *Conversations* Sartre even expressed surprise that through the years philosophy had become more and more important, so important that he had even begun writing philosophy books. Nevertheless, he found that his better books were those concerned not only, but partially, with philosophy. The early influences of philosophy in Sartre's life were, in an indirect manner, via literature. Although his childhood was shaped by a certain amount of philosophy in literature, Sartre nevertheless felt that there was an absence, a lack of philosophy in his early years. In *The Words* Sartre described that a cause for his writing neurosis was not only "the absence of God," but also the absence of a meaningful philosophy of life. As a child he only found a fragmentary purpose for life through reading and writing.

The ethical notions of Good and Evil became concrete reality for the child only during the First World War. In spite of his new ability to differentiate between fiction and reality, he continued to practice ethics as a magical act performed by writing a text. Jean-Paul joined the patriots at the front by imagining his pen a gun.

It was during the Second World War that via socialism and Marxism Sartre came to reject the influence bourgeois literature had on his life. The values found in this type of literature were then repudiated, and instead Sartre began formulating and practicing his own type of Socialism. The formation of Sartre's political philosophy had a direct influence on his writings and on his life. *The Words* was an exercise in increasing awareness of the influence of bourgeois literature on his life, and an attempt to free himself from it completely. It was also an ethical praxis by which he liberated himself and others from the snares of unengaged literature.

The Words does not relate to the period between his teens and his middle age, but from Sartre's references to the years in which he wrote

The Words, it was only in middle age that he succeeded in practicing his socialist philosophy in a radical manner. The political understandings Sartre acquired during the Second World War had not been fully integrated in his daily living till he wrote *The Words*.

In his fifties Sartre had developed into a philosopher who finally freed himself of the values inculcated by his upbringing, but he continued to use the skills he had developed through his education and former literary ambitions.

Characteristically, his method was anti-Freudian, in that it rejected the idea of the unconscious. The past can be deciphered and understood by recalling it. Sartre demonstrated this in his autobiography; without the help of a psychiatrist he analyzed and interpreted his childhood. He remembered intimate moments, happiness, embarrassment, painful events, his desires and attractions, his fears and loneliness. But most important is the interpretation of his early choices.

Sartre interpreted the givens of his childhood in an anti-Freudian manner. He suffered from a "most incomplete Oedipal complex." He was not narcissistic, he just preferred to be at home in a solitary fantasy world of literature. Since he grew up in the isolation of adults, he felt alienated from other children.

In his self-analysis Sartre also considers the absence of positive reciprocal relations with his peer group one of the reasons for his writing neurosis. In *The Freud Scenario* and *Hope Now* he showed that the practice of positive reciprocal relations is essential to self-knowledge, well-being, and social justice.

Analogous to the classical psychoanalytic method, Sartre found it important to express his childhood memories, but in contradistinction to Freud's theory this was important not only from a personal point of view. Through his confession Sartre aimed at changing his own destiny and that of others; those who recognize themselves in Sartre's portrait might also imitate his example.

The Words is a detailed remembrance of his inner development; at the same time it is a denunciation, a purification, of his past. *The Words,* like a magical ritual, has to destroy his bourgeois literary-philosophical practice; only after the autobiographic rites can Sartre truly start a new life full of revolutionary practice.

Whereas in *What Is Literature* Sartre had envisioned literature as a practice, it took more than fifteen years to realize this vision. In *What Is Literature* Sartre described the "choice of freedom" as essential and characteristic for all good writers. When as a child Sartre chose to write, the choice personified his freedom, as well as his desire for freedom. His early and later psychoanalytic method recognized freedom as the foundation of all behavior and choices. When he reached his sixties, he not only continued to believe in and practice freedom as a way of being; he insisted that he would continue to practice freedom in the future as well: "I shall die as I have lived."[106] As I have shown in the section analyzing *The Words*, to a great extent Sartre succeeded in achieving self-liberation through writing his autobiography: After *The Words* most of his work was concerned with concrete daily problems, which he tried to solve by philosophical criticism and political action.

Another theme of *The Words*, God—or more precisely the absence of God—Sartre worked on throughout his life by creating a materialistic philosophy of atheism. Though he remained committed to this materialistic atheism in word and deed throughout his life, one may nevertheless conclude from *Conversations* and *Hope Now* that as his life drew to a close he demonstrated a new openness and more placid attitude toward religious persuasions, and specifically toward Judaism. Sartre, however, persisted in practicing atheism, and did not ask for the Last Sacraments or any other religious ritual at his death bed.

As a child Sartre's fear of death was related to the fear of finality, a fear he tried to overcome by practicing the art of writing. In *The Words* and *Conversations* he acknowledges that the public recognition of his works changed his attitude toward writing; it delivered him from his former obsession of trying to obtain literary immortality and from his writing neurosis. Fame gave him the sense of having attained a kind of immortality. His literary–philosophical practice seems indeed to have been sufficient for overcoming his fear of death, since later in life he faced death with Stoic tranquility and the great anxiety that death caused him in his childhood seemed forgotten.

I will proceed in my analysis of Sartre by revealing patterns of philosophical activity and how these contribute to or diminish consistency and continuity in the life described. One may consider *The Words* the ultimate articulation of Sartre's autobiographical activities. Sartre expressed himself autobiographically in novels, diaries, and letters before he wrote *The Words*, and after he wrote it there were his autobiographical interviews. But *The Words* is and remains his autobiography per se. Here he describes his "final," essential self. Similar to his other autobiographical writings, the descriptions of himself and life situations are not only literary and historical, but also philosophical. His autobiographic works are not only philosophical but also have a practical aim. In all of them Sartre reflects on and interprets changes observed in himself, or they are philosophical attempts to achieve change in himself and others. The portrayals of self are not psychological (i.e., scientific), but philosophical descriptions. All the autobiographic writings confirm the basic idea of Sartre's Existential psychoanalytic method: Human beings are essentially characterized by an inherent freedom. In all of Sartre's autobiographic and biographic writings he shows that freedom makes it possible for human beings to determine, even to create themselves: Human beings were, are, and will be praxis projects.

Though in the course of years Sartre slightly modified his early notion of freedom, practicing freedom was an issue never subject to change, and it was never practiced superficially. Sartre shows that his love of liberty was more than a Bohemian lifestyle; for example, during the Second World War it meant opposing and fighting the French Fascists and the occupation of France by Nazi Germany. Sartre's role as a Marxist fellow traveler was likewise characteristic of his practice of freedom in a dogmatic and austere setting. Last but not least, at the end of his life Sartre did not avoid a confrontation with his lifelong companion Beauvoir and other close friends, and rather expressed freely his latest views about future Leftist politics. Throughout his autobiographic writings Sartre's practice of Existential psychoanalysis uncovers the restraining and suppressive influences individuals and society had on him.

Sartre's interest in autobiographic and biographic writing was not just an exercise in human understanding but a revolutionary practice in itself, because philosophizing about "personal things" is an unpopular, even rebellious act. Although with some exceptions, philosophers from antiquity to the present day describe their understanding of human life in abstractions that do not take into account the concrete history and social situations in which people develop and live.

Sartre's method of describing human life is consonant with the ethical purposes he established for engaged literature in *What Is Literature*. At the very beginning of his career, when he was a child, his writings already had a practical and ethical dimension. For example, during the First World War Sartre had imagined his pen as helping the soldiers defending France. Later in life his writings defended the rights of the poor, the oppressed, and the persecuted. His last interview, *Hope Now*, also had a practical purpose: to attack an undesirable political movement.

It is possible to divide all of Sartre's writings into two major categories: the Existential psychoanalytic (theory and its practical applications in biographical and autobiographical works) and the political (theory and its practical applications in situation-oriented articles, novels, and plays, but also applied in biographic and autobiographic works). These two categories are found in his early and later writings and both are concerned with the development and transformation of human beings and society.

Sartre's childhood segregation from other children and the alienation he continued to experience through the habits he acquired during his childhood seem to have made the grown-up Sartre particularly aware of the need for concrete action in the real world. Though for many years Sartre felt more at home in the literary world of fiction, his activities in the realm of fiction were nevertheless directed toward overcoming alienation and were a quest for positive reciprocal relationships between author and public and among people in general. His works during the years before *The Words* were still products of "magical" action, just as in his childhood; he would change the world through his writings.

What Is Literature envisions reciprocity between author and public, since reading is the synthesis of the reader's perception and the author's text. It requires not only the freedom of an audience, but the author must also endorse freedom through his or her creation. The theoretical and practical importance of reciprocal relationships appear in later works (i.e., *The Words, The Freud Scenario*, and *Hope Now*) as well. However, only after having reached his fifties did Sartre exercise in word and deed his rejection of negative reciprocal relationships while he promoted and was an example of positive reciprocal relationships.

Sartre was likewise consistent in his belief in and practice of atheism. At the age of twelve he had an intuition about the nonexistence of God, and when later at high school he learned about atheism he decided that philosophy had to be enriched with his own materialist atheistic philosophy of man. In *Conversations* Sartre maintains that *The Devil and the Good Lord* was his best work, which is not surprising when one considers Sartre's mission in writing. In *The Devil and the Good Lord* the hero, General Goetz, is able to free himself from a self-chosen deception (i.e., faith in God and the good). It was apparently Goetz's belief in fate that transformed him into a saint, because he threw dice to decide whether to become good or evil. But Goetz had played a foul game: Through a gambler's trick he caused the dice to fall just as he wanted.

Sartre exposes Goetz's religious belief, and that of others as well, as deceptive role-playing. Only Goetz and Hilda escape the different religious delusions of their era, after having caused much suffering to themselves as well as to others through their faith in God. Through *The Words* Sartre believed he had accomplished complete deliverance from his own particular religious delusion: He finally rid himself of his belief in literature, which he compared with belief in the Holy Ghost. When he eventually accomplished his radical project of atheism, practicing his ideas became more important than writing them down.

In his tribute to Gide, "The Living Gide," Sartre described the "problem of God" as "a total problem to which each man brings a solution by his entire life, and the solution which one brings to it reflects the attitude one has chosen towards other men and towards oneself."[107] In Gide Sartre found an exemplary life: Gide is described as having finished the agony and death of God in his own living. Sartre seems to have been as much dedicated to the radical practice of atheism as Gide was; it was important to Sartre not only to develop an atheist theory but to live atheism.

After writing *The Words* Sartre became deeply involved in protest and revolutionary activities. These activities led to his acquaintance and cooperation with Benny Lévy, and ultimately to the publication of *Hope Now*.

Even in the "tragic," final years, Sartre's poor health and blindness did not prevent him from acting according to his philosophical convictions. Cohen-Solal extensively described Sartre's activities during these last years: For example, in 1974 Sartre visited the Stammheim prison, where he met with the German revolutionary leader Andreas Baader, who was imprisoned there. In April 1975 Sartre, Beauvoir, and Lévy went to Portugal, were they met with those involved in "the revolution of the red carnations." On his return to France Sartre gave an interview about this visit to the journal *Libération*. And in 1979 he was part of a delegation petitioning the French president to support refugees from Vietnam and Cambodia.[108] It was obvious that even Sartre's old age and physical handicaps could not deter him from the lifelong practice of his convictions in word and in living.

From *The Words* one may conclude that at an early age Sartre was aware of several inconsistencies in his thought and behavior. One of the inconsistencies in the thoughts of the child philosopher was his awareness of the lack of meaning to life, the absence of a meaningful philosophy of life, but on the other hand his family's idolization puffed him up with pride: He felt indispensable to Heaven and Earth. During Sartre's first individualistic period of writing he was still in search of a meaning for life. Sartre's change from individualism to socialism during the Second World War gave meaning to his life: After having seen children die of hunger it became impossible to write another *Nausea*. However, to overcome his pride at being more indispensable than other people, Sartre would need to become more radical. In his later radical political thought he created meaning in life through a utopian political vision; he envisioned a fraternity in which human beings were equals. Accordingly, everyone was as indispensable as everyone else, and Sartre could finally be a human being like all others.

Another inconsistency concerns his intuition about the absence of God. This intuition might well have originated in the shallow but farcical way Catholicism and Protestantism were "united" in the Schweitzer–Sartre household. Although these faiths stem from a common origin, they contradict each other in their manner of interpretation and practice of religion. Accordingly, Sartre acquired not only a burlesque, but above all an inconsistent image of Christianity. Sartre's later impressions of Catholicism and Protestantism are described in a comparable hilarious and conflicting manner in *The Devil and The Good Lord*. It seems that the child Jean-Paul intuited in a rationalistic frame of mind that inconsistencies cannot go together with a God claiming to be One; His absence became evident through Sartre's lack of a serious religious upbringing, in spite of his catechism lessons.

An inconsistency Sartre observed in himself as a child was the contradiction between the real world and the fictional worlds in which he was at home. Through the First World War he learned that there was real evil and danger that could harm him and others. Though he was part of this real world, he could make believe that he was aloof from it. The war had shown the child that he had lived until then in a fictional world only; he had known evil only through fiction and comic books. His desire to live in the real world was aroused and left him with an inner schism that Sartre diagnosed as one of the origins of his writer's neurosis.

His philosophy of literature as initiated in *What Is Literature* was an attempt to overcome the segregation of being part of a literary fictional world and wanting to take part in the real world of human action. The first period of Sartre's work I consider the individualist period, until the Second World War. In the second, middle period, until *The Words*, Sartre formulated his philosophy and tried to realize his thinking. Only after writing *The Words* did Sartre succeed in overcoming his inner schism through the practice of his philosophy of literature. His writings of this third and last period are the realization of his political and revolutionary thoughts; political action had then become part of his daily life.

According to his own description in *The Words*, as a child Sartre had been obsessively fearful of death; nevertheless, he identified himself with the "immortals," the great writers of former centuries. He considered himself "the dead one" until about the age of twenty. His philosophic way of overcoming his fear of death—without giving up being "dead"—was through accepting death on the condition that it was veiled in a cloak of fame and glory. Therefore, Sartre strove to become like his death and immortal great writers. This is an inconsistent thought pattern for a person afraid of death. Was Sartre really afraid of death as a child? Or was this his way of identifying with the image of his dead father?

In *Conversations* and *Hope Now* it appears as if he never had a problem with death. Then, later in his life, instead of identifying himself as "the dead one," he identifies himself as the one alive, the one in whose life death has no part. Does he forget his former anxiety as a result of having joined the ranks of the immortal writers? Sartre does not explain how this childish, inconsistent method of facing death indeed helped him to rid himself of his fear of death. It is well to remember here that Sartre also related his fear of death to the lack of a meaningful philosophy of life. It might be appropriate to conclude that Sartre's philosophy of practice helped him not only to live in a meaningful manner, but also resolved his childish inconsistent conceptions related to his anxiety over death.

In *What Is Literature* Sartre found that the inconsistencies in the messages of great writers did not prevent their audience from understanding them; these messages were alive because they addressed the readers' repressions. Moreover, Sartre criticized those professional critics who, instead of giving new life to the great writers' texts, void their messages by showing only the internal contradictions between the authors' lives and their writings.

In *Conversations* Sartre indicated that it was during the Second World War that he learned the true meaning of being an individual. Its meaning then became to be embodied in the collective. This new experience contradicted his former understanding. Consequently, he conceived the idea that an individual is always set in a collective and changed his worldview from individualism to socialism. But he continued to search for his own liberal socialism, which then had to be defined and practiced. Sartre continually corrected what he considered his major inconsistency: not practicing his brand of socialism radically enough.

In his interviews with Lévy, Sartre acknowledged some minor inconsistencies in his work, but he found these irrelevant in comparison to his message and its revolutionary impact on life. Continuity in Sartre's thought and its practice in life seems as little problematic to establish consistency, in spite of some minor inconsistencies and discontinuity.

In *The Words* Sartre compares a particular period of his childhood, when he was between nine and eleven years old, to the momentary awareness of a mentally ill person, realizing for an instant that he is a shoemaker and not a prince. At that same age Sartre experienced an interruption in his earliest and most lasting practice: writing. In this period he was sent to school for the first time, and the demands school life made on him relegated his fantasy life to the background. He felt that this short repression of his commitment to writing only strengthened his destiny as a writer.

The skills and experiences Sartre obtained during that period endowed his dream vocation with the contours needed for its realization. His writer's mandate then became his character; he became one with his madness.[109] Sartre did not consider those two years as the negation of his writer's mandate, since the change from fantasy life to school activities was only superficial. His fundamental choice of being a writer imparted continuity to his childhood as well as to his life thereafter.

In his fifties Sartre clarified afresh his commitment to writing. It is not writing as a profession that he censures in *The Words*, but rather a particular brand of writing that he rejected as useless. He is against bourgeois literature, against literature that does not present readers with a critical mirror of themselves, and against literature that is not committed to freedom.

The purpose and content of Sartre's writing became different for him over the years, but he remained committed to his original choice: to be a writer. Whereas Sartre only once changed the focus of his writing from individualistic–bourgeois writing to committed writing during the Second World War, he only gradually radicalized and realized this change of focus. Until he reached the summit of his revolutionary project in *The Words*, Sartre wrote books in the following categories: novels, short stories, drama, philosophy, and criticism—each in its own particular style.

In Sartre's style of writing there is uniformity and continuity with only two exceptions: the styles of *The Reprieve* and *The Words*. In *The Reprieve* Sartre experimented with "the wide screen" technique. He also applied techniques of simultaneity, comparable to the techniques Dos Passos and Virginia Woolf worked with, in order to create the feeling of the September days of 1938, as if "the walls came tumbling down."[110]

In *The Words* Sartre created a similar lack in narrative order. He associated events not chronologically, but around certain themes, such as "Reading" and "Writing." The manner in which Sartre worked on *The Words* was also very different from the way he worked on his other writings. Cohen-Solal, who studied the original versions of the manuscript, finds *The Words* belabored and "the object of many drafts, reformulations, corrections, cuts, revisions. [*The Words* shows] a great deal of patience, the patience of an artisan, such as Sartre had never had before and would never again have with any of his works."[111]

It seems out of the question that Sartre wanted to or would have been able to repeat the "over-worked-phrases" technique of *The Words* in a work like *Hope Now*. This technique, however, has elements in common with Sartre's usual style in that it concentrates on articulating a central message loud and clear. Other minor issues are not considered relevant, and therefore may contradict each other, which allows them to be interpreted in more than one sense.

With the exception of his annual holiday(s) and some ongoing political activities, Sartre's daily life, like his literature and philosophy from the Second World War on, had few changes. He used his freedom mainly for constant reading and writing; continuity in his way of living and thinking was impressively present.

After the Second World War, when Sartre changed his philosophy from individualism to socialism, continuity in his philosophical ideas on psychoanalytic and political issues did not crucially change. He only slightly modified his thoughts, developing them further and making his ideas more complex, although in the end he expressed his ideas with unadorned clarity.

The freedom and sense of self-realization Sartre claims to have achieved through his philosophy and his writer's couch psychoanalysis might be questioned by philosophers, psychoanalysts, and others. Nevertheless, whatever one perceives as Sartre's achievements, for Sartre it had become sufficient to die in the conviction he lived in most of his life: being a free human being.

NOTES

1. Simone de Beauvoir, *Adieux: A Farewell to Sartre* (London: Penguin, 1988), 176.
2. Jean-Paul Sartre, *Witness to My Life: The Letters of J. P. Sartre to Simone de Beauvoir 1926–1939* (New York: Macmillan, 1992); Jean-Paul Sartre, *Quiet Moments in a War: The Letters of J. P. Sartre to Simone de Beauvoir 1940–1963* (New York: Macmillan, 1993).
3. Jean-Paul Sartre, *War Diaries: Notebooks from a Phoney War, November 1939–March 1940*, trans. Q. Hoare (London: Verso, 1984).
4. Simone de Beauvoir, "Introduction" in Sartre, *Quiet Moments in a War: The Letters of J. P. Sartre to Simone de Beauvoir 1940–1963*, xiii.
5. Jean-Paul Sartre, *The Words* (New York: George Braziller, 1964), 251.
6. Ibid., 237, 238.
7. Robert Champigny, "Sartre on Sartre," in *The Philosophy of Jean-Paul Sartre*, ed. P. A. Schillp (La Salle, Ill.: Open Court, 1981), 88.
8. Jean-Paul Sartre, *Life/Situations* (New York, Pantheon Books, 1977), 15.
9. Ibid., 117, 113.
10. Hugh J. Silverman, "Sartre's Words on the Self," in *Jean-Paul Sartre: Contemporary Approaches to His Philosophy*, ed. H. J. Silverman and F. A. Elliston (Pittsburgh, Pa.: Duquesne University Press, 1980), 101, 103.
11. Sartre, *Life/Situations*, 21.
12. Ibid., 48.
13. Douglas Kirsner, *The Schizoid World of Jean-Paul Sartre and R. D. Laing* (St. Lucia: University of Queenland Press, 1976), 64.
14. Jean-Paul Sartre, *Between Existentialism and Marxism* (New York: Pantheon, 1975), 32.
15. Ibid., 121.
16. Sartre, *The Words*, 26.
17. Jeffrey Mehlman, *A Structural Study of Autobiography: Proust, Leiris, Sartre, Levi-Strauss* (London: Cornell University Press, 1974), 153.
18. Ibid., 151.
19. Sartre, *The Words*, 54.
20. Janine Hochland, "Incest: A Theme in Sartre's Literary Work," *Journal of the British Society for Phenomenology* 2 (1970): 99.
21. Kate Fullbrook and Edward Fullbrook, *Simone de Beauvoir and Jean-Paul Sartre* (New York: Harvester Wheatsheaf, 1993), 6.
22. Ibid., 17.

23. Philip M. W. Thody, "Sartre's *Les Mots*: A Defense of Normality," in *Phenomenology and Education*, ed. B. Curtis and W. Mays (London: Methuen, 1978), 112.
24. Sartre, *The Words*, 54.
25. Sartre, *Life/Situations*, 110.
26. Sartre, *The Words*, 21.
27. Sartre, *Life/Situations*, 25, 26.
28. Sartre, *The Words*, 23.
29. Ibid., 208, 209, 222, 230, 254.
30. Rivca Gordon and Haim Gordon, "Sartre's Autobiography and His Early Philosophy," *Journal of the British Society for Phenomenology* 23 (1992): 66–67.
31. Sartre, *The Words*, 102.
32. Ibid., 60, 154, 163, 207.
33. Jean-Paul Sartre, *Saint Genet: Actor and Martyr* (New York: Mentor Books, 1963), 27.
34. Sartre, *The Words*, 40.
35. Ibid., 30, 83, 90.
36. Beauvoir, *Adieux: A Farewell to Sartre*, 333.
37. Sartre, *The Words*, 51.
38. Ibid., 59, 60, 73, 75, 110, 111, 32, 33, 180, 254, 251, 253, 250, 69, 118, 39, 179, 234, 23, 94, 95, 96.
39. Margery L. Collins and Christine Pierce, "Holes and Slime: Sexism in Sartre's Psychoanalysis," *The Philosophical Forum* 5 (1975): 112–127.
40. Sartre, *The Words*, 228, 191, 193, 197, 199, 194.
41. Jane P. Tompkins, "Sartre Resartus: A Reading of *Les Mots*," in *Critical Essays on Jean-Paul Sartre*, ed. R. Wilcocks (Boston, G. K. Hall, 1988), 272.
42. Wallace Fowlie, "Introduction," in J. P. Sartre, *What Is Literature* (New York: Harper and Row, 1965): xv.
43. Hazel E. Barnes, *Sartre* (London: Quartet Books, 1974), 66; Alfred R. Desautels, "The Sartre of Stalag 12D (1940–1941)," *The French Review* 55 (1981): 201–206.
44. Barnes, *Sartre*, 68.
45. Benjamin Suhl, *Jean-Paul Sartre: The Philosopher as a Literary Critic* (New York: Columbia University Press, 1970), 266.
46. Kirsner, *The Schizoid World of Jean-Paul Sartre and R. D. Laing*, 77.
47. Sartre, *What Is Literature*, 18, 52, 27.
48. Iris Murdoch, *Sartre: Romantic Rationalist* (London: Penguin, 1989), 146, 147.
49. Sartre, *Between Existentialism and Marxism*, 11.
50. Sartre, *What Is Literature*, 32, 45, 37, 57, 64, 65, 146, 211, 213, 216, 233, 246, 279, 285, 64.
51. Jean-Baptiste Pontalis, "Preface," in *The Freud Scenario* (Chicago: University of Chicago Press, 1985), xii; Christina Howells, "Sartre and Freud" *French Studies* 33 (1979): 157–176.
52. Hazel E. Barnes, "Sartre's Scenario for Freud," *L'Esprit Createur*, special edition, *Writing Lives: Sartre, Beauvoir and (Auto)Biography* 29 (1989): 64.
53. Ronald D. Laing and David G. Cooper, *Reason and Violence* (New York: Pantheon, 1971), 109, 110.

54. Adrian Mirvish, "Sartre, Reciprocity, Sexuality and Solipsism," *Journal of the British Society for Phenomenology* 25 (1994): 147.

55. Barnes, "Sartre's Scenario for Freud," 61, 62, 53.

56. Jean-Paul Sartre, *The Freud Scenario* (Chicago: University of Chicago Press, 1985), 286.

57. Ernest Jones, *The Life and Work of Sigmund Freud* (Harmondsworth: Penguin Books, 1957).

58. Sigmund Freud, *The Interpretation of Dreams* (New York: Modern Library, 1950), 98–99; Jones, *The Life and Work of Sigmund Freud*, 50.

59. Sigmund Freud, *The History of the Psychoanalytic Movement* (New York: Colliers Books, 1963), 51.

60. Stuart L. Charmé, *Meaning and Myth in the Study of Lives: A Sartrean Perspective* (Philadelphia: University of Pennsylvania Press, 1984), 75.

61. Freud, *The History of the Psychoanalytic Movement*, 51, 55, 56.

62. Jones, *The Life and Work of Sigmund Freud*, 281.

63. Jeffrey Masson, *The Assault on Truth: Freud's Suppression of the Seduction Theory* (New York: Farrar, Straus and Giroux, 1984), 191.

64. Sartre, *The Freud Scenario*, 343.

65. Ibid., 347, 370, 371.

66. Jean-Paul Sartre, *Anti-Semite and Jew* (New York: Grove Press, 1948), 150.

67. Sartre, *The Freud Scenario*, 321, 287.

68. Simone de Beauvoir, "Conversations with Jean-Paul Sartre," in *Adieux: A Farewell to Sartre*, 129–445. The first part of Adieux: A Farewell to Sartre, called "A Farewell to Sartre," is based on Beauvoir's diary during the last ten years of Sartre's life. The second section is based on Beauvoir's conversations with Sartre during the summer and fall of 1974. In my text I refer to this last section plainly as *Conversations*.

69. Hazel E. Barnes, "Beauvoir and Sartre: The Forms of Farewell," *Philosophy and Literature* 9 (1985): 22.

70. Beauvoir, *Adieux: A Farewell to Sartre*, 133, 139, 142, 143, 151, 154, 155, 165, 172, 167, 200, 198, 376, 387, 414, 397, 139, 356, 214, 423, 177, 178, 348, 352, 353, 358, 360, 361, 355.

71. Barnes, "Beauvoir and Sartre: The Forms of Farewell," 22, 31.

72. Beauvoir, *Adieux: A Farewell to Sartre*, 292, 293, 419, 434, 433, 435, 436, 437, 438.

73. Michel Contat and Michel Rybalka, *The Writings of Jean-Paul Sartre: A Bibliographical Life*, vol. 1 (Evanston, Ill.: Northwestern University Press, 1974), 249.

74. Beauvoir, *Adieux: A Farewell to Sartre*, 358, 443, 152, 170, 440, 432.

75. This is at present still an unpublished text, and accordingly I refer to it as "Power and Liberty" rather than as *Power and Liberty*.

76. Arlette Elkaïm-Sartre, "Polémique: La Cérémonie des Adieux," in *Libération*, December 3, 1981, 26, quoted in Ronald Aronson, "Sartre's Last Words," in Jean-Paul Sartre and Benny Lévy, *Hope Now*, trans. A. van den Hoven (Chicago: University of Chicago Press, 1996), 8.

77. Aronson, "Sartre's Last Words," *Hope Now*, 5.

78. Sartre, *Life/Situations*, 31.

79. For documentation on Sartre's recommendation to publish *Hope Now* to the editor-in-chief of the *Nouvel Observateur*, Jean Daniel, see Annie Cohen-Solal, *Sartre: A Life* (London: Minerva, 1991), 514.

80. "A Retrospective on the Context of *Hope Now*," interview by author, Jerusalem, December 1996–January 1997. I thank Professor Lévy for the hours he spoke to me at the Institute of Philosophy and Literature of the University of Paris VII at Jerusalem. I appreciate that he commented on my descriptions of issues he discussed during our first two sessions, and agreed that I tape-record our third, last session. This interview was published in *Sartre Studies International* 4, 1 (1998): 63–75, and was commented on by Ronald Aronson in *Sartre Studies International* 4, 2 (1998): 43–44. Aronson considers that I in the end agree with him, in spite of my criticisms. This, however, seems to me a misreading of the issues I accentuate in the paper.

81. This contradicts Aronson's suggestion that *Hope Now* is best read by remembering that Sartre aimed at achieving multiple meanings with his words, and Aronson thinks that Sartre succeeded in this in *Hope Now* as well. Aronson, "Introduction," in Sartre and Lévy, *Hope Now*, 19.

82. Cohen-Solal, *Sartre: A Life*, 497.

83. Sartre and Lévy, *Hope Now*, 46.

84. Beauvoir, *Adieux: A Farewell to Sartre*, 293.

85. In a conversation between André Gide and Marcel Proust, Gide maintained that Baudelaire might have been homosexual, while Proust tried to convince Gide that Baudelaire was undoubtedly homosexual. See André Gide, *The Journals of André Gide*, vol. 1 (New York, Vintage Books, 1959), 304. Sartre himself raised, though tentatively, the issue of homosexuality in Flaubert's life. See Jean-Paul Sartre, *The Family Idiot*, vol. 2 (Chicago: University of Chicago Press, 1987), 34.

86. Cohen-Solal, *Sartre: A Life*, 500.

87. Beauvoir, *Adieux: A Farewell to Sartre*, 293.

88. Cohen-Solal quotes Sartre as saying that equal relations between him and Lévy were one possibility among others but that equality was of all possibilities "the best one." Cohen-Solal, *Sartre: A Life*, 499.

89. See Lévy's description in "The Final Word": "We are not masters of our acts. I must stop believing that the act is the work of my hands. . . . This is the price at which freedom can begin again." Sartre and Lévy, *Hope Now*, 122 (cf. Rabbi Akiva: "All is foreseen, but freedom of choice is given." Avot 3:15).

90. Sartre and Lévy, *Hope Now*, 101, 104.

91. Sartre, *The Words*, 198.

92. Cohen-Solal, *Sartre: A Life*, 513.

93. Sartre and Lévy, *Hope Now*, 37.

94. Ibid., 110, 54, 53, 90, 107, 47, 54, 66, 101, 102, 107.

95. Sartre, *Life/Situations*, 78.

96. Leo Fretz, "An Interview with Jean-Paul Sartre," in Silverman and Elliston, *Jean-Paul Sartre, Contemporary Approaches to His Philosophy*, 233.

97. Laing and Cooper, *Reason and Violence*.

98. Betty Cannon, *Sartre and Psychoanalysis: An Existentialist Challenge to Clinical Metatheory* (Lawrence, Kan.: University of Kansas Press, 1991), 306.

99. Cohen-Solal, *Sartre: A Life*, 444, 467, 472.

100. Josette Pacaly, *Sartre au miroir: une lecture psychoanalytique de ses écrits biographiques* (Paris: Klincksieck, 1980).

101. Andrew N. Leak, *The Perverted Consciousness: Sexuality and Sartre* (London: Macmillan, 1989), 93, 97, 100.

102. Kirsner, *The Schizoid World of Jean-Paul Sartre and R. D. Laing*, 56, 57.
103. H. Laswell, *Psychopathology and Politics* (Chicago: University of Chicago Press, 1986).
104. Kirsner, *The Schizoid World of Jean-Paul Sartre and R. D. Laing*, 105.
105. Charmé, *Meaning and Myth in the Study of Lives: A Sartrean Perspective*, 107.
106. Beauvoir, *Adieux: A Farewell to Sartre*, 348.
107. Jean-Paul Sartre, *Situations* (New York: Fawcett, 1965), 52.
108. Cohen-Solal, *Sartre: A Life*, 507, 508, 509.
109. Sartre, *The Words*, 254.
110. Contat and Rybalka, *The Writings of Jean-Paul Sartre: A Bibliographical Life*, vol. 1, 113.
111. Cohen-Solal, *Sartre: A Life*, 443.

CHAPTER 7

Epilogue: New Selves for a New Day?

> "But you live your wisdom," said I; "why don't you write your memoirs? Or simply," I added, seeing him smile, "recollections of your travels?"
> "Because I do not want to recollect," he replied. . . . "I don't like looking backwards and I leave my past behind me as the bird leaves his shade to fly away."
>
> André Gide, *The Immoralist*

In this epilogue I reflect on self-renewal or change, and on the likelihood for persons to attain different selves through combining philosophical psychoanalysis with narrative writing. I illuminate these issues through conclusions drawn from former chapters, while comparing these to the dynamics of consistency and continuity in the autobiographies of John Stuart Mill, Søren Kierkegaard, and Bertrand Russell. My treatment of these last mentioned is mainly confined to their autobiographies.

The idea of self-renewal and transformation of the self have been, and still are, ideas that fascinate people. Rites of rebirth and transformation are associated with humanity's earliest narratives; evidence of this particular human intent is found in mythology, early religion, and ancient philosophy.[1] Carl G. Jung considered the theme of destruction and restoration, death and rebirth, as having the significance of an archetype and being part of the "cosmogonic myth."[2]

In *The Politics of Experience*, Laing describes that the journey through death of the so-called normal ego and its rebirth into true sanity actually is what the psychotic experiences. "True sanity entails in one way or another the dissolution of the normal ego, that false self competently adjusted to our alienated social reality; the emergence of the 'inner' archetypal mediators of divine power, and through this death a rebirth, and the eventual re-establishment of a new kind of ego-functioning, the ego now being the servant of the divine, no longer its betrayer." Laing considers such processes of radical change and transformation beneficial and not simply "the effulgence of a pathological process or of a particular alienation." Laing also organized and supervised rebirth events; however, Laing's teachings on this subject seem no longer to be practiced by the analysts of the Philadelphia Association.[3]

In our postmodern world people mainly are interested in progressive adjustment to the conventional norms of their society or community and attempts to improve their socioeconomic status. Moderate change toward such prosaic directions is usually encouraged by the diverse types of mental-health servants. Radical alternating aspirations to self-renewal and change are still fashionable for some individualists and soul-searchers, or are acquired in the exceptional profound therapy, through a religious experience, or involvement in the New Age movement. The hope of obtaining inner, emotional, or character changes through drugs such as Prozac has proven disappointing to many. The chemical-induced changes are experienced as merely a cosmetics for the self, a mere stiffening of feelings and not the transformation of depression into joy or anxiety into tranquility.

The relationship between self-narration, narration, self-renewal, and change coincides with ancient suggestions of self-transformation through personal confessions, or the creative, transforming speech of priests, prophets, and magicians. As intangible worlds were created, upheld, and renewed through words and stories, so narration has been and still is functional in creating national and individual identities. Plato considered that changing the music of a nation determines the state of its affairs; in a similar sense, varying what people think and say about themselves will have not less striking effects.

The psychologist Ira Progoff developed an approach to assist persons in self-narration. In *Life-Study*, Progoff describes the aim of his intensive journal method: He encourages persons to achieve new integrations within themselves through meditation and a journal technique through which one can experience or create a thread of continuity. In *Death and the Rebirth of Psychology*, Progoff describes the holistic depth psychology he developed as the conceptual foundation for his journal method. In accordance with Freudian, Jungian, and other depth psychologies, Progoff's method draws on the memories and imaginations of the narrative subject, while it does not focus primarily on historical facts or critical reflection on the life.[4] Unlike Progoff's and Wollheim's psychologistic perceptions of life-narration, I find that a thread of continuity can be discovered or established by critical reflection on a subject's personal narrative.

In the conclusion to *The Language of Autobiography*, John Sturrock asks where the convergence lies in the about twenty-five autobiographies he studied (including eleven philosophical autobiographies; i.e., Augustine, Abelard, Dante, Descartes, Vico, Hume, Rousseau, Goethe, Mill, Stein, and Sartre). He finds it typical for the autobiographer to have distinguished himself or herself as an individual from an anonymous mass, consisting of persons who seemingly do not have an own story to tell. In addition, Sturrock relates that most autobiographies contain a "dramatic reorientation," a "turning point." These turns and reorientations are more than just rhetorical narrative devices. Changes and transformations "are less narrative 'events' than the intineraries of individuals who have broken with one milieu and entered another and in so doing have affirmed their extreme individuality. The specific autobiographic 'turn' is into independence."[5] Sturrock is careful not to imply independence as the aim of every autobiographer, and he names Augustine and Nietzsche as the exemplary exceptions to the rule. I much appreciate Sturrock's research, but I do not believe that individuation is the significant characteristic of most self-narratives. I find that changes are often not due to personal determination, as this notion seems to me the criterion for individuation. To a certain extent change will occur without what a person wills, desires, or chooses; it happens. Such "turns" I cannot recognize as signifying individuation. In a sense, as Heraclitus already observed, "παντα 'ρει,"everything flows. Change is the norm, repetition the exception. From such a perspective one can define autobiography as an account of diverse personal changes and as a record of how these changes relate to each other. The meanings and intentions of these accounts can be diverging. Some of these accounts may clearly show a pattern of consistency and continuity in spite of including gigantic changes. Nevertheless, fundamental alterations are often taken as evidence of discontinuity or inconsistency within the personal development or personality, particularly so in traditional forms of psychoanalysis.

For example, Søren Kierkegaard writes in his *Diary* that his pseudonymous writings represent various stages of his life. His attempt to present these different stages in one work he finds obstructed through his own belief in the supreme importance of consistency. He considers that if he only had been half so consistent he would be "much better understood. But the Lord takes greater delight in obedience than in the fat of the ram. . . . And consistency is dearer to thought than worldly recognition from society gossips." Kierkegaard characterizes his own consistency as his love for only one idea; that is, "that a man can become what he really *wills*." Kierkegaard describes his true life as writing: "I rise in the morning and thank God—and then I start my work. At a set hour in the evening I stop, and I thank God—and then I go to sleep. And so I live, though not, at certain moments, without fits of melancholy and sadness, yet, in the main, day in and day out in the most blissful enchantment."

When portraying his childhood and youth, Kierkegaard describes his father as the main source for his unhappiness. On the other hand, he finds his father most affectionate and he reveals a deep yearning for him. Essentially he learned from his father the meaning of fatherly love, which he compares with the notion of divine love; it "gave me an idea of the love of our heavenly Father, the only unshakable thing in life, the true Archimedean point."

Kierkegaard also pictures himself as torn to pieces from the inside and without a chance of leading an ordinary happy life because of "the historical continuity of domestic family-life." He describes what rescued him in this desperate situation as follows: "I seized upon the intellectual side of man only and clung to it so closely that the thought of my considerable mental talents was my only consolation, ideas my only joy, human beings objects of indifference." Kierkegaard sees continuity in his life by fulfilling his father's last wish; that is, that he should pass his final theology exam. For Kierkegaard, honoring this wish is fulfilling his earthly destiny.[6]

Another instance of philosophical psychoanalysis revolving around change, consistency, continuity, and intellectual activity is John Stuart Mill's *Autobiography*. In the chapter, "A Crisis in My Mental History," Mill analyzes his depression and describes his recovery. A close reading of how these shifts in his emotional life seem to eventuate allows for a different understanding than the standard psychoanalytic one.

In the introduction to the *Essential Works of John Stuart Mill*, Max Lerner refers to the standard psychoanalytic assessment of Mill. Lerner refers to an article by A. W. Levi, which was published in the *Psychoanalytic Review*, and surmises Mill's crisis as "the result of a repressed death-wish toward his father, that he had harbored a hostility against him during the course of his training, that the unwillingness to recognize the death-wish led to an attrition of his whole feeling-capacity, and that the passage in Marmontel, by resolving his conflict, released his capacity for feeling as well as his fears."[7]

Whereas Mill clearly indicates in his *Autobiography* that he suffered from his father's educational discipline, at the same time he describes his father with profound admiration and respect. There is also gratitude in his words: "If I have accomplished anything, I owe it, among other fortunate circumstances, to the fact that through the early training bestowed on me by my father, I started, I may fairly say, with an advantage of a quarter of a century over my contemporaries."

When in 1821 Mill read Bentham, his happiness became to be a reformer of the world. Five years thereafter he started to question himself about what would happen if the world would no longer need any reformers. Would that make him happy? He discovered in himself a hypothetical *no* to this question. "The end had ceased to charm, and how could there ever again be any interest in the means? I seemed to have nothing left to live for." He describes the depression following his intellectual self-questioning in words from Coleridge's poem "Dejection":

> A stifled, unimpassioned grief,
> Which finds no natural outlet or relief.

He sought relief in his favorite books, without much advantage, until about one year later when he read Marmontel's *Memoires*. In contrast to the Freudian understanding, it seems to me that the paragraph in which Marmontel describes the scene of his father's death does not show any overt or hidden hatred, or any behavior that would suggest that Marmontel had wished his father to die. It illustrates how a "mere boy" takes up the huge responsibility of care for his family in the absence of the paterfamilias. It expresses the continuation of family life and duties in spite of the fact that the father "failed." The death of the father presented the young Marmontel with a heavy task: It imposed on the boy a duty that seemed beyond his strength, yet he embraced it. I propose that Marmontel's example suggested to Mill the possibility of finding a new goal in life, a way of accepting responsibilities; it awakened in Mill a moral imperative. If one compares Mill's description of his father's death with the death scene of Marmontel's father, it seems to me that Mill emotionally identified with Marmontel as a "mere boy." At the time when Mill read Marmontel, he felt unable to take on the responsibility of being a world reformer without the inner guarantee that it would include a happy ending, that it would be a rewarding effort for him.

Mill mentions the death of his father in one sentence, and then contends throughout several pages that his father had not received from the public the honor and appreciation he should have received. He then adds as a personal note, "Though acutely sensible of my own inferiority in the qualities by which he [Mill's father] acquired his personal ascendancy, I had now to try what it might be possible for me to accomplish without him." Years after his crisis we observe Mill acting like Marmontel; that is, continuing the exemplary way his father had set out before him.

Mill describes as symptomatic of his crisis his lack of emotions. But when he identifies with the courageous and ethical choice of the boy Marmontel, he is moved to tears. He writes, "From this moment my burthen grew lighter. The oppression of the thought that all feeling was dead within me, was gone. I was no longer hopeless: I was not a stock or a stone."[8] Though his father had warned against passionate feelings, and even forbidden them, the cultivation of moral feelings through poetry had been part of Mill's childhood education. Some of the poets Mill read in his early years were Cowper, Campbell, and Shakespeare. Mill found further relief from his crisis through reading Wordsworth and temporarily adopted a theory of life similarly to that of Carlyle. Happiness is no longer the main goal in living, but is obtained incidentally, when striving for a moral goal. His new life-orientation was consistent with his intellectual self-questioning and personal experiences; happiness is not the final reward for reforming the world, but the very important by-product of meaningful living.

In the three volumes of autobiography by Bertrand Russell I found an additional example of the theme of change, continuity, and consistency in self-narration, although it seems questionable to Robert H. Bell that one can recognize continuity and consistency in *The Autobiography of Bertrand Russell*. For example, Bell contrasts Russell's life with that of Augustine's *Confessions* and Newman's *Apologia Pro Vita Sua*, because in Russell's life "the symbolic meaning of particular events and the larger pattern of his whole life are not seen as providential." According to Bell, the *Autobiography* of "this perpetually inquiring skeptic is a very puzzling and cryptic work. . . . Russell's *Autobiography* presents a series of revaluations which remain transient and discontinuous. . . . Russell's Logical Atomism, which may account for (or at least describe) the many formal deficiencies of his *Autobiography*, has far graver implications we might call Psychic Atomism." Yet in spite of psychic atomism and skepticism, Bell recognizes that there remained in Russell "a truly spiritual aspiration." This aspiration is traced through Russell's early autobiographic attempts ("Greek Exercises," "Self-Appreciation," *The Pilgrimage of Life*, and *Prisons*). Bell concludes that "the greatest skeptical sage since Voltaire in striking ways remained the child reared by his Calvinist grandmother and never stopped trying to compose spiritual autobiography."[9]

Russell himself did not lose sight of the threads of continuity and consistency in his life. In "Reflections on My Eightieth Birthday" ("Postscript" in his *Autobiography*), Russell sees his life as consisting of two parts that only in his old age appear as united. The first part of his life, leading up to the First World War, he had dedicated to an intellectual search with the aim of finding out what could be known. The second half of his life he had dedicated to creating a better world. Russell does not state explicitly here what it was that caused him, near the end of his life, to experience a consolidation within his life. I suggest that this new homogeneity came with the sense of victory he felt by looking back at eighty, through describing the matters in which he considered himself to have failed as well as recording other issues in which he perceived he succeeded. I believe that Russell experienced an inner homogeneity and personal realization through having written the *Autobiography*. This consideration might be justified by Bell's observation that Russell possessed an autobiographic inclination since childhood.

The wholeness Russell felt in his life, in spite of the splitting experienced around 1914, can also be understood from the prologue to his *Autobiography* and the life-narrative itself. In the "Prologue" Russell describes his life as characterized by three passions: "the longing for love, the search for knowledge, and unbearable pity for the suffering of mankind." Russell dedicated his *Autobiography* "To Edith," together with the poem he wrote for her. The poem reveals that Russell, at the end of his life, felt that he had found in Edith Finch what he had been looking for in former years. Before his marriage to Edith, Russell had been three times married and divorced, and had several extramarital relationships. Russell ascribes great importance to this last—and lasting—marriage (it was "more important than anything in pulling me through the dark apprehensions and premonitions of these two last decades"), but he does not regard this relationship as the cause of a major change in his life. This was in spite of the way he analyzed his childhood and youth, and the romantic dreams he had about love.

Russell describes as a major element in his childhood and youth a sense of terrible loneliness. At a very young age he had lost his parents, and had been brought up by his pious grandmother, Lady Russell. Russell believed that the sense of ecstasy obtained in love could provide an escape from his loneliness. Though Russell found in his last marriage "ecstasy & peace" and "life & love," I believe that long before 1952 he experienced a different ecstasy, which turned him into a less lonely person. I consider that this happened in his so-called conversion experience of 1901.

In the "Prologue" to his *Autobiography*, Russell indicates that his first passion in life is love, but this topic is not found in the "Postscript." In the "Postscript" one finds an evaluation of how he did fare with the other two passions he mentions in the "Prologue" (i.e., knowledge and compassion).

This evaluation does not indicate what it was that divided Russell's life as it were in two. But from the *Autobiography* one knows that what Russell considered "his change" came toward and during the First World War: "The period from 1910 to 1914 was a time of transition. My life before 1910 and my life after 1914 were as sharply separated as Faust's life before and after he met Mephistopheles. I underwent a process of rejuvenation, inaugurated by Ottoline Morrell and continued by the War." This transformation was the only one that really counted for Russell as important, although one can also trace in the *Autobiography* his awareness to how he moved away from the doctrines of Unitarianism, in which he had been brought up. He believed in this type of fundamentalist Christianity until the age of fifteen. At the age of seventeen he considered that there was no life after death, and in 1903, when he was thirty-one, he wrote "A Free Man's Worship." The first pages of "A Free Man's Worship" contain a dialogue between Mephistopheles and Dr. Faustus. Could it be that the ideas found in this Russell piece were realized by him in his private life only years later? Paul Edwards finds "A Free Man's Worship" the result of "an experience Russell had early in 1901." In the *Autobiography* Russell describes this experience as a sort of mystic illumination, and claims that in five minutes he had become a completely different person. Russell had this conversion experience when staying with the Whitehead family. It occurred when he, together with his first wife Alys, returned after a poetry reading to the Whitehead residence and found Mrs. Whitehead in great agony because of a severe bout of pain.

Through this experience Russell understood that his personal experience of loneliness was actually the share of each human being. I believe that this new knowledge probably reduced much of the dreadfulness of his loneliness. He describes this "conversion" as follows:

> Within five minutes I went through some such reflections as the following: the loneliness of the human soul is unendurable; nothing can penetrate it except the highest intensity of the sort of love that religious teachers have preached; whatever does not spring from this motive is harmful, or at best useless; it follows that war is wrong, that public school education is abominable, that the use of force is to be deprecated, and that in human relations one should penetrate to the core of loneliness in each person and speak to that.[10]

Russell adjusted the credo of materialism he presented in "A Free Man's Worship" somewhat over the years, but in 1927 he wrote, "Fundamentally, my view of man's place in the cosmos remains unchanged."[11] Unlike my interpretation of Russell's Faustian change as the outcome of a slow process of freeing himself of his grandmother's beliefs and a process of realizing the ideas he perceived in his "mystic" experience, Ray Monk assigns to D. H. Lawrence the role of Mephistopheles in Russell's development.[12]

Monk attributes paramount importance to Russell's short-lived friendship with Lawrence, a relationship he analyzes also through interpreting Russell's fictional work. In "Devilish Repressions: Bertrand Russell's Use of Fiction as Autobiography," Monk considers the little-known fictional writings of Russell, particularly "Satan in the Suburbs," as "disguised autobiographical revelations. Indeed, it is perhaps, one of the most revealing pieces of autobiography [i.e., "Satan in the Suburbs"] he ever wrote." Monk finds Russell's *Autobiography* "in many ways, a bleak document, a self-portrait of someone who feels entirely cut off from the people around him."[13] This impression ensues from Russell's confessions of loneliness. The considerable selection of Russell's correspondence with friends and acquaintances that Russell inserted at the end of almost each chapter of his autobiography might also have created in Monk a feeling of discontinuity of the narrative and alienation. Yet these letters, and likewise the inserted section from Russell's juvenile journal, "Greek Exercises," reveal much of Russell's real emotions, his intimate relationships, and his private thoughts.

Monk believes that a singular change in Russell occurred through his contact with Lawrence, with bearings on his self-understanding and human understanding in general. But in his *Autobiography* Russell ascribes changes in his understanding of human nature as one of the effects the war had on him: "I had to revise my views on human nature. At that time I was wholly ignorant of psycho-analysis, but I arrived for myself at a view of human passions not unlike that of the psychoanalysts. I arrived at this view in an endeavor to understand popular feeling about the War." Until then Russell had found a deep understanding of human life in Joseph Conrad's novels, and had also been much impressed with Lawrence's insights in human nature.

During the one year of friendship with Lawrence, Russell discovered a different Lawrence from which he dissociated himself, attributing to him a philosophy that "led straight to Auschwitz. . . . He had a mystical philosophy of 'blood' which I disliked. 'There is,' he said, 'another seat of consciousness than the brain and the nerves. There is a blood-consciousness which exist in us independently of the ordinary mental consciousness.'" Gradually Russell came to feel Lawrence as "a positive force for evil," and Lawrence got to feel the same about him.[14] Yet Monk considers that Lawrence, and Lawrence only, had been able to effectively pierce Russell's shell. To the effect that "being 'in close touch' with Lawrence had been *such* a devastating, destructive experience that Russell could not contemplate repeating it: the only options open to him were eternal isolation, a life lived forever behind the prison walls of his self, or oblivion." Monk contends that in "Satan in the Suburbs" Russell tried to some extent to escape his shell by showing what was under it. It was a shell, according to Monk, that Russell had rebuilt and made stronger "than ever, but the horror of being 'in touch' with another—and the fears that that aroused—never quite left him."[15]

I find it objectionable to view the image of Russell that stands out from the *Autobiography* as illusive and the image of Russell as arrived at through Monk's analysis as true. In "Satan in the Suburbs" Russell is believed to have lent a childhood similar to his own to the story's main character, Dr. Mallako, who Monk nevertheless identifies with Lawrence. The narrator of the story—presumably Russell—becomes as it were possessed by the evil of Mallako, and in the end the narrator is committed to a psychiatric hospital. Whatever kind of depth psychology Monk applies in this analysis, the Russell picture he draws from the so-called fictional autobiography seems to me remote from reality. It seems unrelated to the compassionate and socially engaged person one meets through the pages of Russell's self-narrative.

I am impressed with Russell's self-narrative as a sincere work of self-scrutiny in which he describes not only his emotional and social life but also how philosophy shaped his life and how experiences influenced his thinking. The summaries presented in the autobiography's "Prologue" and "Postscript" reflect precisely the threads of continuity and consistency found in the main narrative of the book.

When considering Wollheim's comparison of autobiographic writing to the working-through process in psychoanalysis and psychotherapeutic sessions, the aspiration to attain a "due influence" of the past over the present (i.e., the restoration of memory to its proper function) is not evident in the autobiographies of Augustine, Rousseau, and Sartre. Likewise neither Mill, Kierkegaard, nor Russell felt coerced to more or less repeat what they had experienced or had been taught as children. The purpose in writing these life stories seems to have been different.

Each of these philosophers remembered his childhood and recognized influences of that childhood on his life, but by philosophizing each transformed or even eradicated the influences of the past over the present. In some psychological treatments, rebiographing is used to help patients to interpret their pasts in a different manner by letting them write, for example, narratives of their pasts that interpret matters in a novel way. In the autobiographies discussed here none of the authors intended to interpret the past differently from his own experience of it, or to reinterpret historical evidence. However, what these philosophers share with therapeutic rebiographers is that narrating the life story is experienced as advantageous for themselves or for others.

Both Augustine and Sartre claimed to have made pristine beginnings in their lives as adults, while Rousseau encountered deep changes within himself. Whereas Nietzsche would have considered Augustine's and Sartre's radical new starts as a "poetics of life" appropriate to those who are the poets of their own lives, the Existentialist philosopher–theologian Paul Tillich finds that there are limits to such poetics. He finds that persons need courage for self-affirmation in the face of "finite-freedom." Tillich recognizes an Existential dimension in philosophers such as Augustine, Sartre, and Hegel. However, Tillich finds self-elevation "above the universal process" characteristic of situations is understood as a revolt and a nonexistential interpretation of life: "The latter asserts that man is able to transcend, in knowledge and life, the finitude, the estrangement and the ambiguities of human existence."[16]

Augustine's "revolt" was articulated through his three senses of the past: the past past, the past present, and the past future. These three pasts are not the same; the past present and the past future acquire their meaning and influence from the present and the future (i.e., the present and the future have an influence over the past and imbue it with meaning, not vice versa).

Although Rousseau acknowledged two lasting influences from his childhood as troublesome, even these influences (i.e., the influence of the Romantic novels he read and of his tutor) seem to have been under his control to a personally satisfactory extent through his development of a moral sense and ethical conduct. Rousseau also discovered that in harmony with nature he could attain a different self, his true self.

A traditional psychoanalyst would likely maintain that Augustine, Rousseau, and Sartre established a fallacious consistency with their real selves because a lack of influence of the past over the present, a lack of psychologistic continuity.

Whereas I view consistency as homogeneity in being, in work, and in life, these philosophers, although they appear to transcend the influences of their pasts, nevertheless actually established a consistency with their real selves—that is, the self as they philosophically conceived it. Why must we necessarily accept a Freudian psychoanalytic definition of the self as a universal real self, particularly since scientific evidence for such a universal self seems to be absent?

Augustine's, Rousseau's, and Sartre's in-depth understanding of themselves is in no way inferior to Freudian psychoanalytical understandings. Unlike the Freudian way of attaining continuity, these philosophers did not describe continuity in their lives as a repetition of events (psychoanalytic transference), or as the due influence of events from their childhoods over the present. Nevertheless, events in each of these lives correlate from an intellectual perspective.

Radical changes in the lives are connected with earlier events by a rational interpretation of how these changes occurred. In most instances changes were induced by the application of the philosophers' concepts on how to live. From Freud's and Wollheim's psychoanalytic view the lives of these philosophers may lack continuity, but from a literary, historical, philosophical, and subjective standpoint there is a clear thread of continuity in the writings and lives of Augustine, Rousseau, Sartre, Kierkegaard, Mill, Russell, and other autobiographies discussed in Chapter 2.

Based on the criteria of slavish versus free intellectual activity, and of consistency and continuity, I have tried to demonstrate that philosophical psychoanalysis indeed contributes in a positive sense to constituting and understanding the lives described in philosophical autobiographies. Philosophy and its practice implied consistency and continuity in the lives of the philosophers discussed in this book. Philosophical self-analysis was experienced by these philosophers as making life worthwhile, or was a way of self-expression leading to self-transcendence, wholeness, well-being, comfort, self-justification, vindication, completion, self-realization, self-knowledge, and the like.

Though some Existentialists, like Tillich, may reject the integrity of Augustine's and Sartre's self-transcendence, Tillich and most Existentialists, Pragmatists, Rationalists, Classicists, and other theorists will affirm the great value of philosophy and philosophical psychoanalysis for constituting the self and human well-being.

The bottom line of this study is therefore this: Philosophy was advantageous to the philosophers examined in this qualitative research, and it is likely to be advantageous to many other people as well. However, to grasp this one needs to consider these lives within a philosophical psychoanalytic approach that illuminates patterns of philosophical activity.

In addition, it might be right to conclude that when philosophers and others analyze and write down their philosophical development in the context of their lived experience they might become aware, or more aware, that they changed much, that they became as if different selves. By reflecting on such changes life may receive a new meaning; life itself may become as new.

This seems an encouraging and appropriate concluding word, yet I would like to pose some enduring questions. Is it necessary to recollect one's past and to make through reflections on it new beginnings possible? Is it necessary to look back and by doing so possibly attain more self-knowledge and wisdom in living? Or is wisdom found in putting one's hand to the plow and by refraining from looking back? Or, as Oscar Wilde's life seems to suggest, forget the tortured past in the joy of ecstasy. Or why not consider the words of wisdom Gide lends to Ménalque: "Every joy is like the manna of the desert which corrupts from one day to the next; it is like the fountain of Ameles, whose water, says Plato, could never be kept in any vase. . . . Let every moment carry away with it all that it brought."[17] These questions I leave open-ended, since I believe that there might be a different wisdom for each person and each time.

NOTES

1. Mircea Eliade, *Rites and Symbols of Initiations: The Mysteries of Birth and Rebirth* (New York: Harper and Row, 1958).

2. Carl G. Jung, *Man and His Symbols* (New York: Dell, 1964), 61, 99–100, 124–125.

3. Ronald D. Laing, *The Politics of Experience* (New York: Ballatine Books, 1974), 139, 144–145. For accounts of Laing's activities in rebirthing, see Adrian Laing, *R. D. Laing: A Biography* (New York: Thunder's Mouth Press, 1996), Peter Walker, "Ronnie Laing and Rebirthing," *The Healing Breath: A Journal of Breathwork Practice, Psychology and Spirituality*, available at: <http://www.i-breathe.com/thb31/new_page_5.htm> (last accessed June 2002), and Joy Manne, "R. D. Laing: A Biography," *The Healing Breath: A Journal of Breathwork Practice, Psychology and Spirituality*, available at: <http://www.i-breathe.com/thb31/new_page_6.htm> (last accessed May 2001).

4. Ira Progoff, *Life-Study: Experiencing Creative Lives by the Intensive Journal Method* (New York: Dialogue House Library, 1983), 23, 37, 93. See also <http://www.intensivejournal.org> (last accessed June 2002).

5. John Sturrock, *The Language of Autobiography* (Cambridge: Cambridge University Press, 1993), 290.

6. Søren Kierkegaard, *The Diary of Søren Kierkegaard*, ed. P. P. Rohde (New York: Citadel Press, 1990), 61, 62, 139, 137, 31, 33.

7. John Stuart Mill, *Essential Works of John Stuart Mill*, ed. and intro. M. Lerner (New York: Bantam Books, 1961), xiii.

8. Ibid., 27, 83, 84, 87, 123.

9. Robert H. Bell, "Confession and Concealment in *The Autobiography of Bertrand Russell*," *Biography* 8, 4 (1985): 318, 319, 332.

10. Bertrand Russell, *Autobiography* (London: Unwin, 1989), 557, 9, 238, 149.

11. Bertrand Russell, *Why I Am Not a Christian*, ed. and intro. P. Edwards (New York: Simon and Schuster, 1957), 104.

12. Ray Monk, "Devilish Repressions: Bertrand Russell's Use of Fiction as Autobiography," in *Writing the Lives of Writers*, ed. W. Gould and T. F. Staley (London: Macmillan, 1998), 253.

13. Ibid., 241, 246.

14. Bertrand Russell, *Autobiography*, 240, 245, 243, 245.

15. Ray Monk, "Devilish Repressions: Bertrand Russell's Use of Fiction as Autobiography," 255, 257.

16. Paul Tillich, *The Courage to Be* (New Haven, Conn.: Yale University Press, 1952), 125.

17. André Gide, *The Immoralist* (New York: Vintage Books, 1956), 96.

Bibliography

Abélard, Peter. *The Story of Abélard's Adversities*. Translated by J. T. Muckle. Toronto: Pontifical Institute of Medieval Studies, 1964.

Achenbach, Gerd B. *Philosophische Praxis*. Cologne: Jürgen Dinter, 1984.

Achenbach, Gerd B., and Thomas Macho. *Das Prinzip Heilung*. Cologne: Jürgen Dinter, 1985.

Alighieri, Dante. *The Divine Comedy*. Translated by C. H. Sisson, introduced by D. H. Higgins. Oxford: Oxford University Press, 1998.

———. *Vita Nuova*. Translated and introduced by M. Musa. Oxford: Oxford University Press, 1999.

Almond, Brenda. "Philosophy and the Cult of Irrationalism." In *The Impulse to Philosophise*, edited by A. Phillips Griffiths, 201–217. Cambridge: Cambridge University Press, 1992.

Aronson, Ronald. "Sartre's Last Words." In Jean-Paul Sartre and Benny Lévy, *Hope Now*. Translated by A. van den Hoven, 3–40. Chicago: University of Chicago Press, 1996.

Ashworth, Peter D., Amedeo Giorgi, and André J. J. de Koning, eds. *Qualitative Research in Psychology*. Pittsburgh, Pa.: Duquesne University Press, 1986.

Augustine. *Answer to Skeptics*. Introduced by D. J. Kavanagh. New York: Cima, 1948.

———. *The City of God*. Vol. 1. Edited by R.V.G. Tasker. London: Dent and Sons, 1950.

———. *The Confessions*. Vols. 1 and 2. Translated by W. Watts. Cambridge: Harvard University Press, 1950.

———. *The Happy Life*. Introduced by L. Schopp. New York: Cima, 1948.

———. *The Lord's Sermon on the Mount*. Translated by J. J. Jepson. New York: Newman Press, 1948.

———. *The Retractations*. Translated by M. S. Bogan. Washington, D.C.: Catholic University of America Press, 1947.

Aurelius, Marcus. *The Essential Works of Stoicism*. New York: Bantam, 1965.

Baggini, Julian. "The Biographers: Can We Learn Anything Important from the Biographies of the Great Philosophers?" *The Philosophers' Magazine* 7 (1999): 14–15.

Baiton, Roland H. *The Reformation and the Sixteenth Century*. Boston: Beacon Press, 1956.

Banner, Lois W. "Biography and Autobiography: Intermixing the Genres." *a/b: Auto/Biography Studies* 8, 2 (1993): 159–178.

Barnes, Hazel E. "Beauvoir and Sartre: The Forms of Farewell." *Philosophy and Literature* 9 (1985): 21–40.

———. "Humanistic Existentialism and Contemporary Psychoanalysis." In *Sartre: A Collection of Critical Essays*, edited by E. Kern, 149–160. Englewood Cliffs, N.J.: Prentice Hall, 1962.

———. *Sartre*. London: Quartet Books, 1974.

———. "Sartre's Scenario for Freud." *L'Esprit Createur*, special edition, *Writing Lives: Sartre, Beauvoir and (Auto)Biography* 29 (1989): 52–64.

———. *The Story I Tell Myself: A Venture in Existential Autobiography*. Chicago: University of Chicago Press, 1997.

———. "Who Is the Subject of Autobiography." *Sartre Studies International* 4, 2 (1998): 19–33.

Beauvoir, Simone de. *Adieux: A Farewell to Sartre*. London: Penguin, 1988.

———. "Conversations with Jean-Paul Sartre." In *Adieux: A Farewell to Sartre*, 129–445. London: Penguin, 1988.

Bell, Robert H. "Confession and Concealment in *The Autobiography of Bertrand Russell*." *Biography* 8, 4 (1985): 318–335.

———. "Rousseau: The Prophet of Sincerity." *Biography* 3, 4 (1980): 297–313.

Bernstein, Richard J. *Philosophical Profiles: Essays in a Pragmatic Mode*. Cambridge: Polity Press, 1986.

Boethius. *The Consolation of Philosophy*. Oxford: Oxford University Press, 2000.

Bonner, Gerald. "Pelagianism and Augustine." *Augustinian Studies* 23 (1992): 33–51.

Brockmeier, Jens. "Autobiography, Narrative, and the Freudian Concept of Life History." *Philosophy, Psychiatry & Psychology* 4, 3 (1997): 175–199.

Brockwell, Charles W., Jr. "Augustine's Ideal of Monastic Community: A Paradigm for His Doctrine of the Church." *Augustinian Studies* 8 (1977): 91–109.

Brown, Peter. *Augustine of Hippo*. London: Faber and Faber, 1967.

Bubacz, Bruce S. "Augustine's Illumination Theory and Epistemic Structuring." *Augustinian Studies* 11 (1980): 35–48.

Bubner, Rüdiger. *Modern German Philosophy*. Cambridge: Cambridge University Press, 1981.

Burnaby, John. *Augustine: Later Works*. Philadelphia, Pa.: Westminster Press, 1955.

———. "The 'Retractationes' of Saint Augustine: Self-Criticism or Apologia?" *Augustinus Magister* 1 (1954): 86–92.

Burr, Anna Robeson. *The Autobiography*. Boston: Cambridge University Press, 1909.

Burtt, E. A. "My Path to Philosophy." *Philosophy East and West* 22 (1972): 429–440.

Cannon, Betty. *Sartre and Psychoanalysis: An Existentialist Challenge to Clinical Metatheory*. Lawrence: University of Kansas Press, 1991.

Cavadini, John C. "The Structure and Intention of Augustine's *De trinitate*." *Augustinian Studies* 23 (1992): 103–123.

Cavell, Marcia. "Keeping Time." In *The Analytic Freud: Philosophy and Psychoanalysis*, edited by Michael P. Levine, 85–100. London: Routledge, 2000.

———. *The Psychoanalytic Mind: From Freud to Philosophy*. Cambridge: Harvard University Press, 1993.

Champigny, Robert. "Sartre on Sartre." In *The Philosophy of Jean-Paul Sartre*, edited by P. A. Schilpp, 86–111. La Salle, Ill.: Open Court, 1981.

Charmé, Stuart L. *Meaning and Myth in the Study of Lives: A Sartrean Perspective*. Philadelphia: University of Pennsylvania Press, 1984.

Cohen-Solal, Annie. *Sartre: A Life*. London: Minerva, 1991.

Coleman, Janet. *Ancient and Medieval Memories: Studies in Reconstruction of the Past*. Cambridge: Cambridge University Press, 1992.

Collingwood, R. G. *An Autobiography*. London: Oxford University Press, 1939.

Collins, Margery L., and Christine Pierce. "Holes and Slime: Sexism in Sartre's Psychoanalysis." *The Philosophical Forum* 5 (1975): 112–127.

Contat, Michel, and Michel Rybalka. *The Writings of Jean-Paul Sartre: A Bibliographical Life*. Vol. 1. Evanston, Ill.: Northwestern University Press, 1974.

Cooper, John. "Why Did Augustine Write Books XI–XIII of *The Confessions*?" *Augustinian Studies* 2 (1971): 37–46.

Cooper, Robin, ed. *Thresholds between Philosophy and Psychoanalysis*. London: Free Association Books, 1989.

Cottingham, John. *Philosophy and the Good Life: Reason and the Passions in Greek, Cartesian and Psychoanalytic Ethics*. Cambridge: Cambridge University Press, 1998.

Cranston, Maurice W. *The Noble Savage*. London: Penguin Press, 1991.

Crouse, Robert D. "*In Multa Defluximus: Confessions* X, 29–43, and St. Augustine's Theory of Personality." In *Neoplatonism and Early Christian Thought*, edited by H. J. Blumenthal and R. A. Markus, 181–185. London: Variorum, 1981.

———. "*Recurrens In te unum:* The Pattern of St. Augustine's *Confessions*." *Studia Patristica* 14 (1976): 389–392.

Davis, Michael. *The Autobiography of Philosophy: Rousseau's The Reveries of the Solitary Walker*. Lanham, Md.: Rowan and Littlefield, 1999.

Dent, N.J.H. *A Rousseau Dictionary*. Oxford: Blackwell, 1992.

Derrida, Jacques. *The Ear of the Other: Otobiography, Transference, Translation*. Translated by Peggy Kamuf, edited by Christie V. McDonald. New York: Schocken Books, 1985.

———. *Memoires for Paul de Man*. New York: Columbia University Press, 1986.

Desautels, Alfred R. "The Sartre of Stalag 12D (1940–1941)." *The French Review* 55 (1981): 201–206.

Di Berardino, Angelo. *Patrology*. Vol. 4. Westminster: Christian Classics, 1986.

Dilman, Ilham. "Can Philosophy Speak about Life?" In *The Impulse to Philosophise*, edited by A. Phillips Griffiths, 109–123. Cambridge: Cambridge University Press, 1992.

Dilthey, Wilhelm. *Selected Writings*. Cambridge: Cambridge University Press, 1976.

Donoso, Anton. "Philosophy as Autobiography: A Study of the Person of Miguel de Unamuno." *Personalist* 49 (1968): 183–196.

Duby, George, and Michelle Perrot, eds. *A History of Women in the West*. Vols. 1–5. Cambridge: Harvard University Press, 1992–1994.

Elbaz, Robert. *The Changing Nature of the Self: A Critical Study of the Autobiographic Discourse*. London: Croom Helm, 1988.

Eliade, Mircea. *Rites and Symbols of Initiations: The Mysteries of Birth and Rebirth*. New York: Harper and Row, 1958.

Erasmus, Desiderius. *The Correspondence of Erasmus*. Vol. 4 of *The Collected Works of Erasmus*. Translated by R.A.B. Mynors and D.F.S. Thomson. Toronto: University of Toronto Press, 1977.

Fahnestock, Lee, and Norman MacAfee. "Introduction." In *Quiet Moments in a War: The Letters of J. P. Sartre to Simone de Beauvoir 1940–1963*, edited by Simone de Beauvoir, ix–xi. New York: Macmillan, 1993.

Ferrari, Leo C. "The 'Food of Truth' in Augustine's *Confessions*." *Augustinian Studies* 9 (1978): 1–14.

Fleteren, Frederick van. "Per Speculum et Aenigmate: The Use of I Corinthians 13, 12 in the Writings of Augustine." *Augustinian Studies* 23 (1992): 69–102.

Fowlie, Wallace. "Introduction." In J. P. Sartre, *What Is Literature*, vi–xvi. New York: Harper and Row, 1965.

Freadman, Richard. *Threads of Life: Autobiography and the Will*. Chicago: University of Chicago Press, 2001.

Freud, Sigmund. *The History of the Psychoanalytic Movement*. New York: Colliers Books, 1963.

———. *The Interpretation of Dreams*. New York: Modern Library, 1950.

Fullbrook, Kate, and Edward Fullbrook. *Simone de Beauvoir and Jean-Paul Sartre*. New York: Harvester Wheatsheaf, 1993.

Gibran, Kahlil. *A Self-Portrait*. Translated and introduced by A. R. Ferkis. London: Heineman, 1972.

Gide, André. *The Immoralist*. New York: Vintage Books, 1956.

———. *The Journals of André Gide*. Vol. 1. New York: Vintage Books, 1959.

Gilmore, Allen A. "Augustine and the Critical Method." *Harvard Theological Review* 39 (1946): 141–163.

Gilson, Etienne. *The Christian Philosophy of Saint Augustine*. London: Gollancz, 1961.

Gordon, Rivca, and Haim Gordon. "Sartre's Autobiography and His Early Philosophy." *Journal of the British Society for Phenomenology* 23 (1992): 66–75.

Green, Frederick C. *Jean-Jacques Rousseau: A Critical Study of His Life and Writings*. Cambridge: Cambridge University Press, 1955.

Grimsley, Ronald. *Jean-Jacques Rousseau: A Study in Self-Awareness*. Cardif: University of Wales Press, 1968.

———. *Rousseau and the Religious Quest*. Oxford: Clarendon Press, 1968.

Gutman, Huck. "Rousseau's Confessions: A Technology of the Self." In *Technologies of the Self*, edited by L. H. Martin, H. Gutman, and P. Hutton, 99–121. Amherst: University of Massachusetts Press, 1988.

Halliburton, R. J. "The Inclination to Retirement: The Retreat of Cassiciacum and the 'Monastery' of Tagaste." *Studia Patristica* 5, 80 (1962): 329–340.

Hartle, Ann. *The Modern Self in Rousseau's Confessions: A Reply to St. Augustine*. Notre Dame: University of Notre Dame Press, 1983.

Hartman, Geoffrey H. *Easy Pieces*. New York: Columbia University Press, 1988.

Heil, J. "Augustine's Attack on Skepticism: The *Contra Academicos*." *Harvard Theological Review* 65 (1972): 99–116.

Hochland, Janine. "Incest: A Theme in Sartre's Literary Work." *Journal of the British Society for Phenomenology* 2 (1970): 93–99.

Home, Charles F., ed. *The Sacred Books and Early Literature of the East*. Vol. 6. New York: Parke, Austin, and Lipscomb, 1917.

Horton, John, and Susan Mendus, eds. *After MacIntyre: Critical Perspectives on the Work of Alasdair MacIntyre*. Oxford: Polity Press, 1994.

Howells, Christina. "Sartre and Freud." *French Studies* 33 (1979): 157–176.

Hume, David. "My Own Life." In *Essays: Moral, Political, and Literary*, 1–8. London: Longmans and Green, 1889.

Irwin, Robert. "I Am a False Alarm." *London Review of Books Online*, September 3, 1998. Available at: <http://www.lrb.co.uk/v20nl7/irwi2017.htm> (last accessed January 2001).

Jackson, Susan K. "Claiming the Patent on Autobiographical Fiction." In *Reading La Nouvelle Héloïse Today, Pensée libre* 4, edited by O. Mostefai, 199–210. Ottawa: North American Association for the Study of Jean-Jacques Rousseau, 1993.

Jaspers, Karl. *Plato and Augustine*. New York: Harcourt, Brace, and World, 1957.

Jess, Wilma Gundersdorf von. "Augustine at Ostia: A Disputed Question." *Augustinian Studies* 3 (1973): 159–174.

Johnson, Donovan. "Story and Design in Book Eight of Augustine's *Confessions*." *Biography* 14, 1 (1991): 39–60.

Jolly, Margaretta, ed. *Encyclopedia of Life Writing*. London: Fitzroy Dearborn, 2001.

Jones, Ernest. *The Life and Work of Sigmund Freud*. Harmondsworth: Penguin Books, 1957.

Judt, Tony. "You Say You Had a Revolution." *Tikkun: A Bimonthly Jewish Critique of Politics, Culture and Society* 4 (1989): 115–117.

Jung, Carl G. *Man and His Symbols*. New York: Dell, 1964.

Kanfer, Stefan. "But Is It Not Strange That Elephants Will Yield—and That *The Prophet* Is Still Popular?" *New York Times on the Web*, June 25, 1972. Available at: <http://www.nytimes.corn/books/98/12/13/specials/gibran-elephants.html> (last accessed January 2001).

Kaufman, Peter I. "The Lesson of Conversion: A Note on the Question of Continuity in Augustine's Understanding of Grace and Human Will." *Augustinian Studies* 11 (1980): 49–64.

Kavanagh, Thomas M. *Writing the Truth: Authority and Desire in Rousseau*. London: University of California Press, 1987.

Kelly, Christopher. *Rousseau's Exemplary Life: The "Confessions" as Political Philosophy*. London: Cornell University Press, 1987.

Kennedy, Emmet. *A Cultural History of the French Revolution*. New Haven: Yale University Press, 1989.

Kierkegaard, Søren. *The Diary of Søren Kierkegaard.* Edited by P. P. Rohde. New York: Citadel Press, 1990.

Kirsner, Douglas. *The Schizoid World of Jean-Paul Sartre and R. D. Laing.* St. Lucia: University of Queenland Press, 1976.

Kirwan, Christopher. *Augustine.* London: Routledge, 1989.

Kligerman, Charles. "A Psychoanalytic Study of The *Confessions* of St. Augustine." *Journal of the American Psychoanalytic Association* 5 (1957): 469–484.

Kvale, Steinar. "Psychoanalytic Therapy as Qualitative Research." In *Qualitative Research in Psychology,* edited by Peter D. Ashworth, Amedeo Giorgi, and Andre J. J. de Koning, 155–183. Pittsburgh, Pa.: Duquesne University Press, 1986.

Lafrance, Guy. "L'Éthique de *La Nouvelle Héloïse* et du Vicaire Savoyard." In *Reading La Nouvelle Héloïse Today, Pensée libre* 4, edited by O. Mostefai, 141–150. Ottawa: North American Association for the Study of Jean-Jacques Rousseau, 1993.

Laing, Adrian. *R. D. Laing: A Biography.* New York: Thunder's Mouth Press, 1996.

Laing, Ronald D. *The Politics of Experience.* New York: Ballatine Books, 1974.

———. *The Politics of the Family and Other Essays.* New York: Vintage Books, 1972.

Laing, Ronald D., and David G. Cooper. *Reason and Violence.* New York: Pantheon, 1971.

Leak, Andrew N. *The Perverted Consciousness: Sexuality and Sartre.* London: Macmillan, 1989.

Lear, Jonathan. *Happiness, Death, and the Remainder of Life.* Cambridge: Harvard University Press, 2000.

———. *Love and Its Place in Nature: A Philosophical Interpretation of Freudian Psychoanalyses.* New Haven, Conn.: Yale University Press, 1998.

———. *Open Minded: Working Out the Logic of the Soul.* Cambridge: Harvard University Press, 1998.

Levine, Michael P., ed. *The Analytic Freud: Philosophy and Psychoanalysis.* London: Routledge, 2000.

Lloyd, Genevieve. "The Self as Fiction: Philosophy and Autobiography." *Philosophy and Literature* 10 (1987): 168–185.

Loureiro, Angel G. *The Ethics of Autobiography: Replacing the Subject in Modern Spain.* Nashville, Tenn.: Vanderbilt University Press, 1999.

MacIntyre, Alasdair C. *After Virtue: A Study in Moral Theory.* London: Duckworth, 1981.

———. *Dependent Rational Animals: Why Human Beings Need the Virtues.* La Salle, Ill.: Open Court, 1999.

———. *Marxism and Christianity.* Middlesex: Penguin Books, 1971.

———. *The Unconscious: A Conceptual Analysis.* London: Routledge and Kegan, 1962.

Madden, Edward H., and Marian C. Madden. "Philosophical Biography: The American Scene." *Transactions of the Charles S. Pierce Society: A Quarterly Journal in American Philosophy* 28 (1992): 609–643.

Magees, Bryan. *Confessions of a Philosopher: A Personal Journey through Western Philosophy from Plato to Popper.* New York: Modern Library, 1999.

Man, Paul de. *The Rhetoric of Romanticism*. New York: Columbia University Press, 1984.

Manville, Brook. "Donatism and St. Augustine: The Confessions of a Fourth Century Bishop." *Augustinian Studies* 8 (1977): 125–137.

Markus, Robert Austin. *Saeculum: History and Society in the Theology of St. Augustine*. Cambridge: Cambridge University Press, 1970.

Masson, Jeffrey. *The Assault on Truth: Freud's Suppression of the Seduction Theory*. New York: Farrar, Straus and Giroux, 1984.

Maykut, Pamela, and Richard Morehouse. *Beginning Qualitative Research: A Philosophic and Practical Guide*. London: Falmer Press, 1999.

Mehlman, Jeffrey. *A Structural Study of Autobiography: Proust, Leiris, Sartre, Levi-Strauss*. London: Cornell University Press, 1974.

Mill, John Stuart. *Essential Works of John Stuart Mill*, edited and introduced by M. Lerner. New York: Bantam Books, 1961.

Mirvish, Adrian. "Sartre, Reciprocity, Sexuality and Solipsism." *Journal of the British Society for Phenomenology* 25 (1994): 139–156.

Misch, Georg. *A History of Autobiography in Antiquity*. Vols. 1–2. London: Routledge, 1949–1950.

Moi, Toril. *Simone Beauvoir: The Making of an Intellectual Woman*. Oxford: Blackwell, 1994.

Monk, Ray. "Devilish Repressions: Bertrand Russell's Use of Fiction as Autobiography." In *Writing the Lives of Writers*, edited by W. Gould and T. F. Staley, 239–265. London: Macmillan, 1998.

Morgenstern, Mila. "Rousseau for the Twentieth Century: New Interpretations of the Family." In *Reading La Nouvelle Héloïse Today, Pensée libre* 4, edited by O. Mostefai, 223–235. Ottawa: North American Association for the Study of Jean-Jacques Rousseau, 1993.

Mourant, John A. "Augustine and the Academics." *Recherches Augustiniennes* 4 (1966): 67–96.

———. "The Emergence of a Christian Philosophy in the Dialogues of Augustine." *Augustinian Studies* 1 (1970): 69–88.

Mulhall, Stephen. *Stanley Cavell: Philosophy's Recounting of the Ordinary*. Oxford: Clarendon Press, 1998.

Munteano, Basil. *Solitude et Contradictions de Jean-Jacques Rousseau*. Paris: Nizet, 1975.

Murdoch, Iris. *Sartre: Romantic Rationalist*. London: Penguin, 1989.

Newman, John Henry Cardinal. *Apologia Pro Vita Sua*. New York: Doubleday, 1956.

Niño, Andrés G. "Restoration of the Self: A Therapeutic Paradigm from Augustine's *Confessions*." *Psychotherapy* 27, 1 (1990): 8–18.

O'Connell, Robert J. *The Origin of the Soul in St. Augustine's Later Works*. New York: Fordham University Press, 1987.

O'Donnell, James J. *Augustine Confessions*. Vol. 1. Oxford: Clarendon Press, 1992.

———. *Three Studies in Augustinian Biography*. Internet publication, 1999. Available at: <http://ccat.sas.upenn.edu/jod/> (last accessed August 2000).

O'Meara, John J. "Augustine and Neo-Platonism." *Recherches Augustiennes* 1 (1958): 91–103.

———. *Charter of Christendom: The Significance of the City of God.* New York: Macmillan, 1961.

———. "Introduction." In *St. Augustine: Against the Academics; Ancient Christian Writers,* edited by J. Quasten and J. Plumpe, 3–33. Westminster, Md.: Newman Press, 1950.

———. *The Young Augustine.* Suffolk: Chaucer Press, 1980.

Pelikan, Jaroslav J. *The Mystery of Continuity, Time and History, Memory and Eternity in the Thought of Saint Augustine.* Charlottesville: University Press of Virginia, 1986.

Plato. *Epistles.* Translated by R. G. Bury. Loeb Classical Library. Vol. 9. London: Heinemann, 1929.

Popkin, R. H., Olaso, Ezequiel de, and G. Tonelli, eds. *Skepticism in the Enlightenment.* Dordrecht: Kluwer Academic, 1997.

Progoff, Ira. *Life-Study: Experiencing Creative Lives by the Intensive Journal Method.* New York: Dialogue House Library, 1983.

Rainsford, Dominic, and Tim Woods, eds. *Critical Ethics: Texts, Theory and Responsibility.* New York: St. Martin's Press, 1999.

Reardon, B.M.G. "The Relation of Philosophy to Faith in the Teaching of St. Augustine." *Studia Patristica* 2, 64 (1957): 288–294.

Ricoeur, Paul. "Narrative Identity." In *On Paul Ricoeur: Narrative and Interpretation,* edited by D. Wood, 188–199. London: Routledge, 1991.

Rorty, Amélie Oksenberg. "Rousseau's Therapeutic Experiments." *Philosophy* 66 (1991): 413–434.

———. "Witnessing Philosophers." *Philosophy and Literature* 22, 2 (1998): 309–327.

Rosenthal, Abigail L. *Conversions: A Philosophic Memoir.* Philadelphia, Pa.: Temple University Press, 1994.

Rousseau, Jean-Jacques. *The Confessions of Jean-Jacques Rousseau.* New York: Modern Library, 1945.

———. *The Collected Writings of Rousseau.* Vol. 1, edited by R. D. Masters and C. Kelly. London: University Press of New England, 1990.

———. *The Collected Writings of Rousseau.* Vol. 2, edited by R. D. Masters and C. Kelly. London: University Press of New England, 1992.

———. *Émile.* Translated by B. Foxley. London: Everyman's Library, 1974.

———. *Reveries of the Solitary Walker.* Translated by P. France. London: Penguin, 1979.

Russell, Bertrand. *Autobiography.* London: Unwin, 1989.

———. *Why I Am Not a Christian.* Edited and introduced by P. Edwards. New York: Simon and Schuster, 1957.

Russell, Robert. "The Role of Neoplatonism in St. Augustine's *De Civitate Dei.*" In *Neoplatonism and Early Christian Thought,* edited by H. J. Blumenthal and R. A. Markus, 160–179. London: Variorum, 1981.

Salinas, Oscar. "The Psychological Roots of Augustine's Theories of Good and Evil." *Biography* 15, 4 (1992): 348–370.

Sarbin, Theodore R. "Steps to the Narratory Principle: An Autobiographical Essay." In *Life and Story: Autobiographies for a Narrative Psychology,* edited by D. J. Lee, 7–38. Westport, Conn.: Praeger, 1994.

Sartre, Jean-Paul. *Anti-Semite and Jew.* New York: Grove Press, 1948.

———. *Being and Nothingness*. New York: Washington Square Press, 1966.
———. *Between Existentialism and Marxism*. New York: Pantheon, 1975.
———. *The Family Idiot*. Vol. 2. Chicago: University of Chicago Press, 1987.
———. *The Freud Scenario*. Chicago: University of Chicago Press, 1985.
———. *Life/Situations*. New York: Pantheon, 1977.
———. *Quiet Moments in a War: The Letters of J. P. Sartre to Simone de Beauvoir 1940–1963*. New York: Macmillan, 1993.
———. *Saint Genet: Actor and Martyr*. New York: Mentor Books, 1963.
———. *Situations*. New York: Fawcett, 1965.
———. *War Diaries: Notebooks from a Phoney War, November 1939–March 1940*. Translated by Q. Hoare. London: Verso, 1984.
———. *What Is Literature*. New York: Harper and Row, 1965.
———. *Witness to My Life: The Letters of J. P. Sartre to Simone de Beauvoir 1926–1939*. New York: Macmillan, 1992.
———. *The Words*. New York: George Braziller, 1964.
Sayre, Robert F. *The Examined Self: Benjamin Franklin, Henry James, Henry Adams*. Madison: University of Wisconsin Press, 1988.
Schafer, Roy. *Retelling a Life: Narration and Dialogue in Psychoanalysis*. New York: Basic Books, 1992.
Schaff, Phillip, ed. *A Select Library of Nicene and Post-Nicene Fathers of the Christian Church*. Vol. 3. Edinburgh: T. and T. Clark, 1988.
Scharfstein, Ben-Ami. *The Philosophers: Their Lives and the Nature of Their Thought*. New York: Oxford University Press, 1980.
Schillinger, Liesl. "Pioner of the New Age." *New York Times on the Web*, December 13, 1998. Available at: <http://www.nytimes.corn/books/98/12/13/reviews/981213.13sch.illt.html> (last accessed January 2001).
Schilpp, Paul A. *Reminiscing: Autobiographical Notes*. Carbondale: Southern Illinois University Press, 1995.
Schilpp, Paul A., ed. *The Philosophy of Karl Jaspers*. New York: Tudor, 1957.
Scholem, Gershom. *Kabbalah*. Jerusalem: Keter, 1974.
Schurman, Anna Maria van. *Eucleria, of uitkiezing van Het Beste Deel*. Introduced by S. van der Linde. Leeuwarden: De Tille, 1978.
Schuster, Shlomit C. "Everybody's Philosophical Counselling." *The Philosophers' Magazine* 3 (1998): 44–45.
———. "On Philosophical Self-Diagnosis and Self-Help: A Clarification of the Non-Clinical Practice of Philosophical Counseling." *International Journal of Applied Philosophy* 12, 1 (1998): 37–50.
———. "Philosophical Autobiography." In *Encyclopedia of Life Writing*, edited by M. Jolly, 706–707. London: Fitzroy Dearborn, 2001.
———. "Philosophical Counselling." *Journal of Applied Philosophy* 8, 2 (1991): 219–223.
———. "Philosophical Counseling and Humanistic Psychotherapy." *Journal of Psychology and Judaism* 20, 3 (1996): 247–259.
———. "Philosophical Narratives and Philosophical Counselling." *Journal of the Society for Existential Analysis* 8, 2 (1997): 108–127.
———. "Philosophy as If It Matters: The Practice of Philosophical Counseling." *Critical Review* 6, 4 (1992): 587–599.

———. *Philosophy Practice: An Alternative to Counseling and Psychotherapy*. Westport, Conn.: Praeger, 1999.

———. "The Practice of Sartre's Philosophy in Philosophical Counseling and in Existential Psychotherapy." *Iyyun: The Jerusalem Philosophical Quarterly* 44, 1 (1995): 99–114.

———. "Report on Applying Philosophy in Philosophical Counseling." *International Journal of Applied Philosophy* 9, 2 (1995): 51–55.

———. "Revisiting *Hope Now* with Benny Lévy: A Note on the 1996 English Edition of *Hope Now*." *Sartre Studies International* 4, 1 (1998): 63–75.

———. "Sartre's Freud and the Future of Sartrean Psychoanalysis." *Israel Journal of Psychiatry* 35, 1 (1998): 20–30.

———. "Sartre's 'Words' as a Paradigm for Self-Description in Philosophical Counseling." In *Perspectives in Philosophical Practice*, edited by W. van der Vlist, 20–34. Doorwerth: Dutch Society for Philosophy Practice, 1997.

Schwartz, Joel. *The Sexual Politics of Jean-Jacques Rousseau*. Chicago: University of Chicago Press, 1984.

Sheridan, Alan. *André Gide: A Life in the Present*. Cambridge: Harvard University press, 1999.

Silverman, Hugh J., and F. A. Elliston, eds. *Jean-Paul Sartre: Contemporary Approaches to His Philosophy*. Pittsburgh, Pa.: Duquesne University Press, 1980.

Smith, John E. *Purpose and Thought: The Meaning of Pragmatism*. Chicago: University of Chicago Press, 1978.

Snelling, David. "Subject, Object, World." In *The Analytic Freud*, edited by Michael P. Levine, 101–118. London: Routledge, 2000.

Sontag, Susan. *Styles of Radical Will*. New York: Farrar, Straus, Giroux, 1969.

———. *Under the Sign of Saturn*. New York: Doubleday, 1991.

Sorabji, Richard. *Animal Minds and Human Morals: The Origins of the Western Debate*. Ithaca, N.Y.: Cornell University Press, 1993.

Spengemann, William C. *The Forms of Autobiography: Episodes in the History of a Literary Genre*. New Haven, Conn.: Yale University Press, 1980.

Starobinski, Jean. *Jean-Jacques Rousseau: Transparency and Obstruction*, translated by A. Goldhammer. Chicago: University of Chicago Press, 1971.

Storr, Anthony. *Solitude*. London: Fontana, 1989.

Sturrock, John. *The Language of Autobiography*. Cambridge: Cambridge University Press, 1993.

Suhl, Benjamin. *Jean-Paul Sartre: The Philosopher as a Literary Critic*. New York: Columbia University Press, 1970.

Tauber, Alfred I. *Confessions of a Medicine Man: An Essay in Popular Philosophy*. Cambridge: MIT Press, 1999.

Teske, Roland. "Spirituals and Spiritual Interpretation in Augustine." *Augustinian Studies* 15 (1984): 65–81.

Thody, Philip M. W. "Sartre's *Les Mots*: A Defense of Normality." In *Phenomenology and Education*, edited by B. Curtis and W. Mays, 104–118. London: Methuen, 1978.

Tillich, Paul. *The Courage to Be*. New Haven, Conn.: Yale University Press, 1952.

Toker, Leona, ed. *Commitment in Reflection: Essays in Literature and Moral Philosophy*. New York: Garland, 1994.

Tompkins, Jane P. "Sartre Resartus: A Reading of *Les Mots*." In *Critical Essays on Jean-Paul Sartre*, edited by R. Wilcocks, 272–280. Boston: G. K. Hall, 1988.

Trapè, Agostino. "Saint Augustine." In *Patrology*. Vol. 4, edited by Angelo Di Berardino, 343–403. Westminster: Christian Classics, 1986.

Vallat, Francis, ed. *An Introduction to the Study of Human Rights*. London: Europa, 1972.

Vance, Eugene. "Augustine's *Confessions* and the Grammar of Selfhood." *Genre* 6, 1 (1973): 1–28.

VandeCreek, Larry, Hilary Bender, and Merle R. Jordan. *Research in Pastoral Care and Counseling: Quantitative and Qualitative Approaches*. Decatur, Ga.: Journal of Pastoral Care, 1994.

Veeser, H. Aram, ed. *Confessions of the Critics*. New York: Routledge, 1996.

Verene, Donald P. "The Limits of Argument: Argument and Autobiography." *Philosophy and Rhetoric* 26, 1 (1993): 1–8.

Verheijen, Luc M. J. "The Straw, the Beam, the Tusculan Disputations and the Rule of Saint Augustine: On a Surprising Augustinian Exegesis." *Augustinian Studies* 2 (1971): 17–36.

Wallis, R. T. *Neoplatonism*. London: Duckworth, 1972.

Warner, Martin. "Philosophical Autobiography, St. Augustine and John Stuart Mill." In *Philosophy and Literature*, edited by A. Phillips Griffiths, 189–210. Cambridge: Cambridge University Press, 1984.

Watson, Gerard. "St. Augustine and the Inner Word: The Philosophical Background." *Irish Theological Quarterly* 55 (1989): 81–92.

Watson, James R., ed. *Portraits of American Continental Philosophers*. Bloomington: Indiana University Press, 1999.

Weedon, Chris. *Feminist Practice and Poststructuralist Theory*. Oxford: Basil Blackwell, 1988.

Weil, Simone. *Waiting for God*. New York: Harper and Row, 1973.

Wilkinson, Russell. "Solitaire et Solidaire: Interview with Catherine Camus about Albert Camus' *The First Man*." *Spike Magazine*. Internet journal. Available at: <http://www.spikemagazine.com/0397camu.htm> (last accessed July 2000).

Wollheim, Richard. "On Persons and Their Lives." In *Explaining Emotions*, edited by A. Oksenberg Rorty, 299–321. Berkeley and Los Angeles: University of California Press, 1980.

———. *The Thread of Life*. Cambridge: Cambridge University Press, 1986.

Wright, Elizabeth. *Psychoanalytic Criticism: Theory and Practice*. London: Routledge, 1991.

Wundt, Max. "Ein Wendepunkt in Augustins Entwicklung." *Zeitschrift fur die Neutestamentliche Wissenschaft* 21 (1923): 53–64.

Wyatt, Frederick. "The Narrative in Psychoanalysis: Psychoanalytic Notes on Storytelling, Listening, and Interpreting." In *Narrative Psychology: The Storied Nature of Human Conduct*, edited by T. R. Sarbin, 193–209. New York: Praeger, 1986.

Zeil-Fahlbush, Elisabeth. *Wissen und Handeln: zur Begruendung der praktische Philosophie bei Rousseau*. Bonn: Grundmann, 1979.

Index

ABOUT THE AUTHOR

Shlomit C. Schuster is an independent scholar and lecturer based in Jerusalem. She is the author of *Philosophy Practice: An Alternative to Counseling and Psychotherapy* (Praeger, 1999) and several scholarly articles, as well as the managing editor of the *Journal of Radical Psychology*.